Whose God? Which Tradition?
The Nature of Belief in God

Edited by
D.Z. PHILLIPS
*Formerly Claremont Graduate University, USA
and University of Wales Swansea, UK*

Routledge
Taylor & Francis Group
LONDON AND NEW YORK

First published 2008 by Ashgate Publishing

2 Park Square, Milton Park, Abingdon, Oxon OX14 4RN
605 Third Avenue, New York, NY 10017

Routledge is an imprint of the Taylor & Francis Group, an informa business

First issued in paperback 2021

Copyright © Monica Phillips 2008

D.Z. Phillips has asserted his moral right under the Copyright, Designs and Patents Act, 1988, to be identified as the editor of this work.

All rights reserved. No part of this book may be reprinted or reproduced or utilised in any form or by any electronic, mechanical, or other means, now known or hereafter invented, including photocopying and recording, or in any information storage or retrieval system, without permission in writing from the publishers.

Notice:

Product or corporate names may be trademarks or registered trademarks, and are used only for identification and explanation without intent to infringe.

Publisher's Note

The publisher has gone to great lengths to ensure the quality of this reprint but points out that some imperfections in the original copies may be apparent.

British Library Cataloguing in Publication Data
Claremont Graduate University Philosophy of Religion Conference (2005) Whose God? Which tradition?: the nature of belief in God
 1. Belief and doubt – Congresses 2. God – Proof – Congresses 3. Christianity – Philosophy – Congresses I. Title II. Phillips, D.Z. (Dewi Zephaniah) 212

Library of Congress Cataloging-in-Publication Data
Whose God? which tradition?: the nature of belief in God/edited by D.Z. Phillips.
 p. cm.
 Includes index.
 ISBN 978-0-7546-6018-7 (hardcover: alk. paper) 1. Philosophical theology. 2. Christianity—Philosophy. 3. Belief and doubt. I. Phillips, D.Z. (Dewi Zephaniah)

BT40.W46 2009
210—dc22   2006034964

ISBN: 978-0-7546-6018-7 (hbk)
ISBN: 978-1-03-217997-1 (pbk)
DOI: 10.4324/9781315234090

Contents

Notes on Contributors		*vii*
Preface		*ix*
1	'God' and Grammar: An Introductory Invitation *D.Z. Phillips*	1
	Voices in Discussion *D.Z. Phillips*	18
2	Beyond Subject and Object: NeoThomist Reflections *Fergus Kerr*	21
3	Speaking of the Unknowable God: Dilemmas of the Christian Discourse about God *Anselm Kyongsuk Min*	35
	Voices in Discussion *D.Z. Phillips*	49
4	The 'Grammar' of 'God' and 'Being': Making Sense of Talking about the One True God in Different Metaphysical Traditions *Gyula Klima*	53
	Voices in Discussion *D.Z. Phillips*	78
5	Simplicity and the Talk About God *James F. Ross*	81
	Voices in Discussion *D.Z. Phillips*	92
6	Is God a Moral Agent? *Brian Davies OP*	97
	Voices in Discussion *D.Z. Phillips*	123
7	Anthropomorphism in Catholic Contexts *David B. Burrell CSC*	129

8	Anthropomorphism Protestant Style *Paul Helm*	137
	Voices in Discussion *D.Z. Phillips*	158
9	Is God Timeless, Immutable, Simple and Impassible? Some Brief Comments *Stephen T. Davis*	161
Index		*167*

Notes on Contributors

David B. Burrell CSC is Theodore Hesburgh Professor of Philosophy and Theology at the University of Notre Dame. He has been working since 1982 in comparative issues in philosophical theology in Judaism, Christianity and Islam, as evidenced in *Knowing the Unknowable God: Ibn-Sina, Maimonides, Aquinas* (1986) and *Freedom and Creation in Three Traditions* (1993), *Friendship and Ways to Truth* (2000) and two translations of al-Ghazali: *Al-Ghazali on the Ninety-Nine Beautiful Names of God* (1993) and *Al-Ghazali on Faith in Divine Unity and Trust in Divine Providence* (Book 35 of his Ihya Ulum ad-Din, 2001). With Elena Malits he co-authored *Original Peace* (1998). He is currently completing a translation of the portion of existence from Mulla Sadra's (Sadr al-Din al-Shirazi) *Asfar al-Arbain*, as well as a theological commentary on the book of Job (Brazos Press series).

Brian Davies OP is Professor of Philosophy at Fordham University, New York. His research interests lie in medieval philosophy and philosophy of religion. His books include *The Thought of Thomas Aquinas* (1992), *Aquinas* (2002), *An Introduction to the Philosophy of Religion* (2004) and *The Reality of God and the Problem of Evil* (2006).

Stephen T. Davis is Russell K. Pitzer Professor of Philosophy at Claremont McKenna College, California. He writes mainly in the philosophy of religion and Christian thought. His degrees are from Whitworth College, Washington (BA), Princeton Theological Seminary (MDiv) and the Claremont Graduate University (PhD). He is the author of over 80 academic articles and author and/or editor of 15 books, including *God, Reason, and Theistic Proofs* (1997), *Encountering Evil* (2nd edn, 2001) and *Christian Philosophical Theology* (2006).

Paul Helm is a Teaching Fellow at Regent College, Vancouver, and before that the Professor of the History and Philosophy of Religion, King's College, London, 1993–2000. His several books include *John Calvin's Ideas* (2004), *Faith with Reason* (2000), and *Eternal God: A Study of God without Time* (1989).

Fergus Kerr OP FRSE, Honorary Professor of Modern Roman Catholic Theology at the University of St Andrews, Edinburgh, edits the English Dominican journal *New Blackfriars*. Formerly Regent of Blackfriars Hall, Oxford, his books include *Theology after Wittgenstein* (1986), *After Aquinas: Versions of Thomism* (2002) and *Twentieth-century Catholic Theologians: From Neoscholasticism to Nuptial Mysticism* (2007). He is a Fellow of the Royal Society of Edinburgh.

Gyula Klima is Professor of Philosophy at Fordham University. Prior to this he taught at Yale University and at the University of Notre Dame. His interests include medieval philosophy, metaphysics and logical semantics. He is the author of

The Logic and Metaphysics of John Buridan, Readings in Medieval Philosophy (both forthcoming), John Buridan: *Summulae de Dialectica, an annotated translation with a philosophical introduction* (2001) and *ARS ARTIUM: Essays in Philosophical Semantics, Medieval and Modern* (1988). He has also published over 60 articles in such collections as *Mind, Value and Metaphysics in the Thomistic and Analytic Traditions* (2002), *The Cambridge Companion to Medieval Philosophy* (2003), *Thomas Aquinas: Contemporary Philosophical Perspectives* (2002) and Blackwell's *Companion to Philosophy in the Middle Ages* (2003).

Anselm Kyongsuk Min holds PhDs in theology (Vanderbilt University, Tennessee) and philosophy (Fordham University, New York) and is Professor of Religion at Claremont Graduate University, California. He is the author of, among other things, *Dialectic of Salvation: Issues in Theology of Liberation* (1989), *The Solidarity of Others in a Divided World: A Postmodern Theology After Postmodernism* (2004) and *Paths to the Triune God: An Encounter Between Aquinas and Recent Theologies* (2005). He is now working on a theology of globalization.

D.Z. Phillips was formerly Danforth Professor of Philosophy of Religion at Claremont Graduate University, USA, and Professor of Philosophy Emeritus and Rush Rhees Research Professor Emeritus at the University of Wales, Swansea, UK. Professor Phillips wrote more than 20 books and over 100 articles on topics in philosophy of religion, ethics, philosophy and literature, and the nature of philosophical inquiry. He edited the current work from its beginning to its near completion but died suddenly on 25 July 2006 before final editing procedures had been completed. The loss of Professor Phillips was a terrible misfortune for his family and friends and a devastating blow to the field of philosophy of religion.

James F. Ross is Professor of Philosophy and Law at the University of Pennsylvania, Philadelphia. He is the author of *Philosophical Theology* (1968, reprinted 1979) and *Portraying Analogy* (1982). He has another book forthcoming, *The Hidden Necessities*, on metaphysics, and is completing one on willing belief and rational reliance. He has also written many articles on philosophy of religion, plus reviews and contributions to numerous other works.

Preface

As the first chapter makes clear, the discussions in this book arose from competing contemporary claims about various accounts of religious belief offered by philosophers. Many analytic philosophers of religion have included appeals to orthodoxy in their accounts of religious belief, asserting, confidently, that other analyses, for example, those offered by Wittgensteinian philosophers of religion, obviously do not do justice to the nature of religious belief. If one listened to these voices alone, one would not realize that the accusers have been accused of the very fault they see in others, and that *they* are the ones who distort the nature of religious belief. These accusations have come from Thomistic and Calvinist sources. By giving these voices a major hearing in this book, issues concerning religious belief and philosophical enquiry are opened up in such a way that their outcome can certainly not be taken for granted. The fact that this situation is introduced from a Wittgensteinian point of view, and responded to, at the end of the collection, from the point of view in analytic philosophy being criticized, means that the reader is offered a creative engagement between major traditions in contemporary philosophy of religion.

The papers in the collection were read at the 2005 annual Claremont Conference on the Philosophy of Religion. The conference is supported by the financial generosity of Claremont Graduate University, Claremont McKenna College and Pomona College. Administratively, the conference benefits from the work of Helen Baldwin, Secretary to the Department of Philosophy at the University of Wales, Swansea and Jackie Huntzinger, Secretary to the School of Religion at Claremont Graduate University. The conference also benefits from the support of graduate students at Claremont, ably organized by my research assistant Ray Bitar, to whom I am also grateful for preparing my contribution and the 'Voices in Discussion' for publication from my handwritten manuscripts. The 'Voices' consist of notes taken by me during the conference. They do not claim to be verbatim reports, hence the absence of names, but do claim to give a fairly accurate account of the discussions. Readers, as usual, will have little difficulty in identifying many of the speakers, but contributions from the audience have, on occasions, also been included.

Fergus Kerr was unable to attend the conference due to ill health. I am grateful to my colleague at Claremont, Anselm Min, for introducing his paper, an introduction which led to his valuable contribution to the discussion. Stephen T. Davis's response to criticisms during the conference also enhances the scope of the collection.

No matter which philosophical viewpoint one holds, the present collection should teach philosophers to exercise greater caution in taking for granted that they are always doing conceptual justice to the complexity of religious belief.

D.Z. Phillips
Claremont, May 2005

Postscript

D.Z. Phillips died suddenly on July 25, 2006, before this work went to press. He is responsible for the editing of this work as it appears here. However, special thanks are due to his graduate assistant, Ray Paul Bitar, for completing the various tasks needed to finally publish this work. His diligent commitment to this project proved invaluable.

Chapter 1

'God' and Grammar: An Introductory Invitation

D.Z. Phillips

It is obvious, or should be, that in any theistic context, everything depends on what is meant by 'God'. My own work, in the philosophy of religion, is well known for its view that dominant trends in the subject today distort and confuse the grammar of 'God'.[1] It is equally well known that the counter-charges against me state, with great confidence, that *I* am the one who is guilty of misunderstanding or revising the essential nature of religious belief. Indeed, an appeal to orthodoxy and tradition has been made part of the philosophical arguments of my accusers, as though there were nothing that needed even a cursory argument with respect to the legitimacy of their appeal. My long-standing suspicion of this confidence was, no doubt, the background against which the idea for the 2005 Claremont Conference on Philosophy of Religion came to fruition. It took the July/August 2003 issue of *New Blackfriars*, however, to turn that standing suspicion into a positive intention to address it in an historical/philosophical way.

The issue of *New Blackfriars* consists of essays in memory of Gareth Moore OP, who, in 2001, returned to Blackfriars, Oxford, to teach philosophy. In June 2002, however, he was diagnosed with kidney cancer, and died less than six months later. He had participated in the Claremont conference on four occasions, the last being in 2000.

During his time as Prior of the Belgian Dominican house at Rixensart, near Brussels, Moore had asked Brian Davies OP, by that time teaching at Fordham University, about the state of philosophy of religion in America. After Moore's death it struck Davies that he had never answered this question in any detail. Davies's contribution to the memorial issue of *New Blackfriars* takes the form of a 'Letter from America', in which he draws sharp contrasts between dominant trends in philosophy of religion, and what he takes to be orthodox Christian belief down the centuries. It was this recurring contrast that caught my eye, since 'the modern trend', regarded by Davies as wayward, consisted precisely in those philosophers who accuse me, and other Wittgensteinian philosophers of religion, of distorting Christian belief! But the accusers were now being accused, not by recent Wittgensteinians, but, according to Davies, from the context of classical theistic writing, patristic texts and the works of the giants of the Middle Ages. It is these accusations, from traditions very different from my own, that I wanted to explore further in the present conference by asking, Whose God? Which tradition?

---

1   For the latest expression of this charge, see the early chapters of *Religion and Friendly Fire* (Aldershot: Ashgate, 2004).

Most of this introduction was written before anyone was invited to participate in the conference. This is because it consists of a series of questions I wanted the participants to address. My questions come from a Wittgensteinian context, as does my depiction of how they arise for me. But it is not that context I want to discuss, but the questions themselves. Some of the contributors may have been influenced by Wittgenstein more than others, but, in the main, they come from philosophical traditions very different from my own. I certainly do not expect there to be agreement on all issues. My questions should make that clear. Nevertheless, if what Davies claims can be sustained, a parallel will emerge between Wittgensteinian accounts of religious concepts of belief and the work of Christian thinkers down the centuries. Such a parallel, I confess, would give me personal and philosophical satisfaction, since Wittgensteinians are not reformers of religious belief, but philosophers who seek to give perspicuous representations of what is there already to be seen.

I. The Accusers Accused

Davies refers to philosophers in America whom he regards as talking 'excellent sense about God, or, at least, [as having] a sound grasp of what we cannot say about God'.[2] He refers to the work of David Burrell, Michael Dodds, Germain Guirez, Mark Jordan, Brian Leftow (now at Oxford), Norman Malcolm, Ralph McInerney and James Ross. 'In their different ways,' Davies tells us, 'all these people keep clearly in mind the difference there must be between creature and Creator.'[3] These American authors, Davies writes, 'all have colleagues with the same sensitivity (though of different opinions) working in the context of Europe'.[4] He says that he is thinking 'especially of such authors as Cyril Barrett, David Braine, Ian Crombie, Peter Geach, Herbert McCabe, and D.Z. Phillips'.[5] He also mentions Moore himself.[6]

The importance of all these philosophers, for Davies, is that they do justice to the grammar of 'God'. Ten important features of that grammar must be protected in any philosophical account of 'God'. First, God cannot be said to be part of the world of space or time. Second, God cannot be said to be subject to the limitations which affect spatial and temporal things. Third, it is nonsense to speak of God as an individual, locatable in one place rather than another. Fourth, God cannot be said to be an individual 'in the familiar sense of "individual" where to call something an individual is to think of it as a member of a class of which there could be more than one member, as something with a nature shared by others but different from that of things sharing natures of another kind.'[7] Fifth, there is no distinction between God's identity and God's nature. Sixth, it makes no sense to speak of God changing, as though he passes through successive states. Seventh, God cannot be informed of

---

2 Brian Davies OP, 'Letter from America', *New Blackfriars*, 84//989–90 (July/August 2003): 377.
3 Ibid.
4 Ibid.
5 Ibid.
6 Ibid. See Gareth Moore OP, *Believing in God* (Edinburgh: T&T Clark, 1988).
7 Davies, 'Letter from America', 376.

things, as though he were ignorant of them, and he cannot be caused to have pain. Eighth, God cannot be said to be the source of some things, but not others. Ninth, as Aquinas says, God 'is at work without intermediary in everything that is relative'.[8] Tenth, everything depends on God for its existence, whereas one cannot say that God's existence depends on anything outside itself.

Davies claims that in contrast to these important grammatical features of 'God', which mark essential differences between 'God' and 'creature', much modern American philosophy of religion claims that these features are false when ascribed to God.

> It is false, so we are told, that God is incomprehensible. He is, in fact, something very familiar. He is a person. And he has properties in common with other persons. He changes, learns, and is acted on. He also has beliefs, which alter with the changes in the objects of his beliefs. And he is by no means the source of all that is real in the universe. He is not, for example, the cause of my free actions. These come from me, not from God. He permits them, but they stand to him as an observed item stands to its observer. He is not their maker. He is only their enabler.[9]

In recent American philosophy of religion, Davies mentions Richard Creel, Stephen T. Davis, William Hasker, Nelson Pike, Alvin Plantinga and Nicholas Wolterstorff as holding some or all of these views, but he could have added many others. Had he mentioned European parallels, the name of Richard Swinburne would have to have loomed large.

It would be hard to imagine a greater grammatical contrast than that to which Davies calls our attention. What interested me, as I have said, is the fact that the philosophers he criticizes often use, as part of their philosophical arguments, an appeal to the Christian tradition which they claim to be upholding, in contrast to philosophers whom they claim are distorting or, at least, revising that tradition.

For example, Davies writes, 'Plantinga is a particularly interesting example of the trend to which I am now referring. For he writes in a polemical manner, and he presents himself as a philosophical spokesperson for the Christian community.'[10] Yet, as I know only too well, Plantinga is not alone in that respect. Here is Wolterstorff embracing the same role:

> Phillips understands himself, in his writings, as speaking not religiously but philosophically; and over and over he says that his aim, as philosopher, is not to revise but describe. His description does not hold, however, for how Reformed epistemologists use theistic language; nor, I contend, for how most people use such language. His description holds only for a rather select group of Wittgensteinians and their allies. Yet his words regularly carry the suggestion that he is describing all serious religious use of theistic language. Accordingly, his description is, for most people, a misdescription. And should his discussion succeed in getting some people to think they are using theistic language in his way, when in fact they have been using it in my way, then his discussion threatens to do what he says he wants at all cost to avoid doing; namely, it threatens to function not as description but as revision.[11]

---

8   Aquinas, *De Potentia* III, 7.
9   Davies, 'Letter from America', 377.
10 Ibid., 378.
11 Nicholas Wolterstorff, 'Reformed Epistemology', in *Philosophy of Religion in the 21st Century*, ed. D.Z. Phillips and Timothy Tessin (Basingstoke: Palgrave, 2001), 62–3.

Wittgensteinian philosophy of religion, perhaps more than any other aspect of contemporary philosophy of religion, has been subjected to criticisms such as those of Wolterstorff. In the same vein, Swinburne writes, 'Much of the time Phillips writes as if he were merely analysing religious talk, but he is not; he is recommending a new way of understanding that talk, and he needs to realize this much more fully.'[12] What is more, Swinburne proceeds to suggest how an improved education can help me towards such a realization: 'It's no good reading only Simone Weil – you need to read St. Paul, Irenaeus, and Gregory of Nyssa and Luther and Francis de Sales and so on, and so on. Wittgensteinian Philosphy of religion suffers from a very one-sided diet of examples.'[13] Given such confident criticism, Wolterstorff's, Swinburne's and Plantinga's claim to be spokespersons for the Christian community, what are we to make of Davies's criticisms of such critics? Surveying the American scene, he concludes, 'If there is anything characteristic of modern American philosophy of religion it is the view that God is temporal.'[14] It can be said more generally of such views that they suffer from a distorting anthropomorphism. Swinburne has been aptly called the Cleanthes of twentieth-century philosophy of religion, since, in comparing the Creator and the creature, it is a case of 'the liker the better'. More interestingly, in the light of Swinburne's proposed reading-list, here is Davies's comparison of current anthropomorphism with Christian theological and philosophical traditions.

> I am complaining about a modern trend, one which would have seemed very strange to the majority of classical theistic writers. It would have astonished classical Jewish and Islamic thinkers such as Maimoinides and Avicenna. It would also have astonished most of the Christian patristic writers. And it would have seemed wholly curious to people like St Augustine, St Anselm, Aquinas, Scotus, Ockham, and many other Christian thinkers of the middle ages.[15]

Faced by these competing appeals to tradition, what do we do? Surely, one cannot remain content with competing reading-lists, Davies's versus Swinburne's (if they are competing). Neither is it enough to say, with Wolterstorff, that competing philosophical accounts serve different constituencies, but that one has the majority on its side. The matter cannot be settled by counting heads, since conceptual issues are involved.[16] Davies ends his letter to Moore thus:

> So, Gareth, American philosophy is rich in sound philosophy of God. I have been complaining only about a trend. And I have singled it out only because it is now a prevailing one. Against it, we may set thinkers of such stature as Aquinas, Wittgenstein (whom you especially admired) and [Jonathan] Edwards. So I hope it is nothing more than a trend.[17]

---

12 'Religious Talk: A Mere Viewpoint', review of *Religion Without Explanation*, *The Expository Times* 89 no.3 (1977), 92.

13 Richard Swinburne, 'Philosophical Theism', in Phillips and Tessin, *Philosophy of Religion in the 21st Century*, 17.

14 Davies, 'Letter from America', 380.

15 Ibid.

16 See my exchange with Stephen T. Davis on this issue in *Philosophy of Religion in the 21st Century*, 150.

17 Davies, 'Letter from America', 382.

As his own work in the philosophy of religion testifies, Davies does not, of course, simply hope for the best. He speaks of setting certain thinkers against what he takes to be some modern confusions. What does that 'setting against' come to in philosophy? Is it captured simply by asking, Whose God? Which tradition?

II. Philosophy and Description

What is the hoped-for result if we set one philosopher against another in the philosophy of religion? Surely, not the elimination of all religious and theological differences between and within Catholicism and Protestantism. It would be no part of philosophy's task to resolve these. Nor is there any reason to suppose that they *must* be resolvable. Thus far, Wolterstorff's reference to different constituencies would have a point, although his calculation of minorities would remain problematic. I do not deny that there are forms of religious belief other than those I allude to in my examples,[18] but my examples are not meant to address these differences. They are meant to combat *confusion*. After all, that is what most of my critics think of my views. So the question of how one proceeds from that point remains.

One can see from reactions to my work how fierce the philosophical disagreement can be. While one reviewer, writing of *The Concept of Prayer*, my first book, says, 'the theologian will say that this is prayer as he knows it',[19] and another writes, 'it is clear from the whole tenor of the book that he knows from inside the things he is writing about',[20] a third, reviewing *Religion Without Explanation*, finds 'the view of religion which it presents ... utterly mistaken',[21] a view found by others to be 'extremely dangerous in being reductively attractive and compellingly alluring',[22] 'deeply subversive',[23] and 'sinister'.[24] Little wonder that faced by such differences, an exasperated reviewer of *Faith After Foundationalism* thought I had failed 'to sufficiently answer at least one very crucial question: Who decides and how one does decide when and where religious language is being used efficaciously?'[25]

The philosophical answer to this question is to be found in what Wittgenstein means by 'description' in philosophy. At first, this may seem to make no progress. A disagreement I had with Moore will illustrate why this may be thought.

Moore argued that if, like Wittgenstein, one believes that philosophy's task is essentially descriptive, one can only describe different religious traditions,

---

18 I address this issue in 'Religion in Wittgenstein's Mirror', in *Wittgenstein and Religion* (Basingstoke: Macmillan, 1993).

19 Ronald Preston, 'A Philosopher on Prayer', *The Guardian*, 23 February 1966.

20 A.M. Allchin, 'Talking to God', *Church Times*, 11 February 1966.

21 Hugo Meynell, *The Tablet*, 4 February 1978.

22 James Richmond, '"Religion Without Explanation" – Theology and D.Z. Phillips', *Theology*, January (1980): 63.

23 John Hick, *Disputed Questions in Theology and the Philosophy of Religion* (New Haven, CT: Yale University Press, 1993), 136.

24 Howard Robinson, 'Gareth Moore's Radical Wittgensteinianisn', *New Blackfriars*, 84/989–90 (July/August 2003): 354.

25 T. Werley Stuart, *Journal for the Scientific Study of Religion*, 29/1 (March 1990).

but one cannot arbitrate between them.[26] To attempt to do so would be to move from description to prescription. I had claimed that to worship God out of fear of punishment, or hope of reward, where the punishment and the reward are thought of as externally related to the worship, is a form of confusion. Moore argued that my criticism is not philosophical. Rather, he suggested, I am prescribing, from within a religious sensibility he thinks I share with Wittgenstein; a sensibility to which he, too, is sympathetic. Moore, like myself, found a religion of prudence repugnant, but, he asked, how can it be denied that there are religious traditions of precisely that kind, which cater to the prudential needs of millions? Similarly, it may be argued, Davies finds that he shares a religious sensibility with certain Wittgensteinian philosophers of religion. He mentions Cyril Barrett, Norman Malcolm, Gareth Moore and myself. I am sure he would have no objection to adding Rush Rhees and Peter Winch to the list. But how can he deny that there are different traditions, and that it is these that dominate contemporary philosophy of religion? Shouldn't he content himself with describing the religious differences between them? How can Davies, any more than myself, move from description to prescription?

The attempt to apply the above restriction to Davies and myself is based on a misunderstanding of what Wittgenstein means by 'description'. This has been brought out well in a discussion of criticisms of Gareth Moore's argument.

> I think ... the trouble comes from switching registers when we talk of description. When Wittgenstein talks of description he is showing the role of concepts in our language game. But there is another use of description, a sociological one, which simply refers to what is going on. And one can give a philosophical critique of what is going on by spelling out the implications and surroundings of what is being said. We see that something is a policy, not a faith, so something has gone wrong. So in this way giving a description does have prescriptive force, but this force comes from spelling out what is involved in the actual use of words. It is not the prescription of preference.[27]

It is to providing descriptions, in Wittgenstein's sense of that term, that I invite participants in the conference. Clearly, Davies does not take himself to be simply comparing one theological or religious tradition to another. He is saying that what he calls 'the modern trend' in contemporary philosophy of religion is *confused*. The only difference between us, at this stage, is that it is not sufficient to contrast that confusion with *tradition*. This is because a tradition itself may be confused. There is nothing about confusion which denies it a majority. The mistake of secular reductionist analyses of religion is not that there aren't religious traditions which

---

[26] See Gareth Moore OP, 'Wittgenstein's English Parson: some reflections on the reception of Wittgenstein in the philosophy of religion', in *Religion and Wittgenstein's Legacy*, ed. D.Z. Phillips and Mario von Der Ruhr (Aldershot: Ashgate, 2005): 209–28.

[27] See 'Voices in Discussion,' *Religion and Wittgenstein's Legacy*, ed. D.Z. Phillips and Mario von Der Ruhr (Aldershot: Ashgate, 2005): 248. For my reply to Moore see 'Senses and Sensibilities', *New Blackfriars*, 84/989–90 (July/August 2003): 346–53.

manifest the confusions they identify, but rather, their claim that *all* forms of religious belief are confused.[28]

How is one to tell the difference between genuine religious or theological differences and confusion, if not by drawing out the implications of our words and their surroundings? That is the task facing the papers that follow. After all, any accusation of confusion must have its positive aspects. In tracing out the source of confusion, we bring out, at the same time, the character of what is being confused. It is a matter of striving, through discussion, to answer such questions as 'Why do you say that?' 'How can you use concepts in that way, while ignoring the surroundings in which they have their sense?' In the specific contexts which follow, it is such questions which must be addressed.

III. God and Reference

As I said at the outset, in any theistic context, what we mean by 'God' is a central question. That is the question which needs to be addressed in the second section of the conference – 'Referring to God: Beyond Subject and Object?' In what sense do we *refer* to God? It is easy to present ourselves with too restrictive a context in endeavouring to answer that question. According to Linda Woodhead: I was 'endeavoring to get beyond such a context in the 1960s; beyond the sterile debate between the realists and the non-realists – between those who said that God was a real, verifiable object out there, and those who denied this and said that belief in God was a matter of having a particular attitude towards the world.'[29] But, in 2003, we find Howard Robinson attributing to me this very view. He claims that, according to it,

> Because of the acceptance of Hume and Kant's critique of metaphysics, no religious statements can be accepted as descriptively true, on a par with descriptions of the physical world and the statements of science. Rather they have an entirely different function, being, roughly, expressions of value and attitude towards the world.[30]

When I read Robinson's words, there is a certain irony in Woodhead's view that, in the later essays in *Wittgenstein and Religion*, I 'seem to be fighting battles long since won'.[31] Philosophical confusions rarely disappear once and for all. Their attraction goes deep. In this case, it can be traced to Robinson's conviction that, according to my theory, 'the word "God" is not a name or referring expression'.[32] What is at stake in issues concerning 'reference' and 'God'? Isn't there the feeling behind them that unless 'God' *refers to something*, religious belief becomes a fanciful dream?

According to Swinburne, Hume's objections to inference from the world to God can be put aside once we recognize that 'Hume wrote before scientific inference

---

28 For my criticism see *Religion and the Hermeneutics of Contemplation* (Cambridge: Cambridge University Press, 2001).
29 'Asking Rational Questions', *Church Times*, 11 February 1994.
30 Robinson, 'Gareth Moore's Radical Wittgensteinianisn', 354.
31 'Asking Rational Questions', *Church Times*, 11 February 1994.
32 Robinson, 'Gareth Moore's Radical Wittgensteinianisn', 354.

from things unobservable in the laboratory to the existence of such unobservable entities as photons and protons had become respectable.'[33] But is referring to God like referring to an unobservable entity? The question is whether the grammar of 'entity' remains the same whether it is unobservable or not. As Stephen Williams says, 'there is no doubt that if you throw an object high enough into space it just cannot very well come down because it has left the earth's gravitational sphere and is destined for a sublimer orbit.'[34] On the other hand, Robinson argues, just because 'God' does not refer to a thing among other things, we cannot conclude that the word 'God' does not refer to anything.[35] How is this question to be resolved? Rush Rhees brings out why it is insufficient merely to say that the word 'God' is a substantive:

> If one lays emphasis ... on the fact that 'God' is a substantive, and especially if one goes on ... to say that it is a proper name, then the natural thing will be to assume that meaning the same by 'God' is something like meaning the same by 'the sun' or meaning the same by 'Churchill'. You might even want to use some such phrase as 'stands for' the same. But nothing of that sort will do here. Questions about 'meaning the same' in connection with the names of physical objects are connected with the kind of criteria to which we may appeal in saying that this is the same object – 'that is the same planet as I saw in the south west last night, that is the same car that was standing here this morning.' Supposing someone said 'the word "God" stands for a different object now.' What could that mean? I know what it means to say that 'the Queen' stands for a different person now, and I know what it means to say that St. Mary's Church now is not the St. Mary's Church that was here in So-and-So's day. I know the sort of thing that might be said if I were to question either of these statements. But *nothing* of that sort could be said in connexion with any question about the meaning of 'God'. Now this is not a trivial or inessential matter. It hangs together in very important ways with what I call the grammar of the word 'God'. And it is one reason why I do not think it is helpful just to say that the word is a substantive.[36]

At this point the issue should not degenerate, as it often does, into a purely linguistic dispute over the word 'refer'. It must be remembered that Rhees ends his paper by saying that if the result of his negative analysis is to make anyone think that talking of God amounts to nothing,

> to avoid *that* I might say that the language about God certainly does refer to something. But then I should want to say something about what it is to 'talk about God', and how different this is from talking about the moon or talking about our new house or talking about the Queen. How different the 'talking about' is, I mean. That is a difference in grammar.[37]

---

33 Swinburne, *The Expository Times*, 89 no.3 (1977), 92.

34 Stephen Williams, Review of my *R. S. Thomas: Poet of the Hidden God*, in *Modern Theology*, 5/4 (July 1989): 390.

35 Robinson, 'Gareth Moore's Radical Wittgensteinianisn', 355.

36 'Religion and Language', in Rush Rhees, *On Religion and Philosophy*, ed. D.Z. Phillips, assisted by Mario von der Ruhr (Cambridge: Cambridge University Press, 1977), 45–6.

37 Ibid., 49.

So even if we say that the word 'God' refers to something, it is not as though the grammatical work is not still on our plate. Moreover, it is not as though Rhees does not address this talk. He writes,

> If it was God, then it was the creator of all there is, it was that in which all things live and move and have their being ... Winston Churchill may be Prime Minister and also a company director, but I might come to know him without knowing this. But I could not know God without knowing that he was the Creator and Father of all things. That would be like saying that I might come to know Churchill without knowing that he had face, hands, body, voice, or any of the attributes of a human being.[38]

Rhees's point is that attributes such as 'love' and 'grace' are grammatical attributes; they are part of what we mean by 'God', just as face, hands, body, voice are part of what we mean by 'human being'. Is not this what Davies means by saying 'who God is and what God is are not distinguishable'?[39] But, in that case, does not what we mean by 'God' have to go beyond both 'subject' and 'object'?

IV. Religion, Language and Metaphysics: 'God', 'Being' and 'World'

The subject for the third section of the conference grows naturally out of the conclusions of the second section. If 'God' is not to be conceived of as either 'subject' or 'object', what is the alternative? Robinson recognizes that the rejection of these terms is due to a proper insistence that God is not a thing among things. God belongs to an entirely different order. Robinson insists that 'he is, for example, "pure being", not "a being", as a Thomist might express it and, hence, not "in the universe".'[40] Some have seen an affinity between my work and that of thinkers who have thought of God as 'being as such' or 'the ground of being',[41] but that suggestion is misleading, because the Wittgensteinian tradition which is critical of talk of 'God' as a being among beings is just as critical of the notion of 'being as such'. Such criticism, for Robinson, is indicative of the general antipathy of Wittgensteinianism to metaphysics. Robinson argues that the trouble lies in this antipathy, but in a way very different from contemporary empiricists and reformed epistemologists.

Robinson wants to distinguish between two kinds of Wittgensteinianism. According to the first kind, paying attention to Wittgenstein's arguments against the possibility of a logically private language, 'clears away the "modern" errors of Descartes and the empiricists, leaving the field to an earlier and more traditional metaphysic (Aristotle and Aquinas), fortified by the discoveries of modern logic (Frege)'.[42] Robinson finds Wittgensteinianism of this kind in the work of G. E. M. Anscombe, Brian Davies, Michael Dummett, Peter Geach and Christopher Williams.

---

38 Ibid., 48.
39 Davies, 'Letter From America', 378.
40 Robinson, 'Gareth Moore's Radical Wittgensteinianism', 355.
41 See Adnan Thatcher's review of *Religion Without Explanation*, in *The Baptist Quarterly*, October 1977.
42 Robinson, 'Gareth Moore's Radical Wittgensteinianisn', 354.

There is a second kind of Wittgensteinianism which Robinson finds 'more radical and, from a religious point of view, sinister ... This pedigree guarantees the rejection of all traditional metaphysics, not just the supposedly aberrant subjectivism of the "moderns", represented by Descartes and the empiricists. This is the Wittgensteinianism of D.Z. Phillips and the "Swansea School", and Peter Winch ... This is the view Gareth adopts in *Believing in God*.'[43]

Robinson's critique of this second kind of Wittgensteinianism could not be more extreme. Such views, he believes, 'are normally associated with an extreme liberal Protestantism, and with people who are hanging onto belief by their finger tips, and probably on the way out'.[44] This consequence of being influenced by Wittgenstein should not come as a surprise, since Robinson regarded him 'from first reading, as being more or less a fraud'.[45] As a result, however, Robinson's friendship with Moore created a puzzle for him, for far from being a marginal believer, Moore's 'commitment was to a full-blooded religious life', one in which 'the Wittgensteinian position may very well have played a role in bringing him back to belief'.[46] The purpose of his essay, Robinson tells us, is 'to face up to something I did not face up to in his lifetime, because I found it an embarrassing question, namely, how could someone whose religious commitment and spirituality seemed so firm adopt a position that any normal orthodox person would regard as equivalent to atheism.'[47]

Robinson's conclusions are supposed to follow from a neglect of traditional metaphysics. As a result, 'Believing is simply a matter of certain practices being natural for one.'[48] What this ignores, for Robinson, is the obvious truth that divine reality 'is beyond our concepts'.[49] This, above all, is said to be missed by the Wittgensteinianism Robinson attacks. For as Philip Almond argues, even if one accepts my examples of religious language as paradigmatic, they 'postulate another order of reality 'beyond' this one'.[50] Similarly, Peter Vardy insists that 'Religious language reaches out beyond itself to touch the transcendent ... Aquinas was, above all, a realist ... [and] was never in any doubt that he was seeking to show how language was applied to the ontologically distinct reality that God is.'[51] All this is jettisoned, Vardy argues, when I say that 'different ways of living are not interpretations of anything more ultimate than themselves. It is one of the deepest temptations of philosophy to so regard them.'[52] Vardy responds, 'The religious believer, unless he or she is very sophisticated indeed, is simply going to disagree here.'[53]

43 Ibid.
44 Ibid.
45 Ibid.
46 Ibid. 345–5.
47 Ibid., 355.
48 Ibid., 359.
49 Ibid., 358.
50 Review of *Religion Without Explanation*, *Australasian Journal of Philosophy*, 55/3 (December 1977).
51 Peter Vardy, Review of *Faith After Foundationalism*, *The Heythrop Journal*, 32 no.2 (April 1991), 285.
52 D.Z. Phillips, *Faith After Foundationalism* (New York: Routledge, 1988), 107, 285.
53 Vardy, Review of *Faith After Foundationalism*.

What should be our response to the claim of traditional metaphysics as characterized by these thinkers? It has nothing to do with making sophisticated requirements of believers, but with clarity about language. As we have seen, there is talk of language postulating or reaching out to an order of reality beyond itself. A dispute between Roger Trigg and Peter Winch should help us to see that language cannot be said to do any such thing, either successfully or unsuccessfully.

Trigg argued that Winch had made "Reality ... relative to a language", with the consequence that 'if different languages portray "the world" differently, then there must be different worlds'.[54] Winch's rebuttal of this claim is one which I have never seen refuted. Its consequence is so far-reaching for the metaphysical claim that language points to the transcendent, or postulates it, that it is worth quoting in full.

> Unlike Trigg, I did *not* speak of language as expressing a community's *beliefs* about reality ... it is *speakers* of a language who attempt to say what is true, to describe how things are. They do so *in* the language they speak; and this language attempts no such thing, either successfully or unsuccessfully. Trigg is right to say that, on my view, 'different languages cannot be thought of as different attempts to describe the same reality', but wrong to suppose that the alternative which I must accept is that different languages attempt to describe different realities: they do not attempt to describe anything at all.[55]

Winch proceeds to bring out the incoherence that results from thinking of language itself as a belief or set of beliefs about reality.

> If Tom believes that Harry is in pain and Dick that he is not, then, in the ordinary sense of the word 'belief', Tom and Dick have different beliefs. But according to Trigg's way of speaking, Tom and Dick, because they both speak the same language and mean the same thing by the word 'pain', share a common belief: even though their descriptions of Harry are mutually contradictory – indeed, precisely because they are – they in a sense share a common belief about reality: perhaps that it contains such a thing as pain. But if it is possible to affirm that there is such a thing as pain, it ought to be possible to deny it too. The language in which the denial is couched must be meaningful; and it must mean the same as the language in which what is denied might be affirmed, else the denial would not contradict the affirmation. So to deny that there is such a thing as pain, I must mean by 'pain' just what someone who affirms that there is such a thing means by 'pain'. Hence we are still both speaking the same language and still, according to Trigg's way of thinking, offering the same 'description of reality'. This incoherence illustrates how important it is to recognize that the grammar of a language is not a theory about the nature of reality, even though new factual discoveries and theoretical developments may lead to grammatical changes.[56]

How would Robinson, Almond, Vardy or Trigg meet these logical considerations? None of this means that talk of God being 'beyond the world' is meaningless. What it does mean is that it is to religious language itself that we look to see what saying

---

54 Roger Trigg, *Reason and Commitment* (Cambridge: Cambridge University Press, 1973), 15.

55 Peter Winch, 'Language, Belief and Relativism', in *Trying To Make Sense* (Oxford: Blackwell, 1987), 195–6.

56 Ibid., 196.

that amounts to. Sometimes, certain religious notions, such as the mystery of God, tempt us to think otherwise. This notion does not refer to the limitations of language, since it is in religious language that we find the meaning of mystery in religion. Vardy says that Aquinas 'recognized the difficulty of using language about God, and the whole Summa may well be regarded as an attempt to explore how this language is to be used.'[57] With an important qualification, I would agree. Philosophy does not determine how language about God is to be used. In certain contexts, that is a task for theology. The philosopher is interested in how that language *is* used, and with combating the confusions that arise from mistaking its grammar. This is as true of the notion of mystery as of any other. Welcoming this emphasis in my work, Moore writes, 'The mysteriousness of God, he reminds us, is not a matter of a limitation on our knowing, an epistemological defect; it is not what prevents us from knowing God. God is rather *known* as mysterious, and that God is mysterious is an important element of Christian belief.'[58] Making a similar comment, Fergus Kerr writes, 'It becomes clear that, far from mystery's being what even religious language cannot express, it is precisely what the language of faith articulates all the time ... 'mystery is what faith essentially *includes*' ... It would be difficult to miss the depth of Phillips' understanding the character of Christian faith.'[59] I like to use a simple example to illustrate the point I am trying to make. When someone says, 'Words cannot tell you how grateful I am', that is not an expression of failure to thank due to the limitations of language. That is a precise expression of the form the gratitude takes. Similarly, if a believer says to God, 'You are beyond mortal telling', that is not a failure to worship due to the limitations of language. That is precisely the form the worship takes.

If these lessons about language are appropriated, certain questions arise for the relation of philosophy and religion to the conception of metaphysics I have been addressing. What are the implications of these lessons for the notions of 'pure being' and 'the world'? Further, to what extent does our understanding of belief in God as the Creator of all things depend on the answers we give to that question?

Davies recognizes that one cannot speak of 'the universe' as though it were an object. The same could be said of 'the world'. In that respect, the analogy between them and 'God' goes a long way. Does it make sense to speak of them as 'existing'? Does it make sense to say that the world might not have existed, and that there might have *been* nothing? Is 'nothing' a state which could be said to exist? If not, what sense does it make to ask of the world, as Davies does, 'How come?'[60] He is clear that this question is not a scientific one, but at the beginning of his paper he says that 'belief that there is a God is a natural consequence of basic human curiosity'.[61]

---

57 Vardy, Review of *Faith After Foundationalism*.
58 Gareth Moore OP, Review of *Faith After Foundationalism*, *New Blackfriars*, 71/836 (March 1990): 154.
59 Fergus Kerr OP, Review of *Faith After Foundationalism*, *Philosophical Investigations*, 13/3 (July 1990): 292–3.
60 Davies, 'Letter from America', 372 f.
61 Ibid., 372.

At the end of his paper he says that 'philosophy of God begins in wonder about the existence of things'.[62] Do these two emphases amount to the same thing?

If the question 'How come?' is not a scientific question, is it a philosophical question? The difficulties that arise from giving an affirmative answer to that question are as old as the Presocratics. If we say that the nature of things is x, we can always ask further questions about the reality of x. Plato called the difficulty that of measuring the measure. Plato saw that 'reality' cannot have the unity of a thing.[63] 'Reality' has to do with the sense of things, but can that sense be captured in a form, albeit a religious one?[64]

Davies is clear about the distinction between religious and scientific questions. Is it equally important to distinguish between religious and philosophical questions? How many participants would be happy to assent to the following view?

> For me higher Christianity and true philosophy are one and the same thing. Indeed, since philosophy is love of pursuit of truth and wisdom, and since God is love, truth, and wisdom, it follows that true philosophy and true religion are identical?[65]

Since I do not know their answer to that very important question, I thought it should be addressed in the third session of the conference under the title, 'Religion, Language and Metaphysics: "God", "Being" and "World".' It can certainly be said that science and philosophy investigate reality, and that God is the source of all things. How do these contexts relate to each other? Do they converge? If so, how? Or is it important to recognize important differences between them?

V. Divine Immutability and Simplicity

Davies is in no doubt, as we have seen, that if we do justice to the grammar of 'God', to the essential difference between the Creator and the creature, God cannot be a part of the world of space and time, or subject to its limitations. Yet, having surveyed mainstream American philosophy of religion, Davies concludes, 'If there is anything characteristic of modern American philosophy of religion it is the view that God is temporal'.[66]

Davies gives evidence to show that such a view has been present in American thought for some time. William James, for example, thought of God as locked in

---

62 Ibid., 380.

63 I addressed this issue in the first chapter of *Philosophy's Cool Place* (Ithaca, NY: Cornell University Press, 2000). It is addressed more fully by Rush Rhees in work to which I was indebted. See Rush Rhees, *In Dialogue with the Greeks*, vol. I: *The Presocratics and Reality*; vol. II: *Plato and Dialectic*, ed. D.Z. Phillips (Aldershot: Ashgate, 2004).

64 For a discussion of this issue see the early chapters of my *Religion and Friendly Fire*. For a wider discussion of the issue, especially in relation to Plato, see Rush Rhees, *Wittgenstein and the Possibility of Discourse*, ed. D.Z. Phillips (Cambridge: Cambridge University Press, 1998). A second edition was published by Blackwell in 2005.

65 See Paul T. Fuhrmann's review of *The Concept of Prayer* in the *Columbia Theological Seminary Bulletin*, January 1969.

66 'Letter From America', 380.

a battle of wills with the forces of evil. God struggles, with limited resources, to make the world a better place.[67] For Edgar Sheffield Brightman, God was 'a Person supremely conscious, supremely valuable, and supremely creative, yet limited by both the free choices of other persons and by restrictions within his own nature.'[68] In what sense have such views become something more in contemporary American philosophy of religion? Davies replies, 'They have become common currency.'[69] He proceeds to give well-known examples.

In the Process Thought of Charles Hartshorne, God, though a worthy person, struggles against evil. He grieves, and suffers as we suffer. God improves as time goes on, as qualities are added to the divine life.[70] Alvin Plantinga views God as a person who has to pass moral tests. For example, God can be excused for allowing evil if it can be shown that he was restricted by the free wills of other human beings, so that it was not within his power to create a world containing moral good, but no moral evil.[71] Similarly, William Hasker talks of God as someone who has a reliable character, but who takes risks in creation, because he cannot know how things will turn out.[72] Indeed, according to Nelson Pike, if God were not temporal, he could not have created the world.[73] According to Richard Creel, God must be temporal because he is a privileged observer. If God cannot observe things, as we do, he must be in error.[74] Again, for Nicholas Wolterstorff, a change occurs in God every time someone refers to him, so 'God changes with respect to his knowledge, his memory, and his planning'.[75] Stephen T. Davis raises the question of whether God would be God if he forgot the colour of the shoes Martha Washington was wearing on the day of her wedding to George, or failed to deduce this from other facts.[76] As Brian Davies says, this implies that God can fail in powers of deduction that he possesses, and can suffer from lapses of memory, 'implying that he has a life history to remember'.[77]

---

67 Cf. John E. Smith, *The Spirit of American Philosophy* (rev. edn., New York: Longmans, 1983), 41. See William James, *A Pluralistic Universe* (New York, 1909), 309 ff.

68 Cf. Andrew J. Reck, *Recent American Philosophy* (New York: Pantheon Books, 1964), 331.

69 'Letter From America', 378.

70 Charles Hartshorne, *Omnipotence and Other Theological Mistakes* (Albany: State University of New York Press, 1983), 17 ff.

71 Cf. Alvin Plantinga, *God and Other Minds* (Ithaca, NY: Cornell University Press, 1967), chs 5 and 6; *God, Freedom and Evil* (New York: Harper & Row, 1974), Part I; *The Nature of Necessity* (Oxford: Clarendon Press, 1974); 'Advice to Christian Philosophers', *Faith and Philosophy*, I (1984).

72 William Hasker, *God, Time and Knowledge* (Ithaca, NY: Cornell University Press, 1989), ch. 10.

73 Nelson Pike, *God and Timelessness* (London: Routledge and Kegan Paul, 1970).

74 Richard E. Creel, *Divine Impassability* (Cambridge: Cambridge University Press, 1886), 96.

75 Nicholas Wolterstorff, 'God Everlasting', in Steven M. Cohn and David Shatz (eds), *Contemporary Philosophy of Religion* (New York: Oxford University Press, 1982), 95 ff.

76 Stephen T. Davis, *Logic and the Nature of God* (London: Macmillan, 1983), 4 ff.

77 'Letter From America', 378.

Davies concludes, 'In my view, philosophy of God begins in wonder about the existence of things and it cannot, therefore, end with a finite and mutable divinity.'[78]

Davies's conclusions clearly take us back to the theme of the second session that concerned the incoherence of thinking of God as an object among objects, or as a subject among subjects. What is needed in the fourth session, however, is a discussion of the religious importance and significance of the notion of divine immutability. Similarly, in emphasizing that God is not subject to limitations and change, God is said to be 'simple'. Again, the religious significance of divine simplicity needs to be elucidated. This means, presumably, that there is no distinction between God and his nature. Davies says that, for Plantinga, this is absurd, 'Because, says Plantinga, it entails that God is a property, which cannot be true. In Plantinga's own words: "No property could have created the world; no property could be omniscient, or indeed know anything at all. If God is a property, then he isn't a person but a mere abstract object; he has no knowledge, awareness, power, love or life."'[79] But if Rhees is right in seeing internal relations between love, grace and God[80] – if 'God is love' is one rule for the use of 'God', as 'Generosity is good' is one rule for the use of 'good' – does Plantinga's conclusion follow?

Not that there aren't questions to be asked of notions of divine immutability and simplicity. For example, does it make sense to say that God's power is unlimited, in the sense that he can be said to do anything that is describable without contradiction? This cannot be so, for thousands of activities would disprove God's omnipotence, riding a bicycle, licking a Häagen-Dazs ice cream and learning a language being simply three selected examples. Furthermore, if one says that God's only omnipotence is the omnipotence of love, does this entail any limitation on God's part? The grammar of 'God' cannot be construed as a limitation ascribed to God.[81] For reasons both negative and positive, therefore, the fourth session needs to address the religious impact of the notions of divine immutability and simplicity.

VI. God, Moral Agency and Freedom

Davies admits that the notion of divine temporality is attractive for many reasons, not least the fact that we are finite creatures, and that any understanding we reach in our lives must be an understanding *in time*. If belief in God is to have any relevance to these lives, must not God, too, enter time? One of the main ways in which he needs to do this, it is argued, is by revealing himself to be a moral agent alongside ourselves in our endeavours. This assumption runs through dominant tendencies in contemporary philosophy of religion, and is thought to be necessary if any coherent account is to be given of divine compassion. Nevertheless, Davies argues that the assumption does violence, not only to classical theistic traditions, but also to the

---

78 Ibid., 380.

79 Alvin Plantinga, *Does God Have A Nature?* (Milwaukee: Marquette University Press, 1980), 47; Davies, 'Letter From America', 378.

80 See section III of this introduction.

81 I raise and discuss these questions in *The Problem of Evil and the Problem of God* (London: SCM Press, 2004 and Minneapolis: Fortress Press, 2005).

work of Jonathan Edwards 'who is now commonly deemed to be the father of American philosophy'.[82] Edwards insisted that God did not share what he called, 'the moral Agency of created intelligent beings'. If God is called a moral agent, Edwards insists, it is because he is 'the source of all moral ability and Agency, the fountain and rule of all virtue and moral good'.[83]

Davies admits that the claim that God is the source of all goodness raises the issue of 'how a human free choice can be free while also caused by God'.[84] He points out, however, that this is what Edwards insists on in his 'famous teaching that our freedom is part of what God is doing'.[85] Davies says, 'For some curious reason, this teaching is often taken to be something unique to Edwards and to like-minded Calvinists. As far as I can see, it is the same as what one can find in writers like Aquinas, and it is grounded in the same considerations.'[86] Nevertheless, so counter-intuitive does it appear to many to claim that divine causality and human freedom are compatible, that I thought the fifth session of the conference needed to discuss the special case of God, Moral Agency and Freedom.

There is also another matter that needs to be addressed in this connection. Does saying that God is the source of all goodness imply the denial of the heterogeneity of morals? If not, how is the religious claim related to what appears to be the undeniable reality of the heterogeneity in question?

VII. Anthropomorphism: Catholic and Protestant Perspectives

The sixth session of the conference addresses the issue of anthropomorphism, which marks a sharp divide in the contexts I have discussed. I thought it was important to give some account of the history of the notion in both Catholic and Protestant contexts, although this does not preclude further critical comments on the contemporary situation. Davies is convinced that if we do justice to the grammar of 'God', we cannot think of God, in the language of Matthew Arnold, as if he were 'a magnified and non-natural man'. As Sir William Watson's verse puts it, we cannot end up with 'A god of kindred seed and line,/Man's giant shadow, hailed divine.'[87]

VIII. Invitation

At the beginning of this introduction, I said that although my questions arise out of a Wittgensteinian tradition in philosophy of religion, and out of reactions to it by many of the philosophers Davies discusses, my invitation to the participants is not to discuss that tradition or reactions to it, but the questions themselves. At this point I do not

---

82 'Letter From America', 380.
83 Jonathan Edwards, *Freedom of the Will*, quoted from *Jonathan Edwards: Basic Writings*, Elizabeth Winslow (New York: New American Library, 1966), 222.
84 'Letter From America', 376.
85 Ibid., 381.
86 Ibid.
87 Ibid., 380.

need to repeat why, given the present trends in contemporary philosophy of religion, discussion of these questions is so important: Referring to God: Beyond Subject and Object?; Religion, Language and Metaphysics: 'God', 'Being' and 'World'; Divine Simplicity and Immutability; God, Moral Agency and Freedom; Anthropomorphism: Catholic and Protestant Perspectives – all, hopefully, responding to this introductory invitation to strive to be clear about the grammar of 'God'.

Voices in Discussion

D.Z. Phillips

A: I do not know how C can speak of *the* grammar of God in a regulative way. He and I differ on a number of issues, but I do not think my point of view can be ruled out by his invoking of a regulative use.

B: I agree. You will notice that in my paper I never speak of *the* grammar of God and neither do I do so in my "Letter from America". If we are to be true to a Wittgensteinian perspective you would expect a variety to be observed. Ironically Phillips, as a Wittgensteinian, seems to be suffering from a one-sided diet of examples.

C: May I remind you of Conant's excellent distinction between two senses of 'description'. In the one case, description is understood sociologically, and that simply refers to 'what goes on'. That may be confused. But 'description' in Wittgenstein's sense means showing the location of concepts in our language-game. That has prescriptive force in that it will bring confusions of those concepts, to life, but this is still not the prescription of preference.

B: Even so, what goes on is varied and therefore does not exhibit a single grammar. Isn't there a craving for generality in what you say? For example, isn't this shown in your rejection of Moore's appeal to a religious sensibility different from your own?

C: I think you extrapolate too much from my saying that we are discussing the grammar of religious belief. That simply indicates the character, namely, the conceptual character, of the issue being raised. It doesn't follow that I must be saying that there is only *the* grammar of religious belief. Interest in grammatical questions does not entail that there is only one grammar to be interested in. Whether there are grammatical differences between or within specific religions will show itself in the actual use of the words in them. But apart from such grammatical differences, there is also grammatical confusion. In my disagreement with Moore I did argue, and still would, that you cannot worship God out of self-interest – in the hope of reward or fear of punishment. It simply would not be worship. Another example is the frequent defence used by apologists in the problem of evil, when they say suffering is necessary in order to give us an opportunity to exercise our moral responsibilities with respect to it. But if anyone regarded people in distress in that instrumental way, it would be the negation of anything you would call moral responsibility with respect to them.

D: I sympathize with those who find some of your grammatical observations too restrictive. For example, I find this in what you say about mystery. You seem to deny any epistemic dimensions to mysteries. But what do you make of mysteries such as that of the Incarnation and the Trinity? Is there nothing to reflect on here? Haven't there been deep theological and philosophical speculations about them?

C: I confess that I cannot discuss the details about the theological disputations surrounding these notions, but I think you'd agree that in all traditions the mysteries are 'givens' not 'demonstrable' by knowledge or proof by reason alone. I characterized them as lights or illuminations offered to believers in terms of which they are invited to live their lives. But perhaps I can illustrate my point by an example of how mystery is of religious importance. If we listen to Hume or those influenced by him, religious believers of a certain kind are confused, and he offers an account of how they came to be confused. On the side of Reformed epistemology, you have explanations of why people don't believe – their faculties aren't working properly. So both sides offer explanations for the state of the other, but according to a certain conception of grace as a mystery that is to be guilty of pride, hubris. We should say that it is a mystery that one has been able, by the grace of God, to believe; and it is a mystery why this hasn't been the case for others. Here is a religious non-epistemic account of mystery.

D: But all mysteries may not be of the same kind. There may be some mysteries which will be resolved when we come to know what we don't know now. After all, there is a distinction between the faith by which we travel now, and the sight we are promised in the fulfilment of it.

C: I do want to resist turning religious mysteries into epistemological mysteries, where mystery is contingent. So when a believer is taught of faith culminating after death in sight, I do not take that to mean we pass from one situation dominated conceptually by something thought to be inferior, namely faith, into another, thought to be superior, called sight. It is a matter of spiritual fulfilment in God. Now, of course, there is the issue of what that means. The only promise made to believers is that they will be where God is, so everything depends on the grammar of God's reality. Sometimes it sounds like an earthly meeting. G.E.M. Anscombe, it is reported, said that she looked forward to having conversations with Christ – as though you'd have philosophical difficulties cleared up. Rush Rhees, by contrast, said he wouldn't take a philosophical difficulty to Jesus. He didn't think he'd be interested. He'd probably say 'Go and sin no more'!

Anyway, I want to keep 'mystery' as a conceptual category in its own right. We are told that we can feed on the mysteries. They are supposed to be food for the soul.

As for the notion of seeing *all* things clearly, that has implications in a wider context. What would a complete unified account be of all things? Rhees says that the Hebrews were a remarkable people but limited, like all others. It is difficult to see anything like secular literature there; what did music mean (cf. the way Chopin's music opens up possibilities of the human spirit); as for architecture, there is little compared with Greece and Egypt. Rhees was not saying that these things should be included. His whole point is that the greatness of the Hebrews depends on them not being there. But it means there is much that is missing. And there is little point in looking for 'completeness' anywhere – that very notion is confused.

E: When you say that 'Words can't tell you how grateful I am' is not a report of failure to thank, but a form of 'thanking', the point is well taken. On the other hand, there is also the admission here of inadequacy of language. And where God is concerned, our language is always inadequate. Even in the case of the expression of love for another person, can't our expression of love be inadequate?

C: Of course, but that is another context. A person may say, 'I made a hopeless job of telling her how much I loved her.' But that is not the context I was thinking of. 'Words can't tell you how much I love you' is an expression of love. If we take such expressions as inadequate, this can sometimes have comic results. If it were proper to negate the expression for a better one, 'Words can't tell you how grateful I am to you' would become, 'Words can tell you how grateful I am'!

Where God is concerned, 'You are beyond mortal telling' is appropriate as an expression because the believer is always unworthy before God. But his words do not fail to express that. That is what they do express.

F: I think what the discussion, and future discussions, will show is that, as Brian Davies says, one of the central issues is the difference between God as creator and human beings as creatures.

Chapter 2

Beyond Subject and Object: NeoThomist Reflections

Fergus Kerr

If you came into Roman Catholic theology in the 1950s, as I did as a Dominican friar, though this was customary for all seminarians and ordinands from about 1860 and mandatory from the Code of Canon Law in 1917, you started with courses on logic, cosmology (Wolff's *cosmologia generalis*: motion, nature, cause and so on; in our case with Aristotle's *Physics* the primary text) and rational psychology, *psychologia rationalis* (also Wolff's creation, not that his name was ever mentioned).

It's the last of these that concerns me here. The purpose of *psychologia rationalis*, as a glance at the textbooks (in Latin or latterly in vernacular languages) would soon confirm, was to relieve the student of a certain conception of the 'subject', of 'subjectivity', of 'the subject/object relation', indeed of 'subjectivism' ('idealism', 'relativism', 'Modernism' in the sense condemned by the Vatican in 1907), which it was assumed (rightly!) most of us carried over as baggage from the culture, or would find we accepted and were indeed gripped by as soon as we began to think 'philosophically'. Relieved of this 'subject/object' talk, in regard to ourselves, we had no inclination at a later stage, as we advanced into natural theology and then into Christian dogmatics, to speak of God as 'subject'. On the contrary, it was perfectly natural to speak of God, or one's neighbour, as *objectum* of one's act of charity, and so on.

I

In those days, however, the subject/object relation was of great interest in Christian theology more generally, outside the confines of Roman Catholic seminaries. The book everyone read was James Brown, *Subject and Object in Modern Theology*.[1]

None of the multiple copies in Edinburgh University divinity school library has been checked out since 1991. Perhaps no one reads this book now, which would not be very surprising, since it was one of the first to appear in the so-called Library of Philosophy and Theology, planned as 'a meeting-place for the thought of contemporary theologians and philosophers, Continental and Anglo-Saxon, yet without partisan or *a priori* assumptions about the way in which such a meeting may best be used' (5–6).

The general editor of the series, Ronald Gregor Smith, refers to what he seems to regard as a happy state of affairs in the previous generation when philosophical theology was carried out by theologians who had undergone intensive training in

---

1 London: SCM Press, 1955.

the then dominant idealist school in metaphysics (I guess he would have agreed that philosophers then had a better grasp of, or anyway a lot more interest in, Christian theology, than they commonly have today). By 1950, however, Gregor Smith says, 'the strong blasts of ... dogmatic theology blowing down from Switzerland upon Europe and America' (Karl Barth, he means), and 'the immense changes which have overtaken philosophy, especially in Britain' ('the linguistic philosophy' he mentions over the page, note the definitive article) have brought about a 'revolution' in the work required of theologians and philosophers: 'Philosophy and theology alike are being compelled to face their traditional problems in such a radical way that the question even arises: are our traditional problems the real ones?' 'We live', Gregor Smith concludes, 'in a post-liberal, post-idealist, atomic age in theology' (5).

So what's new, one may ask. That sentence might have been written today. We live in a post-liberal age, non-realist some might say, rather than post-idealist; postmodernist most would no doubt say, rather than 'atomic' – all much the same thing, we might agree. The chairs have been rearranged on the deck, that's all.

Some of the chairs may now be empty or the occupants left undisturbed. Gregor Smith promised books involving 'the existentialist theology' associated with the Lutheran New Testament scholar Rudolf Bultmann, little read nowadays by philosophically minded theologians; secondly, Dietrich Bonhoeffer's unfinished work on ethics (certainly still read); and, lastly, work on philosophical theology 'from the standpoint of the philosophers of logical analysis' (*New Essays in Philosophical Theology*, edited by Antony Flew and Alasdair MacIntyre),[2] no doubt seldom consulted now.

Some of the authors examined by James Brown are now (I think) much less read by theologians than they were then: Brown devotes a whole chapter to Martin Buber, 'The subject-object and I-thou' (postmodernist theologians now read Emmanuel Levinas). Paul Tillich is the focus of his interest in the concluding chapter, much less written about nowadays. For the rest, however, the book revolves round Kierkegaard (two of the seven chapters and frequently referred to in the others), Heidegger (one chapter: 'The Subject Makes Itself') and Karl Barth (one chapter: 'God. "Indissolubly Subject"'). And Kant frames the whole discussion.

Obviously Kierkegaard, Heidegger and Barth are far too important in the history of 'the Subject–Object relation' (as Brown calls it) for anything useful or fruitful to be said in the compass of this paper. Let me confine myself to much less demanding matters.

II

First, let me rehearse what James Brown says about the subject/object relation.

It seems amazing to us now that philosophers did not hit on this until the time of Kant. The distinction and relation of subject and object are implicit – 'immanent' – in language; the philosophies of ancient Greece and of the Middle Ages worked with 'some consciousness of this fundamental structure of human thought'; from

---

2   London: SCM Press, 1955.

Descartes to Hume philosophers were concerned with the distinction between mind and matter; 'still it was only in Kant that the modern formulation of the relation clearly emerged and that the terminology in which we still discuss the problems of the relationship was fixed' (19). Thus Brown, so far.

There is a history. As Brown says, 'it comes to us as a surprise', perhaps; but in the use of the terms 'subjective/objective' since Kant reverses the use of these terms in the work of the medieval Schoolmen. For the latter, the *subjectum* was the concrete object of thought, something about which some property may be predicated, the subject matter of a judgement, as we might say; whereas the *objectum*, typically, meant the special interest engaged in some action, including 'mental actions'.

Without making a song and dance about it, let us recall that the first occasion on which Thomas Aquinas uses this pair of terms in the *Summa Theologiae* (*ST*) shows us what Brown means to remind us of. Thomas is arguing that the *subjectum* of theology is God: 'what a science discusses is its subject', *illud est subjectum scientiae de quo est sermo in scientia* (*ST* I.1.7). He is arguing firstly against those who would say that since we cannot say what God is (strict apophaticism) God cannot be the 'subject' in theological discussion; and secondly against those who would say that the subject-matter of theology is the Trinity and the sacraments, the works of redemption, or Christ and the Church.

Thomas appeals to the following principle: 'A subject is to a science as an object is to a [psychological] power or training' (Thomas Gilby's translation), '*sic enim se habet subjectum ad scientiam sicut objectum ad potentiam vel habitum*'.

Much more might be said, obviously; but the basic point is clear: for Aquinas, here, the 'subject' is the matter under discussion, the object of thought or action or whatever, the subject-matter, as we might say; whereas the 'object' is the correlative to some capacity in the human agent to act in this or that way, or to a settled bent to do so, a *habitus*, – the object as that for which the human agent acts. 'The *objectum* of a [human] power or skill,' as Aquinas goes on to say, 'is that under the description of which things are related to that power or skill; as, for example, a man or a stone is related to eyesight in that both are coloured – being coloured is the proper *objectum* of the sense of sight' (*ST* I.1.7)

Just as Brown says, the medieval sense of the *subjectum/objectum* pair is effectively the reverse of the modern sense. For the medievals the *subjectum* is what we should call the object of thought or action, independent of our knowledge or existence; whereas the *objectum* is whatever it may be as seen or heard or thought by the human agent, there being no *objectum* except in what we might call subjective experience.

The medievals did not live in the same world as we seem to do: they were not 'subjects', as we appear to be, inhabiting a world of 'objects', assumed to be 'out there', independently of our attending to or being attracted by them.

It was only when Latin gave way to German, Brown reminds us, that the reversal took place. This first happened, he says, in the philosophy of Christian Wolff. Initially, Brown says, the new meanings, in philosophical jargon, of *subjektivisch* and *objektivisch* were found strange.

In due course, the pair was translated, or anyway settled down in English, by Samuel Taylor Coleridge. Brown cites a splendid passage from *Biographia Literaria*:

> All knowledge rests upon the coincidence of an object with a subject ... The sum of all that is merely objective we will henceforth call nature ... the sum of all that is subjective we may comprehend in the name of the self, of intelligence ... Intelligence is conceived of as exclusively representative, nature as exclusively represented; the one as conscious, the other as without consciousness ... During the act of knowledge itself, the objective and the subjective are so instantly united, that we cannot determine to which of the two priority belongs ... self-consciousness is not a kind of being, but a kind of knowing.[3]

– all this from chapter XII: 'A perusal of requests and premonitions concerning the perusal or omission of the chapter that follows' – the chapter that precedes the famous one on the imagination.

As Brown points out, Coleridge is well aware that the subject/object distinction comes in with Kant and that we are in epistemology, not metaphysics or ontology. (Kant died in 1804; *Biographia Literaria* was published in 1817.)

This way of talking took root and spread very quickly, to the extent that we now take it for granted. 'Subjective and objective have become two departments of reality, of which different qualities and characteristics can be predicated' (24). What was innovation in Coleridge's philosophical terminology soon became one of our most basic assumptions, unexamined and seemingly requiring no examination. Things and human activities are more or less subjective or objective now according to whether they partake more or less of the nature of intelligence, mind or the 'subject' on the one hand, or more or less of matter, presented to the mind, as it were from outside, 'objects' in the modern sense.

As Brown also notes, sometimes the subjective means 'anything and everything which a feeling and a thinking creature experiences in itself' – that which is 'deepest' in experience; and sometimes it means 'all convictions extending beyond the immediate existence of the facts ... a species of mere trimming' (24–5). The subjective, for us, is either what is deepest, most inward, most personal, or what is shallowest and most superficial.

The distinction which is so familiar to us now, between objects and the self (Coleridge's word), did not drop down from heaven – it has a history. We do not need James Brown's book to tell us this; but he did a good job in his day, opening up the possibility for reflection that the modern subject/object relation may not be quite as unavoidable, and in conformity with the way the world is, as it seems.

---

3   See, for example, Samuel Taylor Coleridge, *Biographia Literaria or Biographical Sketches of My Literary Life and Opinions*, Everyman's University Library, ed. George Watson (London: J.M. Dent & Sons, 1975), 144–5.

III

Anyone who studied English literature as well as philosophy back in the 1950s would no doubt have read such books as *The Rise of the Novel: Studies of Defoe, Richardson, and Fielding* by Ian Watt.[4] This is, of course, a classic. Coleridge is cited, though not in connection with the introduction of the Kantian subject/object distinction.

Watt makes two or three references to philosophy, one in particular to Descartes, ascribing to him (no doubt correctly as to the *Wirkungsgeschichte* whatever about his own intention) the origin of 'the problem of how the individual mind can know anything that is external to itself', the dualism which 'dramatizes the opposition between different ways of looking at reality', but which easily leads to 'complete rejection of the reality either of the ego or of the external world' (Hogarth edition, 295).

These extremes do not occur in the novel, or anyway not in the novels Watt discusses. For him, in a richly documented and instructive discussion, the rise of the middle class, with changes in the economy, layout of private accommodation in their homes etc., including the new ease of communication by letter and many other factors, created the environment in which the authors of *Robinson Crusoe*, *Pamela* and *Tom Jones* wrote.

The letter, for example, was 'an opportunity for a much fouler [sic!] and more unreserved expression of the writer's own private feelings than oral converse usually affords', such that Richardson's narrative mode, to take an instance, 'may also be regarded as a reflection of a much larger change in outlook – the transition from the objective, social, and public orientation of the classical world to the subjective, individualist, and private orientation of the life and literature of the last two hundred years' (ibid., 176).

In due course, Watt contends, the rise of individualism weakened communal and traditional relationships, offering the individual 'a more conscious and selective pattern of social life to replace the more diffuse, and as it were involuntary, social cohesions' (ibid., 177), at the risk of fostering a certain idea of private and egocentric subjectivity, at best (however) opening the way to the value we place on 'personal relationships', without which we could not imagine ordinary everyday living in our culture. (Watt, of course, does not claim to look outside western and indeed English middle-class culture.)

Much more might be said; what needs to be noted, however, is this much more complex background to the 'invention' of the modern concept of the 'subject' than theorizings by philosophers, including Descartes. Clearly, the modern concept of the self should be subjected to questioning in a socio-economic perspective (who has all this 'privacy', these 'personal relationships', this 'freedom of choice' and so on). On the other hand, this is an experience of the self, which is so central in our Western culture that we can only with great difficulty imagine ourselves without it. (Consider the loss of self in Zen Buddhist ascetical practices, or the loss of self in Alzheimer's disease, in John Bayley's shameless account of Iris Murdoch's deterioration.)

---

[4] London: Chatto & Windus, 1957; Hogarth Press, 1987.

IV

What does a modern theologian make of the subject/object relation?

Consider *God and Rationality* by Thomas F. Torrance,[5] the first book that came to hand. The 'subject/object relation' is listed in the index of subjects. (Torrance is generally regarded as the most eminent Scottish theologian of the twentieth century and among the half-dozen most eminent Presbyterian theologians.)

The first mention in the book is to 'the unfortunate Cartesian split between subject and object, in which the observing and thinking subject was thrown back upon himself as the one centre of certainty in a sea of doubt' (8).

In the context Torrance is combating the notion that 'scepticism belongs to the essence of the scientific attitude'. The point I draw attention to here is, however, only the attitude to the subject/object split. A certain moralism comes into play: 'we must think out more carefully and stringently the interrelation of object and subject and build into our thinking remedies for the inveterate preoccupation with ourselves from which we all suffer' (52).

Who exactly are 'we' here? We need to adopt the mode of objectivity appropriate to the situation, Torrance goes on to say; for example: 'Thus I adopt toward another person quite a different mode of rationality from that which I adopt toward my desk, because his nature is different from that of a desk' (52). It would be 'irrational or unscientific' to treat someone like a block of wood or to treat a desk as if it were a human being. This has implications, which are 'profound and far-reaching', specifically in theology: 'it would be utter nonsense for me to try to know God in the mode in which I know a creature or to treat Him as if He were a star' (ibid.).

Fine. But this talk of 'treating' people like desks or desks as people takes us back to debates that raged in philosophy about 'things and persons' which were surely quite artificial. What possibility is being imagined here? What thing might someone be treated as? What else could a person be other than a person? What is all this talk of 'treating as'?[6]

However shaky the argument here, anyway, Torrance is out to discredit the 'axiomatic assumption' in the 'new theology' (J.A.T. Robinson, H.A. Williams, Paul Van Buren, Werner Pelz, Thomas Altizer and William Hamilton are named on page 29; but we must not forget 'the so-called "new theology" in the Roman Church', which, 'under the influence of phenomenology' is going the same way, see page 20): the assumption, that is to say, of a radical dualism between God and the world, such that any notion is rejected according to which God is present and active in our existence in space and time, thus ruling out the possibility that incarnation, atonement and resurrection could be anything but 'symbolic'; and, more to the point here, the assumption that the subject is thrown back on himself, 'so that all his thinking is poised upon his own *sacro egoismo*, while the content of divine revelation is reduced to the conceptions and artefacts that are creatively produced out of his own self-understanding' (55).

---

5   Edinburgh: T&T Clark, 1971.

6   See, for example, Stanley Cavell, *The Claim of Reason* (New York: Oxford University Press, 1979), 372 for some further reflection.

In short, according to Torrance reflecting on modern Christian theology, there has been an 'eclipse of the object by the interposition of ourselves, the obscuring of God through our own subjectivity' (54).

According to Torrance there is no way of our being 'emancipated from imprisonment in ourselves', no way of learning 'to distinguish the reality of God from our own subjective states and conditions', other than by 'following Jesus Christ': he is 'the one point in our human and historical existence where we may be lifted out of ourselves and escape the self-incarcerating processes of human subjectivism' (54–5).

There is plenty more to this effect in Torrance's book. He studied with Karl Barth in Basle and would not be unhappy about being called a 'Barthian'. For Torrance, and I think for many other theologians, talk of the subject/object duality is inseparable from talk of 'the threat of impersonalizing objectivism and determinism' (science), and thus of a reaction into 'the prison-house of [one's] own in-turned subjectivity' (81–2), rescue from which can come only by turning straight to the Christian gospel, thus by repentance and conversion. For Torrance, that is to say, there would be no way of freeing ourselves of the bad effects of the dominance of subject/object relation in philosophy other than submission to and the practice of Christian discipleship. There is nothing that philosophy might usefully do.

However, there are, or were, Christian theologians with more time for philosophical intervention – the neoThomists for example. Yet they too – we also – accepted the authority of the subject/object duality in our culture, including something like Torrance's moralistic assumptions that this duality tempts us into, imprisons us in, a duality of objectivism and subjectivism which, inter alia, sets thinking about God, from the outset, off on the wrong track.

We might go to Karl Barth himself. In the lengthy discussion of Descartes in the third volume of *Church Dogmatics* (1932 originally),[7] he writes of our having to 'cross the bridge from mere consciousness ... to the recognition of existence' (347), thus displaying the hold on his mind of the picture of the human mind as trapped on one side of a chasm, with getting to know anything whatsoever as a perilous leap across. Rather than Cartesian reliance on the certainty of self-consciousness, however, Barth proposes sheer obedience to the authority of divine revelation. It is 'as and because we believe in God that we believe ... that we are ... and that the world which surrounds us also is' (362).

In other words, it is because we believe in God that we believe in the existence of the world and indeed in the existence of ourselves. Descartes did not go nearly far enough. We can be certain of the 'presupposition' that we are real only because God has been revealed to us as our Creator. The gap between subject and object, self and reality, created by modern philosophy, something that Barth accepts, is bridged only by appeal to divine command; there is nothing for a philosopher to do.

---

7   Vol. III/1 (Edinburgh: T&T Clark, 1958).

V

In the Roman Catholic tradition, however, much more is expected of philosophy. After 1879, with Pope Leo XIII's encyclical *Aeterni Patris*, the authorities in the Roman Catholic Church insisted with increasing vigour that no one, and certainly no candidate for ordination to the priesthood, should be permitted to study Christian doctrine before undergoing a serious course in 'Thomistic philosophy'. By the revised code of canon law that came into effect in 1917, every ordinand was required to study *philosophia thomistica* for three years before reading a word or, more likely, hearing a single lecture, on a theological subject (including Scripture).

In the medieval universities nobody studied theology who had not already studied the *artes liberales*. (One of the disasters for Christian theology in Scotland is that theology is now a first degree.) In the patristic age, if we go back to the likes of Justin Martyr, Clement of Alexandria and so on, it is obvious that interaction with Hellenistic philosophy has always been essential in Catholic Christian theological practice. We needn't linger over this but it seems to me that the role of philosophy in the patristic period and then again in the Middle Ages was different – different, anyway, from what happened in the late nineteenth and early twentieth centuries, when the mandatory study of philosophy *secundum mentem Sancti Thomae* was chiefly to inoculate Catholic clergy and theologians against the temptations of 'modern philosophy', 'philosophy of consciousness', 'Cartesianism', German idealism and so on.

By the way, it may be noted that the nineteenth century was punctuated by immensely impressive and at the time very influential 'programmes' to rethink Catholic Christian doctrine in the light of modern philosophy: Georg Hermes in the light of Kant; Anton Günther in the light of Hegel; Antonio Rosmini-Serbati in the light of idealism more generally, to mention the most prominent. All of these projects, sooner or later, ran into hostility from the pastors of the Church and seminary professors responsible for maintaining the traditional faith of the Catholic Christianity. By the 1920s it was established that the only way to keep Catholic doctrine sound, orthodox, pure and so forth, was to ensure that no one was ever allowed to teach theology unless he was trained in Thomistic philosophy. (The only woman I can think of trained in neoThomism, with two doctorates from the Dominican-run faculty at the University of Fribourg, was Mary Daly, the American theologian, whose work eventually went in a very different direction.)

Specifically, then, mandatory exposure to Thomistic philosophy was to free would-be Catholic theologians from the assumption that scepticism about knowledge of the external world is a reasonable thought, a temptation that needs to be exposed, a case that needs to be refuted; and the correlative idea that nobody but God knows what I think or feel unless I disclose it deliberately.

When Heidegger famously remarks that, contrary to what Kant said, the scandal in philosophy is not that philosophers have not yet come up with an argument for the existence of the external world but that anyone ever supposed there was any need for such an argument in the first place, he was speaking almost as the young seminarian he briefly was – raising the problem in any first-year neoThomistic course, as to whether the 'subject' could have knowledge of 'external reality'.

The key idea, for the first-year neoThomist, was to understand the thesis that 'the soul, in a way, is all', *anima est quodammodo omnia*; or, putting it epistemologically, to accept the thesis that *intellectus in actu est intelligibile in actu*, 'intelligence actualized is intelligibility actualized'.

In short: in any instance of cognition the subject and the object are identical. The picture of the subject (the self, the 'I' and such) over against the object (the world, reality and so on), with a gap to be bridged between what is in one's head and what is 'out there in the real world', needs to be rejected.

The best that my tutor in *psychologia rationalis* (Cornelius Ernst, who attended some of Wittgenstein's last lectures at Cambridge) could propose was, citing Wittgenstein, that 'we should yield to the temptation to use this picture; while, however, investigating how the application of this picture looks, '*wie die Anwendung dieses Bildes aussieht*'.[8] Ruminating about it, in discussion, we should find that, while plausible enough in certain circumstances perhaps, for the most part the picture of the self as subject having to cross a chasm to encounter the world as object turns out to be pretty empty.

VI

In connection with knowledge, one of Thomas Aquinas's most frequently repeated axioms is to the effect that 'the soul is in all things' (always citing Aristotle), 'the intellect in act is the thing understood in act' (seemingly his own pet formula), as noted above.

According to Eleonore Stump in *Aquinas*,[9] this should not be translated into such 'startling formulations' as she quotes from the eminent Canadian Thomist Joseph Owens (writing of Aristotle as it happens): 'you *are* the things perceived or known' (273).

For Stump, Aquinas's theological *a priori* (as she would agree), to the effect that the human soul is created such as to become one with things as they disclose their intelligibility in the actualizing of our knowing and of their being known, does not amount, in any strong sense, to 'cognition by assimilation', or 'mind/world identity'. Rather, when he says that 'the intellect is all things', Aquinas is speaking in the same register as we are when we say, for example: 'It won't be long before all our reference books will be on CD-readers' – or so Stump maintains, deflatingly (275).

Thomists of Joseph Owens's generation would, however, be familiar with much stronger readings.

Bernard Lonergan, for example, speaks frequently, in a now classic study, *Verbum: Word and Idea in Aquinas*[10] of 'knowing by identity', of Thomas Aquinas's 'theorem of immaterial assimilation' and suchlike.

Lonergan appeals to the distinction Aquinas makes between what he regarded as the Platonist conception of knowledge on the model of confrontation and his

---

8   *Philosophical Investigations* (Oxford: Blackwell, 1953), §374.
9   London and New York: Routledge, 2003.
10 Notre Dame, IN: University of Notre Dame Press, 1967; material first published as articles in the 1940s.

own conception of knowledge as a kind of assimilation (*Summa contra Gentiles*, book II, section 98).

Lonergan extends this distinction somewhat, contending that the confrontation model is at work in the conception of knowledge in Plato, Plotinus, Augustine, medieval Augustinians and modern 'dogmatic realists' (85, 192–3 etc.).

The story goes as follows. For the Platonist, knowing is primarily a confrontation in the sense that it presupposes the duality of knower and known, so that knowing consists in an additional, subsequent movement. In the medieval Augustinians, so Lonergan says, knowing as confrontation reappears in the doctrine of intuitive cognition of material and singular existents.

Later, Lonergan extends this into the claim that the history of philosophy is littered with this picture of knowing as 'taking a look'. This is a very natural picture, he thinks. Suppose I wonder whether you have a colour television set but do not know: how can I come to know except by popping in and taking a look at your set when it is switched on? Then I know what previously I did not know. In this case, as in many others, before I took a look, I did not know and after I have taken a look, I know. I take the example from Hugo Meynell, *The Theology of Bernard Lonergan*.[11]

Conceiving of knowing on the analogy of taking a look is thus very natural. Lonergan will go on, however, to argue but we easily overlook the fact that what we know is known in judgement, in the exercise of intellect, discursively, not attained simply by taking a good look at what is 'out there', as we fancy. It is not to the purpose here to follow him into that argument, obviously as it stands in need of unravelling.

For the Aristotelian, so Lonergan's claim goes, confrontation is secondary. Primarily and essentially, knowing is perfection, act, identity. There is, as he will put it, an isomorphism obtaining between the structure of knowing and the structure of the known. Knowing consists in an act, or related set of acts, and the known is the related set of contents of these acts, he will say, which means that the pattern of the relations between the acts is similar in form to the pattern of the relations between the contents of the acts. This premise is analytic, he will say.

Isomorphism is not identity, obviously. John Haldane, for example, speaks of Aquinas's theory of knowledge as a 'mind/world identity theory'.[12]

Norman Kretzmann seems to go further than Stump, seeing our access to the world, for Aquinas, as 'utterly direct, to the point of formal identity between the extra-mental object and the actually cognizing faculty'.[13]

Others are only wistful. Charles Taylor, for instance, argues against 'representationalist' theories of the mind/world relationship: views that presuppose a gap between our minds and things in the world and seek to bridge it by positing intermediate entities such as mental images, sense data, raw feels and so on. Sometimes he appeals to the premodern view, thinking of Aristotle, not explicitly of Aquinas, according to which one comes to know something by the mind's becoming one with the object of thought. Thought and thing collaborate, so to speak,

---

11 Atlanta, GA: Scholars Press, 1986, 1.
12 See 'The life of signs', *The Review of Metaphysics*, 47 (1994): 451–70.
13 See his chapter 'Philosophy of Mind', in Norman Kretzmann and Eleonore Stump (eds), *The Cambridge Companion to Aquinas* (Cambridge: Cambridge University Press, 1993).

rather than confront each other, with the mind's having to impose intelligibility on inherently unintelligible objects. Aristotle sometimes sounds like supporting representationalism, Taylor says; but, on the contrary, his model of how knowledge happens is participational: 'being informed by the same _eidos_, the mind participates in the being of the object known rather than simply depicting it'. However, Taylor concludes, this philosophy of mind depends totally on the philosophy of forms, and once that has collapsed, as he seems to assume it has, the account becomes 'untenable' and 'almost unintelligible'.[14]

Similarly, Hilary Putnam speaks not of representationalism, but of the 'tempting idea that there has to be an "interface" between our conceptual powers and the external world'. In modern philosophy, and when we begin to think about these questions, it seems overwhelmingly obvious that what goes on in our heads is separated by a chasm from what is there in the world outside. We are strongly tempted to think that 'our conceptual powers cannot reach all the way to the objects themselves'.[15]

Looking for a way out of this 'egocentric predicament', Putnam appeals to a statement by John McDowell: 'We need to stand firm on the idea that the structure of elements that constitutes a thought, and the structure of elements that constitutes something that is the case, can be the very same thing.'[16]

This claim seems to echo Lonergan's knower/known isomorphism; though I doubt McDowell has ever read Lonergan.

G.E.M. Anscombe, maintaining that, since Frege, we have come to see that 'thoughts are characterized by what they are of, with no substantive being of their own', argues that the medieval concept of intentional existence, brought to the fore by Brentano, 'may even be making a come-back, a reappearance in modern dress' – but, she warns, 'these matters are still very dark'. Nonetheless, the confusions of modern philosophy in this matter may be so intractable that we should survey 'the obscurities of the scholastic _esse intelligibile_, whose actuality is the same thing as the actual occurrence of a thought of such-and-such, with a not totally unfavourable eye'.[17]

VII

For Thomas Aquinas, the knower enables the thing known to become intelligible, thus enabling the thing to enter the domain of meaning, so to speak, while the thing's becoming intelligible activates the mind's capacities, and allows the mind to pass from potentiality to actuality. Knowing, we may say, is a new way of being on the knower's part; being known is a new way of being on the object known's part. Knowing is the coming to fulfilment of the human being's intellectual powers; simultaneously, it is the world's intelligibility being realized.

Philosophers are not likely to be persuaded by mantra-like repetitions of the axiom '_anima est quodammodo omnia_'; the human mind is – in a certain way – identical with the world, as the world is – in a certain way – identical with the human mind.

---

14 See _Philosophical Arguments_ (Cambridge, MA: Harvard University Press, 1995), 3.
15 See _Words and Life_ (Cambridge, MA: Harvard University Press, 1994), 282.
16 See _Mind and World_ (Cambridge, MA: Harvard University Press, 1994), 27.
17 See _Collected Papers_ (Oxford: Basil Blackwell, 1981), vol. 1, 85.

Thomas likes to cite this axiom, from Aristotle, though no doubt a more ancient, even religious picture of the human being as microcosm lies somewhere in the remoter background. The intractable question, noted by Anscombe, is, obviously, exactly what we might mean by the qualification 'in a certain way'.

On the whole, I think it is fair to say, in neoThomistic literature, the axiom was taken to mean that there is no gap between mind and world, thought and things, that needs to be bridged, either by idealist/empiricist representations or (as with Barth) by divine intervention. There was no need to take the discussion any further. Perhaps this was because, in the end, Aquinas's view of how our minds are related to the world is interwoven with his doctrine of God: no epistemology without theology, as rational animals we belong to the world which God created for us and we cannot but find it intelligible. Aquinas's (perhaps we should now think naive) confidence that things are indeed as they seem, most of the time anyway, and that there is no veil between the world and our minds, springs from, indeed is identical with, his belief that the world to which we belong is the world that belongs to God.

On the modern view we think of having a mind and being a person very much in terms of the 'subject', the 'I' as privileged and unified locus of self-consciousness, facing an array of objects out there (including other human beings) which one apprehends initially in images, impressions, sense data or other representations of them which we make, or they force on us.

In contrast, Aquinas has a non-subject-centred conception of the self: the objects out there in the world become intelligible in the act of awakening the intellectual acts on our part which manifest our intelligence.

Instead of being objects out there, either opposing us blankly or inertly waiting for us to look at them, so to speak, in our first-person perspective, it is the world that has priority, in the sense that objects elicit and configure the powers of the soul (as Thomas would say): 'With us, to understand is in a way to be passive' (*ST* I.79.2). Indeed, citing Aristotle, Thomas contends that the human mind is 'at first like a clean tablet [*tabula rasa*] on which nothing is written'. Certainly, we have to 'assign on the part of the intellect some power to make things actually intelligible'; but this capacity, which we are inclined to regard as primary or all-important since it seems to fall to us to impose intelligibility on things, is, according to Thomas (as to Aristotle before him), secondary. The intellect is a 'passive force' (*ST* I.79.2 ad 3).

In short, the difference between the prevailing modern conception of the self and that which we find in Thomas may be put in terms of a contrast between the modern 'subjectivist-observing' and the premodern 'objective-participant' perspective.

The contrast between a 'subjective-individualist' conception of persons and an 'objective-participant' conception is drawn by Christopher Gill in *Personality in Greek Epic, Tragedy and Philosophy: the Self in Dialogue*.[18] He finds the latter in ancient Greek philosophy and literature; but, citing Alasdair MacIntyre, Gill allows that 'medieval Christianity' can be seen as embodying one version of an objective-participant conception of human persons, in contrast with the 'more familiar type of Christian theorizing about personal identity' that he finds in the post-Cartesian soul–body dualism of Richard Swinburne. However that may be, it seems justifiable

---

18 Oxford: Clarendon Press, 1996.

to suggest that Thomas has a 'non-subject-centred' approach to human experience in the sense that he never pictures the mind as projecting significance on intrinsically unintelligible and valueless objects, but always rather as the actualization of intellectual capacities by potentially significant objects, according to the axiom '*intellectus in actu est intelligibile in actu*': our intellectual capacities actualized *are* the world's intelligibility realized.

VIII

Our experience of things is not a confrontation with something utterly alien, but a way of absorbing, and being absorbed by, the world to which we naturally belong. The mind does not primarily depict, reflect or mirror the world; rather, it assimilates the world as it is assimilated to the world.

That is an easy claim to make but, of course, very hard to explain as a philosophical account of our way of knowing, and our way thus of actually being in the world. Much else perhaps needs to be in place.

Aquinas takes for granted this non-subject-centred way of being in the world. We are inclined to begin with the mind, asking how our mental acts relate to the world; he begins on the contrary with the external objects which evoke intellectual activity on our part, and thus bring to fulfilment the capacities with which we are endowed.

We are inclined to assume that the objects of our knowledge remain totally unaffected. To be known, for an object unaware of it, is as if nothing had happened. This surely misses something. On Thomas's view, articulating as it does the doctrine of creation in terms of the metaphysics of participation, the object, in being known by the subject, is brought more clearly into the light and to that extent its nature and destiny are fulfilled.

It is easy to see how our minds are affected, changed, enriched and so on by absorbing what comes to view in the world. But for Thomas it makes sense to hold that, even if there were no human minds, things would still be 'true' – in relation, that is, to God's mind (for example *Quaestiones disputatae de veritate* q.1). He does not look at the world and see it as simply all that is the case, in itself; rather, he sees the world, and things in it, as destined to a certain fulfilment, with appointed ends, modes and opportunities. It is perhaps not too much to say that Thomas sees the way that things are in terms of the way that they ought to be. Certainly, he does not picture knowing as the subject's projecting value and intelligibility upon raw data. Rather, we exist at all only by participation in being (the doctrine of creation) and, since minds are what we are, we participate, by exercising our intellectual capacities, and of course to a very limited extent, in God's own knowledge of the world.

In short, is Thomas Aquinas's mind/world identity view of knowledge a possible way of recovering from what are perceived as still deeply entrenched and widely influential modern philosophical myths about the self and about our cognitive situation in the world? And secondly, is the thought that I am so much at home in the world that, in a certain way, in the event of meaning, I may be said to be the world, and the world to be in me, a thought that can be entertained apart from something like Thomas's characteristic emphasis on the doctrine of creation?

Many people, certainly philosophers, regard the world as inherently hostile or at least indifferent to human beings: unsurprisingly they have no difficulty in postulating some kind of screen between the mind and the world, a confrontation, perhaps a voluntaristic imposition of concepts on raw and hopelessly unreachable objects.

Others, with a naturalistic epistemology rooted in evolutionary theory, might argue that, biologically, we are animals in tune with the surrounding environment and it is not at all odd that our minds and the objects with which we deal ordinarily match perfectly. There need be no kind of theism in the background to make some such view plausible.

Others, in certain non-Christian religious traditions, which for Aquinas would have been represented typically by the Manicheanism against which he develops his theology of the goodness of being, might be inclined to posit some kind of veil between the mind and the world. Indeed, they might be inclined to say that the real world is radically inaccessible to the human mind.

For Thomas, in contrast to such views, human beings are created in God's image and likeness, and, more particularly, are born such that our minds are connaturally open to the world that reveals itself to us and even reveals itself as created. Well aware of alternative epistemologies, it seems likely that Thomas saw the mind/world identity theory not as an isolated instance of good philosophy, but as a philosophical conception that confirmed his perhaps optimistic and anthropocentric sense of how creatures of every kind, and certainly creatures of the human kind, are at home as participants in the world that is God's creation.

In the end, as always, Thomas relates everything back to God: as the image of God we too are each the source of our actions, as having free will and control of our actions (*ST* I-II, prologue). 'We receive knowledge from natural things', Aquinas says (for example *ST* I.14 ad 3), 'of which God, by his knowledge, is the cause': unsurprisingly, since we are born to know what there is and to love its goodness, on Thomas's view, our relationship with what there is – 'being' – would seem to him better expressed as identity than as either confrontation or inference from intervening entities.

In short, epistemology is not separable from theology. Aquinas was not conducting a speculative inquiry into human understanding for its own sake, or merely conjuring up polemics to discredit rival theories. In the end, he was interested in the activity of the human mind only in order to elucidate the way in which human beings imitate God.

The discussion goes even more deeply into darker matters than modern epistemology ever reaches.

There is no doubt that 'the subject/object relation' has been, and still is, central in recent Christian theological discussion (section I). The terms reversed their meaning in modern times; the subject/object relation is not the only possible way of thinking of ourselves in the world (section II). We might think the notion of subjectivity is much more intelligible and valuable in the context, say, of recent literature (section III). Leaving aside the discussions by Kierkegaard and Buber we see in modern theologians such as Torrance and Barth what the subject/object split is supposed to mean (section IV). Rational psychology as mandatory in neoThomistic philosophy highlights the thesis that the world and I are one in the act of knowing (section V). This thesis has given rise to a range of interpretations (section VI). One wonders, however, if this way of dealing with the subject/object or knower/known relationship does not rely on the Christian doctrine of creation (section VII).

Chapter 3

Speaking of the Unknowable God: Dilemmas of the Christian Discourse about God

Anselm Kyongsuk Min

In this paper I would like to begin with comments on the two points that Fr Kerr is making, the contrast he draws between modern and premodern approaches to knowledge as a contrast between a subjectivist, observer approach and an objectivist, participant approach, and his derivation of the Thomistic ontology of knowledge as participation from a theology of creation. I go on to show how St Thomas's theology of creation makes it possible to both speak of God in human language and preserve God's transcendent incomprehensibility, that is, to speak of God without committing anthropomorphism. I conclude with brief comments on the relation between metaphysics and the grammar of 'God', an issue that D.Z. Phillips raises in his inaugural essay of this volume.

Knowledge as Participation within a Theology of Creation

Kerr provides both an insightful survey of the many ways in which the subject-object relation was conceived in modern philosophy from Descartes to Coleridge, based on James Brown's *Subject and Object in Modern Theology*, and a perceptive review of the ways in which Protestants and Roman Catholics tried to cope, through a return to the Word of God and the revival of Thomism respectively, with the theological and epistemological consequences of the radical modern dualism of subject and object such as idolatry of human subjectivity and theological scepticism.

He goes on to make two points with regard to the position of St Thomas. One is that, for St Thomas, knowledge is not, as it is for much of modern thought, a confrontation between two mutually hostile, alien and isolated entities called subject and object, a veil that has to be removed or a gap that has to be filled, but a mode of union, assimilation and participation between two entities who are mutually ontologically oriented, between a subject and an object between whom there is, to use Lonergan's term, a structural isomorphism. This isomorphism or mutual ordering of the knower and the known has been indicated by the ancient Aristotelian axiom that St Thomas so often repeats, that the soul is 'in some way all things [*quoddammodo omnia*]' and that the intellect in act is the same as the intelligible in act. Knowledge is not an attempt on the part of a subject to dominate an object by imposing an intelligibility that has no ontological basis in the structure of the object as such; rather, it is a mode of union between two entities that primordially belong together and are mutually connatural, in such a way that the knower enables the intrinsically intelligible thing to become actually intelligible while the thing's becoming intelligible activates the mind's capacities. It is a process of mutual ontological enrichment, not a process of domination, suspicion or opposition. If the premodern Thomistic view regards knowledge as a process of objective participation, the modern view regards knowledge as a process of subjective observation. The recovery of St Thomas in this regard is one way of overcoming the modern dualism of subject and object.

The other point Professor Kerr makes, rather briefly, is that this participatory view of knowledge is inseparable from a theology of creation. That is to say, the structural isomorphism of the knower and the known is the result of creation in which God has endowed her creatures with isomorphic structures so that eventually they can all imitate and participate in God.

Now I would like to make a comment on the first point and add an elaboration on the second.

With regard to the first point, I am inclined to think that the contrast between the medieval Thomistic view of knowledge as assimilation and participation and the modern view of knowledge as domination and opposition veils a deeper contrast, the contrast between two fundamentally different approaches to reality as such. The medieval objectivist view is based on a contemplative approach, while the modern subjectivist view is based on an activist approach. The activist approach looks upon reality as something to be acted upon and transformed by the assertion of human subjectivity. To the activist, therefore, the world necessarily appears an object to be manipulated and presents itself to us only in its aspect that is particularly relevant to our subjective, human purposes and goals. It appears only in its instrumental value and only in its useful aspect, never as something intrinsically valuable and something possessed of its own integrity and depth. This approach is necessarily anthropocentric and utilitarian. It is based on an anthropology of action, of the human being as an agent in history, as distinct from the classical anthropology of thought, of the human being as a thinker or knower of being.[1] In relation to history, its typical claim is that history is not something given but something *made* by humans, that human beings are the *subjects* of history. In relation to knowledge, it is necessarily projectionist; its typical claim is that the world is what human subjectivity constitutes and interprets it to be.

The contemplative approach, on the other hand, looks upon reality as something *given* in its basic structures and orientations prior to the intervention of human subjectivity, and only seeks to comprehend and appreciate reality as a whole as it truly is in its ultimacy and depth by actualizing the intrinsic intelligibility already there. The part of the human being is not to impose his own subjectivity on the world and remake it altogether in his own image but to remain open to the self-disclosure of the world in its objectivity, totality, ultimacy and depth. It does not believe that human subjectivity is the constitutive source of the intelligibility of the world as moderns tend to claim. If human beings can constitute the world at all, it is only because they have already been themselves constituted to constitute the world and because the world itself has already been constituted so as to correspond to human constitution.

---

1   See my *Dialectic of Salvation* (Albany: State University of New York Press, 1989), 27–8, 163–9.

Contemplation takes reality as given, tries to know or contemplate it in all its aspects and implications, and enjoys both reality and our knowledge of that reality as an end in itself. This does not mean that human beings cannot or should not act on the world for the purpose of changing and transforming it, but it does mean that with regard to the basic structures, conditions and dynamics of the world, human beings are far more passive than active. Whatever we can do through action is limited by the basic conditions of life we have not created ourselves. A constructive action is possible only under the given ontological conditions of life and only in actualizing the potentialities already given in those conditions, just as all empirical knowledge is no more than the actualization of the mutual ordering of the activity of the intellect and the intelligible structure of the object. Whenever we act by violating such conditions, we are the first ones to suffer, as we now begin to realize in our ecological relation to nature. In a fundamental sense we do not, as modern homocentrism has claimed, either 'make' or 'constitute' the world.

In the case of St Thomas, this contemplative approach takes the form of a theology that is essentially theocentric, not anthropocentric. Its basic concern is to contemplate God as the ultimate origin and end of all things and all things in relation to God or *sub ratione Dei*. As such, it does not absolutize either nature as in much premodern culture or history as in the modern but God alone, relating both nature and history to God and thereby relativizing both.

In short, the relation between subject and object is not merely an epistemological issue; it is an issue involving fundamental attitudes toward reality as a whole. Clearly, overcoming the radical dualism of subject and object in modern philosophy, as the later Heidegger took pains to point out, requires a shift from the activist modern approach to a more contemplative approach to reality while also accommodating the practical necessity of transformative action within an essentially contemplative approach.

It is also important, however, to realize that this shift from the contemplative to the activist approach at the dawn of modernity took place for definite historical reasons. The modern Western era was an era of the colonial conquest of oceans and continents, the rise of contending nationalisms, the development of industrial capitalism and its technological conquest of nature, the overt struggle of the social classes for oppression and liberation, and the globalization of these struggles against other human groups and against nature in late twentieth century. The struggles unleashed by Western modernity have been awakening, reinforcing and highlighting the activist, aggressive, domineering, utilitarian sides of human nature, of which the many theories of human knowledge as constitution, interpretation and projection are the philosophical reflections. As this activist homocentrism wreaks its havoc on humanity in terms of the many global wars of destruction, the globalization of social conflicts and the massive destruction of nature, movements have been springing up demanding more harmonious, less aggressive and more cosmological perspectives and attitudes toward one another and the cosmos as a whole. With the return to a more cosmological and less anthropocentric view we have also seen a massive critique of Western modernity for its basic exploitative homocentrism and the lie it really is, as witness the writings of the later Heidegger, postmodernists, ecofeminists, ecological theologians, process thinkers and much Asian religious thought.

This does not mean that we can simply return to the premodern harmony of subject and object, the structural isomorphism of the knower and the known, without further ado. What is necessary, in my view, is to find a way not of eliminating the activist dimension of knowledge altogether, which is no longer possible, but of subordinating its role within a basically contemplative perspective, a way of maintaining a tension between action and contemplation within the unity of human existence and within the unity of humanity and nature. Without action aimed at social liberation and transformation, contemplation tends to breed indifference to evil and suffering in the name of the eternal; without a contemplative vision of the basic unity of all beings, action tends to reduce all reality – including humanity – to objects of human exploitation and reduce human life to a struggle for mutual domination.[2]

This also poses a challenging task to the Thomistic ontology of knowledge. It is important, indeed, to affirm the ontological unity of the knower and the known, the intellect and the object and elaborate the ontology of participation and assimilation. Without this ontology of participation human knowledge reduces itself to a purely ad hoc, subjectivist, projectionist action of the homocentric subject. In the contemporary world, however, the knower and the known rarely encounter each other in the peace of primordial harmony. Their relation is mediated by all the complexities of contemporary history reflected in cultural and religious pluralism, sociology and archaeology of knowledge, philosophy of science and the ideologies of power and domination. The Thomistic ontology of knowledge as participation needs to enter into dialogue with all of these contemporary mediators and disturbers of the ontological mutuality of the knower and the known and to acquire concreteness and relevance commensurate with the complexities of the contemporary epistemological situation. Thomism cannot remain content with the mere ahistorical affirmation of an ontology of participation, but must go on to develop that ontology in response to today's critical challenges. What we need is a Jacques Maritain for the twenty-first century.

Kerr's second point is that St Thomas's ontology of knowledge as participation is derivative from his theology of creation. Let me now elaborate a little on this theology. St Thomas begins by distinguishing among the truth of the human intellect, the truth of things and the truth of God. The human intellect is true when it is conformed to the object understood, which occurs when the intellect possesses the likeness or form of the object. The intellect, however, does not know this conformity when it apprehends the nature or form of the thing, but only when it *judges* that a thing corresponds to the form which it apprehends of the thing by composing and dividing or affirming and negating. The truth of the human mind formally lies in the judgment of the intellect, in apprehending a thing *as* it *is*, not in sense perception as such or in the intellectual apprehension of what a thing is. The truth of the human intellect is derivative from its conformity with the nature of things as they are, from which it receives its knowledge and which thus constitutes the 'principle' of

---

2   For an elaboration of the contrast between the contemplative and the activist approaches to reality and its relevance to contemporary theology, see Anselm K. Min, *Paths to the Triune God: An Encounter between Aquinas and Recent Theologies* (Notre Dame, IN: University of Notre Dame Press, 2005), ch. 7 ('Toward a Dialectic of Prophetic and Sapiential Theology: A Postcritical Retrieval of Aquinas').

human truth. The human intellect is not free to 'constitute' objects according to its own a priori subjectivity; it is bound by the objective nature of things.[3]

Just as the human intellect derives its truth from its relation of conformity with the nature of things, so things derive their truth from their conformity with the source of their being. Artificial things are true if they conform to and express the likeness [*similitudo*] of the forms in the mind of their maker, as a house is true if it conforms to the blueprint in the mind of its architect. In the same way all created things, natural or artificial, are products of the divine intellect, and are true if they express the likeness of the species in the divine intellect. Creatures as creatures, including artificial things, intrinsically [*per se*] depend on God for their very being [*esse*], while their dependence on the human mind for their knowability is accidental, not essential; they will continue to exist without the human mind. In this ontological sense things are simply or 'absolutely' [*absolute*] true when they conform to the divine mind, and true only accidentally or in a qualified sense when they conform to the human mind. Things are true in the simple or proper sense if they express their proper natures or forms according to the preconceptions in the divine mind, that is, if their existence conforms to their essence as originally conceived according to their idea or exemplar in the divine mind. Given the teleological understanding of natures and forms, this also means that things are true insofar as they fulfil the end to which they were ordained by the divine intellect and thereby imitate the divine source of their being. Ontologically, this reference of created beings to the divine intellect is prior to their reference to the human intellect that knows them. It is precisely the reference to the divine mind that makes them knowable by the human mind while they remain intrinsically knowable even without the existence of the human mind.[4]

As creator of all things the divine intellect by its essence contains the likeness of all things [*similitudo omnium rerum secundum suam essentiam*]. The blueprints or ideas of all things pre-exist in the mind of the creator, as the likeness of a house pre-exists in the mind of the architect. It is this blueprint or idea to which the nature of created things must conform and in which they must participate each according to its nature in order to be true. The divine idea is both the ultimate *ratio* in the sense of the principle of all speculative knowledge and the ultimate exemplar in the sense of the principle for the making of things. Now this divine idea is identical with the divine essence. God primarily knows her own essence and all other things as so many participations in her essence according to varying degrees of likeness to the divine blueprint. Truth in the sense of the conformity or equation of intellect and being or subject and object is realized to a supereminent degree in God as creator of all things. God's being is not only conformed to her intellect but *is* the very act of her intellect, and her act of understanding is the cause and measure of all things and all other minds. In this sense God is truth itself, the sovereign and first truth. The human mind derives its truth from its conformity to the nature of things, which in turn derive their truth from their conformity to the divine idea. There are as many truths as there are created intellects, and as many truths even in one intellect as there are things known. There are also as many forms or essences as there are things.

---

3   *Summa theologiae* [*ST*] I.16.2; I.16.5; *Quaestiones disputatae de veritate* 1, 8.
4   *ST* I.16.1; I.16.2; I.16.5; *De veritate* I, 1; I, 7.

However, both the truth of the human intellect and the truth of things ultimately derive from their conformity and assimilation to the one primary truth, which is the divine mind. The truth of the divine mind is the one truth to which all things are assimilated according to their essences and by which all things are true. The divine mind measures all things without being measured by them.

Truth, therefore, resides properly and primarily in the divine intellect and properly but only secondarily in the human intellect. The relation to the divine intellect is essential to the truth of things insofar as the divine intellect keeps bringing them into being [*esse*], while their relation to the human intellect is accidental. By their form through which things have their acts of existing, things both imitate the art of the divine intellect, which is their measure, and bring about a true apprehension of themselves in the human intellect so that the human mind can conform to the truth of things. Furthermore, it is the divine mind that has so ordered the human mind itself as to tend to truth as its own nature, end and good precisely by knowing the form of things. The truth of things, the truth of the human intellect, and their mutual orientation and connaturality derive from the teleological providence of the divine creator. All truths come from the one divine truth.[5]

For St Thomas, then, the theory of knowledge as participation in the isomorphic structure of the knower and the known is derivative from his theology of creation. Knowledge and truth are not something purely neutral, impartial or static. Rather, by knowing the natures and forms of things by which things fulfil their ends and participate in God, the human mind also fulfils its nature and end and participates in the teleological movement of the universe. For St Thomas, all things have been created in the image of God. To be created is not only to be a creature with an essence proper to itself but also to refer beyond itself to God by imaging, imitating, resembling and participating in God, whose creative wisdom and love sustains and structures the teleological movement of all creation. Non-intellectual things participate in God's activity simply by existing and living. Intellectual creatures participate in God's form by knowing and loving. The just participate in God's life by faith and charity which make them God's children through grace. The blessed participate in God's eternal life through the beatific vision of divine glory. To know is to know the truth of things, and to know the truth of things is to know things in the light of the supreme, first and ultimate truth which is God, which in turn is to participate in the teleological dynamics of creaturely participation in God.

Furthermore, for St Thomas, this creation of all things in the image of God is mediated through Christ, the eternal Word of the Father, who is the perfect image of the Father and therefore also the perfect exemplar, blueprint or model for all created things. This divine Word is the eternal law or plan for the divine government of the universe in which the Holy Spirit directs all things to their proper acts and ends each according to its own nature. All created things bear the imprint of the eternal law as an intrinsic principle of their being and acting. The law of nature or natural law is an imitation or participation in the eternal law that is the eternal Word and Son. Things have their truth only insofar as they imitate this eternal law and exemplar, Christ. It is the presence of this creative divine Logos or Word that guarantees

---

5   *ST* I.15.1; I.15.2; I.16.5; I.16.6; *De veritate* I, 4; I, 7; I, 8; III, 1.

the mutual connaturality and harmony between the knower and the known, the structural isomorphism of the Logos of the human knower and the Logos of the object to be known, and provides the theological basis of truth as the transcendental, universal characteristic of all beings, which in turn makes particular empirical acts of knowledge possible.[6]

Speaking of the Unknowable God

It is also this theology of creation that makes it possible for us both to truly speak of God in the only language we have, which is human language, and to speak of God in the way worthy of God, that is, without violating God's transcendent incomprehensibility without which we commit anthropomorphism and reduce God to a human projection.

Ever since Heidegger's critique of the ancient philosophy of substance and the ontotheological constitution of metaphysics, there has been a universal rejection of any idea of God who basically remains one object among others even when endowed with all the usual divine perfections. Such an idea is a product of human projection and an object of human idolatry, about which David Burrell's assertion in this volume is quite apropos: 'the more notions of the divinity tend towards idolatry, the more we will find them opposing one another like tribal gods,' leading to exclusivism and conflict of religions. No wonder, therefore, that every modern theology begins with the disclaimer that God is not an object among other objects. God is rather the ground of being, being itself (Tillich) or the ground of both being and our knowledge of being (Rahner). Behind this critique of the rather widespread anthropomorphic, ontotheological idea of God lies the perception that God is somehow a qualitatively different kind of being, which constitutes as it were the grammar of all talk about God. If God is truly God, God cannot be just another human being, however magnified or glorified she might be.

Is there anything in the theology of St Thomas which makes such an anthropomorphic conception of God in principle impossible? I don't think anyone modestly familiar with his theology would have any problem finding that his theology is fundamentally incompatible with any anthropomorphic conception of God. His stricture against anthropomorphism is much more decisive and definitive than similar strictures in many other theologians and philosophers. The fundamental stricture is based on the idea that God is a being in whom essence and existence coincide, whose very essence is to exist, who exists by her own essence and therefore can also create, that is, communicate the act of existing, the most profound act of all actuality, to all other entities and empower them to exist by participation. This distinction between creator and creature, between a being who exists by essence as the *ipsum esse per se subsistens* from which all the classical divine perfections follow, and all other beings who can exist only by participation, is the most universal, most fundamental and most radical division there can be. All other distinctions between finite individuals,

---

6   For an elaboration of this Trinitarian account of creation, see Min, *Paths to the Triune God*, ch. 1 ('Reason and Creation in Theology and Faith').

species and genera infinitely pale in significance by comparison. No one should confuse God as an infinite being, a being who exists by his own essence, with all other beings who are finite and can exist only by participation. God is not simply one being among other beings, an 'object' opposed to other 'subjects' or a subject opposed other objects, all existing at the same level. God is infinitely other than other entities, different from them all not just categorically but transcendentally. God always remains the 'light' or horizon in which we come to know and judge of all other things, not an 'object' – not even the highest object that can be known in itself – because she is the light in which all other things can be comprehended as objects. God exists indeed beyond the distinction and opposition of subject and object.

The task of a Christian philosophy or theology of God, however, is not simply to protect God against anthropomorphism; it also includes the much more difficult and complicated task of authorizing us to truly speak of God, although without being anthropomorphic. This requires analysis of the nature and limits of human knowledge in relation to the knowledge of God and reflection on this human knowledge in light of the doctrine of creation. Avoiding anthropomorphism is praiseworthy but not very consoling for human beings who can only know and speak as human beings can and therefore must so know and speak of God yet without falling into anthropomorphism. The alternative to anthropomorphism is not sheer silence or apophaticism. The task of theology, therefore, goes beyond mere strictures against anthropomorphism to defining the conditions which both prevent anthropomorphism and enable us to truly speak of God at the same time.

For St Thomas, the proper object of human knowledge, and therefore human predication, is the essence of material things. Because of the hylomorphic composition of the human knower – and, remember, one can only know according to one's nature – the basic paradigm of human knowledge remains that of sensible things and their relations in the world, precisely the source of the ontotheological constitution of metaphysics. Our knowledge of God 'does not transcend the genus of the knowledge gathered from sensible things'.[7] At best, we know God as we know the cause from its effects, from God's effects in nature as in philosophical knowledge or from God's effects in grace as in faith.[8] These effects indeed bear traces of likenesses to God, but such likeness is so imperfect as to be 'absolutely inadequate [*omnino insufficiens*] to manifest God's substance'.[9] The cognitive way to the essences of purely spiritual entities and, a fortiori, that of God, the sole purely actual entity, is permanently barred to the human intellect. The only way, therefore, available for the human being limited to the human mode of knowing is to infer to God from his effects and images in the material world by way of causality, negation and eminence, the so-called analogical way.

For St Thomas, creating means not only bringing into existence things that are not, but also empowering them to exist precisely by resembling, imitating and participating in God as her images and effects, that is, by reflecting something of the logic of the divine Word and the love of the Holy Spirit to the glory of the Father.

---

7 *Summa contra Gentiles* [*SCG*] 3, 47; also *Compendium Theologiae* I, 105.
8 See *ST* I.1.7.
9 *SCG* 1, 8.

Through creation the triune God empowers us to reflect and know God as far as creatures can reveal her as her images and effects. It is not our own power but precisely the creative power of God and the grace of divine motion that enables us to know and refer to God. Our language too can, to that extent, refer to God as the source and exemplar of our existence. Our knowledge of God as creator is really directed to God, not to a counterfeit or a figment of the human imagination.

This, however, is to know God only on the basis of her created effects and images and therefore only in relation to us as her effects and images, but not in herself or her essence. From God's effects and images we can indeed demonstrate that God exists, but this is a matter of only knowing that the judgment that God exists is true, not of having an intellectual intuition into the divine essence or act of existing which would make God's existence self-evident, precisely St Thomas's critique of the ontological argument.[10] Insofar as God remains the creator in whom essence and existence coincide and thus at an infinite distance from her finite creation, human knowledge and language will always remain infinitely inadequate to its divine object to which it is indeed empowered to point beyond itself but without ever being able to comprehend God in her proper essence with the same certainty and immediacy with which it can comprehend the essence of another material object to which human knowledge and human language are connatural. Any complacent reference to God, without the nagging self-questioning by a reverent, worshipful sense of God's transcendent incomprehensibility, will be not only naive anthropomorphism but also self-idolatrous anthropocentrism.

For St Thomas, in this life 'what God is not [*quid non est*] is clearer to us than what God is [*quid est*]', for God is above what we may say or think of him [*quod sit supra illud quod de Deo dicimus vel cogitamus*]'.[11] God surpasses all things 'infinitely according to every mode of transcendence [*in infinitum secundum omnimodum excessum*]'.[12] In fact, 'what is ultimate in human knowledge of God' is the Socratic confession that 'one knows that he does not know God, because he knows that what God is exceeds everything that we can understand of him'.[13] As long as we live in this world, even with the revelation of grace we cannot know what God is, and we are only 'united to him as to one unknown [*quasi ignoto*]'.[14] This incomprehensibility of God's essence is such that it does not cease even in the beatific vision, because God does not cease to be infinite any more than finite intellects cease to be finite. As Karl Rahner used to argue, divine incomprehensibility 'does not really decrease, but increases, in the vision of God'.[15] The *lumen gloriae* does not remove the gap between finite and infinite. God always remains more, radically and infinitely more, *semper major*.

---

10   *ST* I.3.4 ad 2; I.2.1.
11   *ST* I.1.9; also *SCG* 1, 5.
12   *ST* II-II.81.4.
13   *De Potentia* 7, 5 ad 14.
14   *ST* I.12.13 ad 1.
15   Karl Rahner, 'Thomas Aquinas on the Incomprehensibility of God', *Journal of Religion*, Special Supplement S109 (1978): 107–25; also his *Theological Investigations* 16, trans. David Morland (New York: Seabury, 1979), 244–54.

By creating and empowering us as her images and effects to imitate, resemble and participate in her, the triune God authorizes us to know her precisely as human beings and refer to her in human language, which is the way of causality. The infinite transcendence of God, however, also requires that we negate and exclude all the material and finite 'modes of signification' from all the attributes predicated of God, which is the way of negation. We affirm of God only the signified reality of all the perfections that are not intrinsically material or finite, such as being, unity, goodness, truth, wisdom, vitality and so on, and do so to a supereminent, infinite degree, pointing to something whose essence we can never comprehend, like an arrow shot into the dark, which is the way of eminence. It is crucial to insist that analogical attribution requires all three steps. Without the way of causality we are reduced to utter silence about God. Without the way of negation we are reduced to sheer anthropomorphism by reducing God to a mythological idol or an ideological projection. Without the way of eminence we are reduced to either silence or anthropomorphism, and fail to truly speak of the infinite God in her infinity in either case.[16]

Christian existence is inevitably caught in a tension between the need to do justice to God as God, and therefore to God in her genuine transcendence, and the need to speak of and worship God as a community using human language, which always remains more or less ontotheological. To give up on the first will be to give up on God and substitute human projections and idols, but to give up on the second will be to give up on what makes Christian faith Christian: namely, the faith that the inaccessible, transcendent God has nevertheless come close to us precisely in our human nature and therefore in our human mode of knowing and speaking. The hypostatic union of the human and the divine in Christ intensifies this epistemological and existential tension.

The union between the human and the divine in Christ means that the human is united to the divine and expresses and refers to something of the divine. Insofar as this union is so intimate as to be hypostatic or personal, there is even a sharing of proper characteristics [*communicatio idiomatum*]; what Christ does in his human nature such as preaching, healing, dying on the cross and rising from the dead can legitimately be predicated of the divine nature and divine person, the eternal Son and Word of the Father. It is legitimate to say that the divine Son died on the cross when the human Jesus did. The grace of hypostatic union makes it possible and necessary for the human nature of Christ to really express, reveal and refer to the divine person of the eternal Word. It is crucial to remember, however, that the relation between the human and the divine in Christ is precisely one of union, not identity. The human and the divine cannot be identical without self-contradiction, but they *can* be united and even united so intimately as to be hypostatic, not by virtue of any power on the part of the human but precisely by virtue of the divine grace of hypostatic union, which is what Christian faith teaches. Humans cannot unite themselves with God by their own power, but *God* can unite herself even personally with the human in order to share her love and goodness.

It is not only that it is divine grace which makes it possible for the human nature of Christ to express and refer to the divine, but also that the – infinite – distinction

---

16 See Min, *Paths to the Triune God*, chs 5 and 6.

and distance between the human and the divine remains despite the personal union. To deny this is to be guilty of Monophysitism. The union does not make the human nature cease to be human and finite any more than it makes the divine nature cease to be divine and infinite. Each nature remains in its full integrity and distinction. The self-transcendent reference of the human to the divine in Christ is itself the effect of the divine grace of hypostatic union, which makes it possible for the human to refer to the divine beyond itself but does so without cancelling the infinite difference between the divine and the human. The human nature reveals the divine precisely according to the human mode, which means that such revelation does not amount to an intuition into the divine essence but remains a 'pointing to' without ever becoming a 'seeing'.

The hypostatic union only assures us that it is the eternal Father *himself*, not merely an image or concept of the Father, that is truly revealed in the human experiences of Christ, but the Father is *himself* revealed precisely in the *human* nature of Christ, not in his own divine nature. One does not 'see' the eternal Father when one sees Jesus. If John's Gospel tells us that 'he who has seen me has seen the Father' (14:8), this seeing is seeing proper to faith, not to an intellectual or sensible intuition, and therefore an experience of Christ's humanity pointing beyond itself to the divine, an experience of the self-transcendence of the human to the divine and an experience of the self-transcendence of the divine to the human. The reference of the human to the divine in the incarnation, therefore, is one of intrinsic and infinite tension, not of complacent identity; the hypostatic union both preserves and overcomes the distance between the human and the divine.

This tension comes to a scandalous expression on the cross. Finding the eternal Son of God *in* the figure of a crucified criminal of an earthly empire indeed boggles the mind and intensifies to the extreme the tension of the human and the divine in the hypostatic union, the paradigmatic case of the relation between the finite and the infinite and therefore of all human knowledge and speech about God in Christian faith. For Kierkegaard this tension requires the 'crucifixion of the understanding'. All anthropomorphism founders on the rock of the crucified God. It is the analogy of being made most intense and tensive when sublated [*aufgehoben*] into an analogy of faith. It is no wonder that one is always tempted to avoid the tension by falling either into the easy, anthropomorphic Monophysitism of seeing only the divine in Christ, identifying it immediately with the human and seeing the divine in the human without negation and transcendence, or into the easy, dualistic Nestorianism of separating the human and the divine into two persons and seeing only the human person in Christ without also recognizing its hypostatic union with the divine.[17]

---

17 Min, *Paths to the Triune God*, ch. 7. For some of the best commentaries on the use of analogy in Aquinas and contemporary theology (Barth, Balthasar, Rahner, Jungel and Kasper), see Joseph Palakeel, *The Use of Analogy in Theological Discourse: An Investigation in Ecumenical Perspective* (Rome: Editrice Ponificia Universita Gregoriana, 1995) and Gregory P. Rocca OP, *Speaking the Incomprehensible God: Thomas Aquinas on the Interplay of Positive and Negative Theology* (Washington DC: The Catholic University of America Press, 2004).

The Christian therefore can only try to maintain an ongoing tension between the two poles of their faith. According to Rahner, all our statements about God are caught in an irreducible tension between their categorical or historical origin on the one hand and their self-transcendence to God to which they point on the other. Such a tension is not a secondary product of our logic trying to avoid univocity and equivocity, but a primordial tension which we *are* as spiritual subjects who can have a history only through transcendence and can transcend only through history. As the condition of the possibility of all categorical experience, transcendence is more original than categorical, univocal concepts. Analogy in its most primordial sense is none other than this transcendental movement of the spirit itself; it is not a subsequent midpoint, a hybrid, between univocity and equivocity, which are deficient modes of the more original analogical relationship to transcendence. Analogy indicates the tension between our categorical existence and the incomprehensibility of God. We *exist* the analogical tension between historicity and transcendence.[18]

I submit that the whole theological corpus of St Thomas is a living testimony to this analogical tension that constitutes our very existence and therefore also our knowledge and language. I also suggest that the anthropomorphic crisis of much contemporary philosophy of religion in the analytic tradition is really due to the absence of the analogical sensibility and the failure to maintain the analogical tension.

The Grammar and Metaphysics of 'God'

The 'grammar' of God in St Thomas is based on this metaphysical analysis of the structure of being in God and other entities. Through a very comprehensive and extremely sophisticated metaphysical analysis Aquinas shows the infinite transcendence of God over all finite beings and provides the ontological basis for the grammar of God or the laws that govern our speech about God. We speak of God in a certain way because God is or exists in a certain way. It is not that God is in a certain way because we speak of God in a certain way. The grammar or linguistic logic of God is derivative from the ontologic of God, not the other way round. If, as Phillips interprets Rush Rhees, 'love' and 'grace' are 'grammatical' attributes of God, that is, part of what we mean by 'God', it is so only because God is a certain kind of being to which such attributes are deemed essential. Without an analysis of this ontologic the grammar of God becomes baseless, arbitrary, something merely asserted, without justification. It is not enough to condemn a theory, for example, the finitist process theory of God, for violating the grammar of God; it is also necessary to provide a metaphysical analysis of that theory and show how that theory fails to do justice to the being of God and thereby violates the grammar of God. The grammar of something depends on the metaphysical analysis of the kind of being it is. Different kinds of beings require different kinds of grammar.

To be sure, this ontologic must also be nurtured in a community of faith, but a community of faith as a community of human beings also has a capacity for self-

---

18 Karl Rahner, *Foundations of Christian Faith: an Introduction to the Idea of Christianity* (New York: Seabury, 1978), 71–3.

reflection and self-criticism. It does not accept something simply because it has been there in its tradition; it can be there in the first place only because the community has found it in some way acceptable in an ongoing dialectic between its own growing self-consciousness and the validity of the content of its faith. This also means that there is no one grammar of God simply given for all times and places. It is itself dependent on the different historical experiences of the many different religious communities of humankind. The Christian grammar of 'God' is not something simply intuitively given, but a result of a long process of communal and philosophical reflection. As Rush Rhees is quoted as saying in Phillips's inaugural essay, grammars can and do change through 'new factual discoveries and theoretical developments'. An appeal to a mere intuitive sense of difference between God and creatures, unsupported by a sense of historical and philosophical development, is liable to hide all kinds of naive assumptions.

D.Z. Phillips raises the question of whether it makes sense to talk about the inadequacy of language when it is precisely within language that the transcendence, the mystery of God, is recognized and celebrated. As Jean Luc Marion, Jacques Derrida and Catherine Pickstock all agree, it is precisely in the liturgy or prayer that we speak to God precisely as transcendent, the equivalent of the affirmation, negation and eminence that constitute the way of analogy. It is important, however, to note that when we speak of the inadequacy of language in relation to God, we are speaking of the inadequacy of language to express what God is *in her essence* as distinct from what she is known to be on the basis of her created effects and signs, and that the experience of God in prayer and liturgy is not the direct vision of the divine essence, which remains inaccessible to our vision and therefore to our knowledge and language, not only in this world but also in the next. The divine essence is not reducible to the linguistic context, which can at best reveal God precisely as transcending that context, which is not quite the same as comprehending and expressing God in the fullness of her essence.

The issue is not whether worship fails because of the limitation of language, but whether language itself fails to express God in her essence. For Aquinas and the classical tradition, all human language is inadequate to express the essence of God because there is no proportion between the subject, the human knower, and the object, the divine essence. The success of worship is itself dependent on the recognition of this inadequacy. In worship we speak and appeal to God and praise him precisely as holy, transcendent, infinitely other than a created being, and thus beyond the ability of any human language to express adequately. The sense of the holy, of the 'you alone are holy [*tu solus sanctus*]', increases insofar as our worship maintains the tension between the inevitable use of human language in the liturgy and the admission of its own inadequacy to its holy object, between the affirmation of God in human language and the negation and elevation of that affirmation beyond the human. Speaking of God means 'knowing' God indeed but knowing God precisely *as* unknowable in her essence. Without the element of negation worship lapses into pure human discourse among equals; without the element of affirmation there is no human worship. The success of worship is itself dependent on the recognition of its own linguistic inadequacy, on its ability to speak of God precisely *as* unknowable.

That 'words cannot express how grateful I am' is indeed a statement of gratitude, as Phillips argues, not a failure to express gratitude due to the limitation of language; but it is essential to note that the success of the expression of gratitude does depend on the admission that words cannot express how grateful one is. The issue here again is not whether the statement succeeds or fails as an expression of gratitude, but whether this expression of gratitude contains precisely as an intrinsic element the expression of the inability to express the fullness of gratitude. The successful expression of gratitude does not depend on the ability of words to express the fullness of gratitude, but precisely on its opposite, their inability to do so: that is, on the simultaneous affirmation of the intention to express gratitude and negation of the ability to adequately do so. It is parasitic on recognition of this inability; it uses words precisely as incapable of expressing the fullness of gratitude. The success of the expression of gratitude, therefore, does not deny but presupposes the inability of words to express gratitude adequately.

Voices in Discussion

D.Z. Phillips

E: Fergus Kerr has brought out well for us the difference between a modern and premodern conception of knowledge. In the modern context, the relation between the knower and the known is one between two alienated objects between which a bridge has to be built. On the premodern conception, the relation between the knower and the known is one of assimilation and orientation. There is a structural isomorphism between the knower and the known. So the first is the active approach (one of praxis and so on), whereas the other is a contemplative approach to the world. On the active approach, what is known is an object to be manipulated. It is of no value initially. The value it has is one given by us as we project value and meaning on to the world as agents. Things have a certain utilitarian aspect. On the contemplative approach, reality is a 'given' and the possibility of being known by the subject depends on the structural reality it already has as a creation by God. We do not make the world. The world is independent of anything we care to think about it. We discover the nature of the world when we discover the structure it already has. There is a shift from the dualism of the modern conception to the contemplation of the world as it is. For Christians, this 'knowing' is in the image of the triune God, and Christ is the perfect exemplar of all created responses to the world. All this is an expression of the divine law and governance of the world.

In Heidegger, we find a critique of onto-theology. There is an insistence that God is not one being among others, but being itself or the ground of being. That insistence is clear in Aquinas. God is not an object among objects. God is 'infinitely other'. The grammar of God is shown through this metaphysical analysis. We speak as we do about God because God is a certain way. What is 'given' is not arbitrary. True, for believers, it is given to a community of faith, but it is also a community of reflective people.

But where God is concerned, our language is radically inadequate. We do not know God as he is, but only through his effects. God is not known as he is even in the beatific vision. The liturgy, too, is not a divine vision. This is because there is a lack of proportionality between the knower and the known. So there is always a tension in our language between that which affirms and that which negates in our relation to God, and that tension is primordial.

C: I want to ask about the structural character of the world which makes thought about it possible. Take, for example, counting. We can say 'There are seven sheep in a field.' But suppose there were a tribe that didn't count. Instead, they speak in terms of 'many', 'not many', 'not enough' and so on. Are you saying that the objects in the field, the sheep, make it necessary, in some sense, that we count them so that even if, in fact, they aren't counted, they exist with the property of 'countability'?

E: He couldn't count the sheep unless they were capable of being counted. The knower discovers something about the character of what is known. That is the conception that is lost in modernity. Epistemic access depends on the nature of what is known.

G: After all, take geometrical truths. Aren't they true before the actual practice of geometry? The truths are not temporal.

H: Can we go back to premodern conceptions? Why is it not possible to begin with human agencies and their activities and to see that their very agency in science and elsewhere as the route by which we acquire new insights about religion?

B: Aquinas is full of talk of agency. Human agency is where one has to begin even if we want to talk about God. But he does not end there.

D: The issue being raised here is the central philosophical issue of the natural fittingness or otherwise of the human mind and the world. If you say it is fitting, what sort of thesis is that? It is certainly not a scientific hypothesis, since any attempt to treat it as such presupposes what is being questioned.

E: What is in question for Aquinas is insight into the nature of things. The belief in creation justifies belief in the order of things and was, in fact, a stimulus for scientists to investigate that order. But, theologically, the order is a 'given' by God.

G: Of course, one can always invoke the prospect of the Demon who is deceiving us all the time.

C: The questions of truth that have been raised side-step the earlier question I was raising about the recourse to a structural account of reality. Of course, if one is counting, it will be either true or false that there are seven sheep in the field. What I was asking was whether the activity of counting, in which the sense of the true or false answers to the question – 'How many sheep there are in the field?' – have their sense, is itself determined by the structure of the world, such that given the structure, counting had to develop among human beings.

It has been put to me that this is too strong a demand. For example, although there is a natural development from an acorn to an oak, it does not follow that the acorn must become an oak. In fact, we know that millions don't; they are crushed or prevented from developing in some other way. But it is still the case that without the acorn, the oak cannot emerge. Moreover, if asked what the oak emerges from, the answer is acorns.

The analogy is not a good one. With the acorn and the oak we have a natural development which we have observed. If the acorn doesn't develop into an oak, we ask what went wrong, and we come up with the appropriate explanation. But if a tribe does not have the practice of counting, can we say that something has gone wrong? Can we say that they have not developed as they ought to develop? Science did not develop among some so-called primitive peoples. Some early anthropologists said that this fact showed that they were at an early stage of human development.

Science is more rational than magic. The latter may be challenged as to whether it achieves better results than the former. But the tribe is not trying to solve our scientific problems; it doesn't have those problems.

Given all this, what does it mean to say that science depends on the independent structure of the world, or that counting does? What more does it say than that when science and counting do develop, such-and-such calculations etc. are made possible. But these activities are not underwritten by a structural necessity that makes them happen.

E: But I want to distinguish between the premodern and modern conceptions. In the modern conception, the modes of reasoning are looked at as our representations of the world, but in the premodern view – what I have called the contemplative view – the representations presuppose the structures of the world which make them possible. We discover truths about the nature of things, and those natures are part of the structures of the world. If the world were chaotic we couldn't have an orderly investigation of it. The order of the world is presupposed by our investigations.

C: But what does the appeal to the structure of the world add to saying that if you conducted such-and-such investigations you would get such-and-such results? Because this doesn't show that such investigations are themselves determined by the structure of the world. What are you going to say if those investigations do not occur?

G: Then we can say that they are potentialities in the world.

C: So it leads to the idea of a structure full of potentialities before they develop?

G: But since the potentialities are true of the structure, they are necessary possibilities that belong to the structure of the world.

I: But to speak of a necessary possibility is to say that the possibility will in fact be realized. So that begs the question, since the issue being raised is whether the mode of reasoning is determined by a structure of the world which underlines it.

E: You can't count the sheep unless the sheep have a nature that is countable.

C: It is true that unless physical objects were stable over time you couldn't count them. But it doesn't follow that stability is the foundation of the activity of counting. It is not as though the sheep prior to the activity of counting had the property of being 'countable'. Counting is an activity. If it is applied to natural objects certain questions and answers are made possible through such an application, such as, 'How many sheep are in the field?' But it is the application of mathematics to natural objects which makes such calculations possible, not the discovery of a property called 'countability' in the sheep.

J: But how would D.Z. Phillips speak of the relation between the scientific explanation of diseases by reference to germs and talk of spirit possession?

C: It would depend on what the talk of spirits amounted to. It may turn out that certain aspects of that talk are in fact in conflict with theoretical explanations and would be superseded or overthrown by them, but this need not be the case. The belief in spirits need not be a theory at all. This doesn't mean that there can't be conflict between them. One may erode the other. Take the example of a tribe who believe in a holy mountain. Explorers discover gold in the mountain and the tribe gets to know of it. Soon fights and disputes break out as people clamber to possess the gold. The mountain's holiness does not survive the utilitarian manipulation of it. Does this show that the belief in the holiness of the mountain has been falsified? No. It shows how one kind of interest in the world can erode that way of thinking. Not that it must erode it, but that it can. Would it make sense to say that the mountain still retained a property called 'holiness'?

E: I still want to say that the contemplative attitude to the world is interested in 'how the world is', whether it is intelligible and so on. This interest has dangers because it can lead to complacency in face of the need to change. That is why I became interested in Hegelianism. It seemed to seek to do justice to historical change and development. In the end, however, I concluded that Hegel is reductionist. He reduces reality to our own modes of thought and does not do justice to the central desire to know how things are in themselves; an enterprise to which Aquinas does justice.

Chapter 4

The 'Grammar' of 'God' and 'Being': Making Sense of Talking about the One True God in Different Metaphysical Traditions

Gyula Klima

Introduction: Is There a 'Grammar' of 'God'?

Is there a grammar of the name 'God'? In an obvious and trivial sense there certainly is. This term, being a part of the English language, has to obey the grammatical rules of that language. So, for example, by consulting the relevant textbooks and dictionaries we can establish that 'God' is a noun, so it can function as the subject or predicate of simple categorical sentences, but it cannot, for example, function as a verb or a preposition.

But perhaps it can, or at least *could*. After all, as our medieval colleagues often emphasized: *nomina sunt ad placitum* – names are conventional; we use them at will, as we please. For example, the 'creators' of the popular search engine Google managed to introduce its name into our language in 1998, and they then succeeded in turning the name into a commonly used verb just two years later.[1] So what could prevent anyone from starting to use the word 'God' in a similar way, and from forming verbal derivatives from it analogous to, say, 'googled' and 'googling'? Apparently, nothing.

But then again, does this mean that I can go ahead and use the word just *any* way *I* want? Would that yield anything but some strange stares from my audience? Most probably, my using the word in some odd way would simply be taken as a sign of my linguistic (or some other sort of) incompetence. So, even if we obviously *can* use a word any way we wish, not just any such use would be regarded as acceptable.

---

1   'Rarely do we know the exact circumstances surrounding the coining of a brand new word. But in the case of googol, a mathematical term for the number represented by a one followed by 100 zeroes, or 10^{100}, we know exactly who coined it. In 1940, Mathematician Edward Kasner asked his nephew, nine-year-old Milton Sirotta, to come up with a name for such a big number. Sirotta came up with googol and also suggested the term googolplex for an even bigger number. Kasner assigned that term the value of ten to the googol power. The name of the search engine and software company, Google, is a deliberate variant of the mathematical term. The company's founders, Larry Page and Sergey Brin, came up with the name in 1998. They altered the spelling for trademark purposes. The verb to google, meaning to search for something on the World Wide Web, particularly to search using the Google search engine, is from the corporate trademark and dates to 2000.' <http://www.wordorigins.org/wordorg.htm>. Last updated 15 August 2004, © 1997–2004, by David Wilton. *Se non è vero è ben trovato.*

But then, *whose* usage is it that should count as acceptable or, indeed, as setting the standard for acceptable usage? And why is this question important from a philosophical point of view?

Clearly, the philosophical relevance of the question consists in the fact that different uses of the same word may express its different senses. And the same word being used by different philosophers in different senses can easily lead to equivocations in their debates, yielding the well-known phenomenon of philosophers talking past each other, committing the fallacy of *ignoratio elenchi*.

So, in order to avoid the misunderstandings and mere verbal quibbles characteristic of this situation, philosophers have to clarify their meaning, and have to agree on what they would regard as the proper sense of the terms causing the confusion. But is there such a thing as 'the proper sense' of a term and, if so, who or what establishes it?

If we can use a term in some improper sense (as I would be using 'God' if I started using it as a verb), then it has to have some proper sense, for we call the improper sense 'improper' only as opposed to what we take to be 'proper'. But just because the term has to have *some* proper sense, it does not follow that the term has only *one* proper sense. It would be ridiculous, for example, to try to rule out the several verbal senses of the word 'bat' as improper (as in talking about batting an eye or the batting average of a baseball player) on the grounds that *the* proper sense of the word is that in which we use it to talk about certain flying mammals. So, of course, the same term may have several, equally legitimate and proper uses and senses in the same language, provided that the term in question is equivocal, or when at least it is not purely univocal. And, equally obviously, what establishes any of these uses and senses as proper and acceptable is the existence of the well-established common usage of that term in that sense, an existing linguistic tradition that in better dictionaries is also supported by citations of authoritative texts clearly illustrating, or even explicitly establishing, the sense in question.

Thus, although it is clearly within my power to use any word in any odd, idiosyncratic way I wish, I can only do so at the risk of disqualifying myself as a competent speaker of the language, at least with regard to some proper usage of the term in question. Of course, this is not to say that I cannot legitimately use a term in some improper way, say, for the sake of humour, irony, poetic expression and so on. But these 'secondary language-games' presuppose my competence in the 'primary language-game' of understanding and being able to use the term in its proper sense or senses in the first place. Thus, to 'participate in the game' of speaking the language, I first must be able to align my usage with an existing linguistic tradition, which then of course I can also influence in my own ways, if I manage to establish some authority concerning some uses of some terms.

The philosophically relevant lesson of these (rather trivial) points seems to be the following. In the first place, although (nay, *because*) linguistic usage is conventional, it cannot be entirely arbitrary. One can only qualify as a competent user of the language by aligning one's usage with an established linguistic tradition, based on some commonly accepted authoritative usage. In the second place, joining a linguistic community as a competent speaker consists precisely in conforming to the authoritative usage of that community. However, even within the same language as well as across different languages there are various linguistic communities with various standards for usage based on various types of authorities, and, even within what may be identified as one and the same community concerning the usage of certain parts of their language or languages, modifications (indeed, *schisms*) may develop over time. Therefore, rational conversation within the same language and within the same linguistic community is inevitably exposed to the contingencies of this dynamic of emerging and falling linguistic authorities and correspondingly changing meaning and usage. To be sure, this is nothing to despair about. One only has to be constantly aware of and reflect on this dynamic in order to keep rational discourse across the board possible.

So, with respect to 'the grammar' of 'God' and its equivalents in other languages, when questions arise as to 'Whose God?' and according to 'Which tradition?' philosophers of religion are talking about, then it is precisely this phenomenon that we need to reflect on. In view of the foregoing, therefore, these reflections should begin with what we should regard as the proper authoritative uses of the term, at least insofar as they are relevant to the particular issues we are considering.

Linguistic Authority, Imposition, Sense and Reference

To be sure, talking about some 'linguistic authority' above, I certainly didn't mean a policeman with a baton in his right hand and a dictionary in his left one. A linguistic authority is just anybody whose usage is regarded in some community of speakers as authoritative, as setting the standard for some proper sense of some phrase in that usage. The usage setting this standard may be provided in the form of an explicit definition, as for example Boethius's definitions of 'person' (*substantia individua intellectualis naturae*; an individual substance of intellectual nature) or 'eternity' (*interminabilis vitae tota simul perfecta possessio*; the perfect possession of an interminable life, the whole, together) were regarded in the Middle Ages, or may be taken to be embedded in authoritative, axiomatic statements, as for example Aristotle's descriptions of unity (*unum est ens indivisum*; what is one is an undivided being) or goodness (*bonum est quod omnia appetunt*; the good is what everything desires), which, being transcendentals, are strictly speaking indefinable.

One of the foremost authorities for Western Christianity's usage of 'God' and its equivalents ('*Deus*', '*Dieu*', '*Gott*', '*Isten*' and so forth) spelled with a capital letter is certainly St Augustine. In his *On Christian Doctrine*, Book I, Chapter 7, he describes what 'all men understand by the term "God"' as follows:

> For when the one supreme God of gods is thought of, even by those who believe that there are other gods, and who call them by that name, and worship them as gods, their thought takes the form of an endeavour to reach the conception of a nature, than which nothing more excellent or more exalted exists. And since men are moved by different kinds of pleasures, partly by those which pertain to the bodily senses, partly by those which pertain to the intellect and soul, those of them who are in bondage to sense think that either the heavens, or what appears to be most brilliant in the heavens, or the universe itself, is God of gods: or if they try to get beyond the universe, they picture to themselves something of dazzling brightness, and think of it vaguely as infinite, or of the most beautiful form conceivable; or they represent it in the form of the human body, if they think that superior

to all others. Or if they think that there is no one God supreme above the rest, but that there are many or even innumerable gods of equal rank, still these too they conceive as possessed of shape and form, according to what each man thinks the pattern of excellence. Those, on the other hand, who endeavour by an effort of the intelligence to reach a conception of God, place Him above all visible and bodily natures, and even above all intelligent and spiritual natures that are subject to change. All, however, strive emulously to exalt the excellence of God: nor could any one be found to believe that any being to whom there exists a superior is God. And so all concur in believing that God is that which excels in dignity all other objects.[2]

As Augustine concludes in this passage, the idea of 'God' with a capital 'G', that is, when the term is used to refer to what people take to be the God of gods, is that of something that is absolutely better than everything else. Now, it is important to notice here that under this characterization of the intended sense of the term, it can only apply to one object. For if something is better than everything else, absolutely speaking, then there cannot be another such thing, given the irreflexivity and transitivity of the relation 'is better than'. For if there were two such things, say **a** and **b**, then **a** would have to be better than **b**, and **b** would have to be better than **a**. But then, by the transitivity of 'is better than', **a** would have to be better than **a**, which is impossible because of the irreflexivity of the same relation.[3] So, there can only be one 'God of gods', which at once establishes that whoever is talking about other 'gods' is not talking about the same God. Therefore, the word with a capital 'G' is only properly used if it is intended to refer to the God of a monotheistic religion, given that the uniqueness of its intended referent is built into its intended meaning (for those who are willing to accept Augustine's text as at least linguistically authoritative).

---

2   "Deum omnes intellegunt, quo nihil melius. Nam cum ille unus cogitatur deorum Deus, ab his etiam qui alios et suspicantur et vocant et colunt deos sive in caelo sive in terra, ita cogitatur ut aliquid quo nihil sit melius atque sublimius illa cogitatio conetur attingere. Sane quoniam diversis moventur bonis, partim eis quae ad corporis sensum, partim eis quae ad animi intellegentiam pertinent, illi qui dediti sunt corporis sensibus, aut ipsum caelum aut quod in caelo fulgentissimum vident, aut ipsum mundum Deum deorum esse arbitrantur. Aut, si extra mundum ire contendunt, aliquid lucidum imaginantur idque vel infinitum vel ea forma quae optima videtur, inani suspicione constituunt, aut humani corporis figuram cogitant, si eam ceteris anteponunt. Quod si unum Deum deorum esse non putant et potius multos aut innumerabiles aequalis ordinis deos, etiam eos tamen prout cuique aliquid corporis videtur excellere, ita figuratos animo tenent. Illi autem qui per intellegentiam pergunt videre quod Deus est, omnibus eum naturis visibilibus et corporalibus, intellegibilibus vero et spiritalibus, omnibus mutabilibus praeferunt. Omnes tamen certatim pro excellentia Dei dimicant, nec quisquam inveniri potest qui hoc Deum credat esse quo est aliquid melius. Itaque omnes hoc Deum esse consentiunt quod ceteris rebus omnibus anteponunt." Translated by the Rev. Professor J.F. Shaw; excerpted from *Nicene and Post-Nicene Fathers*, series 1, vol. 2; edited by Philip Schaff (New York: The Christian Literature Publishing Co., 1890).

3   Cf. "Non enim possibile est esse duo summe bona. Quod enim per superabundantiam dicitur, in uno tantum invenitur. Deus autem est summum bonum, ut ostensum est. Deus igitur est unus." – "There cannot be two things that are supremely good. For what is predicated in the superlative, applies only to one. But God is the supreme good, as has been shown. Therefore, there is one God." (When not indicated otherwise, translations are mine.) Aquinas, *Summa contra Gentiles* I, 42, 2.

Still, it is important to note here that this does not turn the name into a grammatically *proper noun*. A proper noun has a unique referent because it is given to one individual in an act of name-giving, or as our medieval colleagues would put it, an *act of imposition* (*impositio*), directly targeting that individual as the intended referent of the name. Indeed, this is the reason why if the same name happens to be given to several persons as a result of several impositions, the persons will be named by that name homonymously. A common term, on the other hand, is not imposed on one object: as far as its imposition is concerned, it might apply to several individuals, for the name-giver is not giving it to one individual with the intention of referring only to that individual. This is precisely why it could apply to several individuals univocally, whether there actually are, or just can be, several individuals it applies to or not. Still, it can be the case that the specification of the meaning of the name along with other semantic principles implies that there cannot be more than one thing to which the name applies. This is the case with the name 'God' as its intended meaning is specified by Augustine.[4]

But then, if the name in the intended sense can apply only to one object, it seems to follow that whoever is talking about God must be talking about the same God. Therefore, at least *all monotheistic religions must be talking about the same God*. But then, if the sense in which the term is used is nothing but what its users understand by it (if, that is, it is the same as the conception they form in their mind when they use the term with understanding), does this mean that all monotheistic believers must have the same conception of God? Or, conversely, does it mean that believers in polytheistic religions cannot use the term in the same sense, and therefore cannot have the same concept of God, and therefore cannot even talk about the same God?

Sense, Reference and Use

Let me begin with this last question first, because it raises most obviously the issue of the difference in sense and reference of the term 'God' with a capital 'G' (that in Augustine's intended sense is not properly applicable in the plural form) and the lower case 'god' (that is properly used in plural form).

On standard semantic accounts of sense and reference, sense determines reference (intension determines extension, connotation determines denotation and so forth). And on pure semantic grounds this is how it should be. After all, a term is supposed to refer to what satisfies the conditions of its applicability specified by its sense. So, if a term has different senses, it may refer to different sorts of things in accordance with those different senses. But the same sense of the same term determines the same reference. Therefore, difference in reference should indicate difference in sense. So, if in one of its senses only one thing can satisfy the conditions of the term's applicability, then in that sense it can refer only to that one thing, even if it is not a singular term by imposition. But then, if the term is used to refer to something else, then it can only be used in a different sense. So, it may seem that the pagan Romans whose beliefs Augustine recalled in this passage must have used the term '*deus*' in

---

4   Cf. Aquinas, *Summa Theologiae* I.13.9.

a sense that is different from Augustine's intended sense of the same term when he is talking about the God of gods, and so it may seem that they just did not have the same conception that Augustine presents here, despite what he says about what *all* people understand by the name.

However, in actual situations of actual uses of a term, including both proper and improper uses, pragmatic factors complicating this simple semantic picture also have to be taken into account. For different users may have different degrees of competence, different, occasionally conflicting authoritative paradigms to follow, different intentions on different occasions and so on. Furthermore, even when they are willing and able to use the term properly and competently, they are not logically omniscient, that is, they may not be aware of all implications of the term in the sense they intend to use it, or they may be just ignorant or mistaken about whether some thing satisfies its conditions of applicability, and thus they may simply misapply it. All these pragmatic factors will then alter the simple semantic picture according to which a given sense of a given term determines what the term stands for.

In fact, medieval logicians were very much aware both of the immense variability of sense (*singificatio*) and of the context-dependence of reference (*suppositio*) in actual use, which they deliberately built into their *semantic* theory itself. So, it should not be surprising that medieval theologians, trained in this type of semantic theory, were also extremely sensitive to these issues.

Thus when Aquinas in q.13, a.10 of the first part of the *Summa Theologiae* addresses the issue of various uses of the term 'God', he contrasts the proper (*per naturam*) use of the term with its metaphorical (*per participationem*) and putative (*secundum opinionem*) uses.[5] According to Aquinas's determination of the question, these different uses express different, yet not unrelated senses of the same term. The primary, proper sense of the term is expressed when it is used to signify true divine nature and thus to refer to what has this divine nature. This is the way Christians use the term to talk about the Christian God. The metaphorical sense of the term is expressed when we improperly call something or someone 'a god' or 'divine' on account of some excellence, imitating divine perfection. Finally, the putative sense of the term is expressed when it is used to refer to what other people believe to be God, but what the speaker would not believe to be God. This is the way Christians talk about 'the gods of the pagans', intending the term to be used *not* in its proper sense, to signify divine nature, but improperly, to signify what other people (according to the Christians mistakenly) believe to be divine nature. This is how it happens, then, that believers of different religions – indeed, even believers of different *monotheistic* religions – take believers of other religions to talk not about God, properly speaking, but about something else, describable in the putative sense as '*their* God' or 'their gods' (as in the Psalms, quoted by Aquinas, 'all the gods of the pagans are demons').

---

5   The English phrases in this sentence are not, strictly speaking, translations of the Latin phrases that follow them in parentheses. But I hope the subsequent discussion will justify the use of these 'smoother' English expressions, as properly conveying the intended sense of Aquinas's distinctions. The strict translations would be 'according to nature', 'according to participation' and 'according to opinion' respectively.

However, this is also the way pagan Romans would use the term to talk about 'that God of the Christians or Jews', while they would talk about Jupiter or Mars as being the true Gods, in the proper sense of the word.[6] This is precisely why the pagan and the Christian can genuinely contradict each other: they both intend the same proper sense of the term in which it signifies true divine nature when for instance they say 'Jupiter is God' and 'Jupiter is not God'. Indeed, the Christian may further express his denial by saying 'that God of yours is not God'. In this sentence, the complex subject term ('that God of yours') carries the putative sense of the term 'God', referring to a Roman god, say Jupiter, whereas in the predicate it expresses the proper sense of the term, intending to signify true divine nature. But the Roman might also retort by the exact same sentence, although this time the subject in the putative sense of the term would refer to the Christian's God, whereas in the predicate it would intend to signify again true divine nature as it did when the Christian uttered it.

So the pagan and the Christian can (and in the predicate of this sentence do) use the same term in the same sense, for otherwise they could not contradict each other. Still, they obviously do not have the same conception of divinity; indeed, that is *precisely* the reason why they contradict each other.

Metaphysical Theories vs Semantical Rules

Accordingly, it seems that it is possible for different users to use the same term in the same sense, yet to have rather different conceptions about what is signified by the term in that sense. Despite possible intuitions to the contrary, this happens regularly. Consider for instance the term 'gold'. This term was imposed to signify the true nature of gold, whatever it is. Therefore, when something merely looks like gold, but is revealed not to have the true nature of gold, such as fool's gold (iron sulfide), then it is immediately declared not to be gold. This is something all competent users of the term know, regardless of what conceptions they have of exactly what it is that is signified by the term. Thus, the ordinary gold-digger, the alchemist, as well as the modern chemist mean the same by the term 'gold' properly speaking: namely, the true nature of gold, even if the first may have only some vague and obscure idea about what the true nature of gold is, the second may have a totally mistaken idea about it and the third perhaps possesses an articulate conception that adequately represents that nature. Still, it is the same nature – no matter what they may vaguely comprehend, mistakenly believe or strictly know about it – that they all signify when they use the term properly, as opposed to using it to indicate what they take to be the other's inarticulate or mistaken conception.

So, if we assume that the modern chemist is right about the nature of gold when he thinks of it as the element of atomic number 79, and the alchemist is wrong when he thinks of it as a mixed body composed of the four Aristotelian elements in a certain way, then it would be a mistake to describe the situation by saying that it is only the

---

6   In this paper, the capitalized word is meant to express the proper sense; the same in quotes, in lower case or in the possessive construction is meant to express the putative sense. The word in single quotes is just referring to itself. This I believe squares quite well with the general usage of these forms of expression.

modern chemist who is capable of talking about genuine gold, whereas the alchemist is only able to talk about something else, given his mistaken conception about the true nature of gold. For they can obviously contradict each other when they both use the term 'gold' in the proper sense in order to signify the true nature of gold, say, in the sentences 'What the gold-digger found is gold' and 'What the gold-digger found is not gold', provided they disagree over the gold-digger's recent find. But, of course, this disagreement can be genuine only if the predicates of these sentences signify the same, namely, the true nature of gold. However, besides this disagreement over the factual issue whether the gold-digger's find actually possesses this true nature or not, they have a further *metaphysical* or *scientific* disagreement over what constitutes this true nature. Indeed, they can properly express their metaphysical disagreement only if they use the term 'gold' in the same sense, to refer to the same kind of thing, when they say 'Gold is a mixed body composed of water, earth, fire and air' and 'No, gold is not composed of those things, gold is an element', respectively, for otherwise, if they were to use the term in different senses, to refer to different things, then they would not contradict each other.

So, their metaphysical disagreement is possible only on the basis of a previous semantic agreement: they both have to have the same, simple, 'pre-theoretic' concept of gold, indeed, a concept that they share with the gold-digger, on the basis of which they are all able to conceive of and hence signify the same nature, and thereby to refer to the same kind of thing that has the same nature. But the chemist and the alchemist also have their own articulate, theoretical concepts of the same nature, which they employ in their substantive metaphysical and physical theories to characterize in a more articulate fashion the kind of thing having that nature, allowing them to theorize about it in a scientific context.

On the other hand, it may also happen that, say, a die-hard alchemist takes the claim that gold is a mixed body to be established by Aristotle's authority in such a way that it is *regulative* of the proper sense of term 'gold'. Thus, for him, the claim that gold is a mixed body is *not* a (possibly falsifiable) *metaphysical* or *scientific theory* about the nature of gold, but the expression of a *semantical rule* governing the strict, proper usage of the term. In fact, we might say that nowadays the claim that gold is the element of atomic number 79 has pretty much the same status: any sample of gold that a jeweller would regard as genuine gold, the chemist would rather describe as an alloy containing a certain percentage of pure gold. And anything that is not made up from atoms having 79 protons, no matter how much it would otherwise be like gold (say, 'twin-earth gold'), would not be called 'gold' by the chemist. So, in the chemist's usage, this claim now has the status of a *semantic rule* regulating strict scientific usage, and no longer the status of a possibly refutable scientific theory. In *this* case, if these theorists both take their respective theories as *regulative* of the proper sense of the term 'gold', then even if they predicate the same term of the same subject, they no longer properly contradict each other, since each of them will take the term in what each regards as its proper sense to express radically different concepts, with radically different implications, embedded in a radically different web of interrelated concepts. Thus, instead of being two theorists in genuine disagreement, risking different hypotheses about the nature of a thing commonly grasped by them by means of a vague common concept that is expressed by them in a common language, they should rather be described as two people speaking different languages constituted by their different semantical rules.[7]

To be sure, even this situation does not have to lead to a complete communication breakdown, but it will certainly render communication more complicated, especially given the fact that it is occurring only implicitly, not in obviously different languages. But this is precisely the kind of situation facing anyone trying to communicate about God or about the gods of different religious traditions or even in conversations with atheists.

Proper Sense and Constitutive Reference vs Putative Sense and Parasitic Reference

A typical feature of conversations in this situation is what I characterized elsewhere as 'parasitic reference'.[8] In this type of conversations, the interlocutors do not share their fundamental beliefs about the objects they refer to, although they take many of these beliefs to be fundamental in the sense that sharing those beliefs is *semantically regulative* of the *proper* sense of the names they use to refer to those objects. Accordingly, they believe that whoever does not share these fundamental, regulative beliefs cannot properly refer to the same intended referent. This, however, does not have to mean that those who do not share their beliefs absolutely cannot refer to their intended referent at all. To be sure, it is only the believers who are willing to refer to their intended referent *constitutively*, that is, using the term in what they take to be its proper sense *constituted* by their regulative beliefs. Thus, the believers' referring to their intended referent constitutively implies the belief that the referent satisfies the term's conditions of applicability specified by its proper sense, regulated by their fundamental, semantically regulative beliefs. Therefore, their constitutive reference commits believers to all the implications of their regulative beliefs concerning their intended referent. Still, the non-believers, or believers of other faiths, can also refer to the believers' intended referent *parasitically*, that is, without holding those beliefs, but at the same time understanding that the believers are targeting their intended referent as something they believe is properly picked out by the term in what they take to be its proper sense constituted by those beliefs. So, the non-believer in this case is exploiting the believers' beliefs to refer to their intended referent, but without

---

7 Perhaps, I should note here just for the record that this does not mean that both these theorists are or can be right about the nature of gold, or that there is no way they can contradict each other, for of course understanding is possible across different languages and different conceptual frameworks. It is just not as straightforward as it is in the case of two people holding contradictory opinions expressed in the same language within the same conceptual framework, using the same term in the same sense.

8 G. Klima, "Saint Anselm's Proof: A Problem of Reference, Intentional Identity and Mutual Understanding", in G. Hintikka (ed.), *Medieval Philosophy and Modern Times*, Proceedings of "Medieval and Modern Philosophy of Religion", Boston University, 25–27 August 1992 (Dordrecht: Kluwer Academic Publishers, 2000), 69–88; G. Klima, "On whether *id quo nihil maius cogitari potest* is in the understanding", *Proceedings of the Society for Medieval Logic and Metaphysics*, <http://www.fordham.edu/gsas/phil/klima/SMLM/PSMLM1.pdf>, 1 (2001): 70–80; G. Klima, "Conceptual Closure in Anselm's Proof: Reply to Tony Roark", *History and Philosophy of Logic*, 24 (2003): 131–4.

sharing those beliefs, and thus, *without any commitment to the implications of these semantically regulative beliefs* concerning the intended referent. This is possible because the non-believer of the given faith may use the same term in what he takes to be its *putative sense*, which he may even explicitly mark, for example, by quotation marks, or by the use of some other construction indicating the ascription of the regulative beliefs to the believers, but at the same time distancing himself from these beliefs. Examples of this sort would be phrases like 'Augustine's God' uttered by an atheist, 'the Roman gods' uttered by a Christian or 'the Aristotelian elements' uttered by a modern chemist and so on.

This is how it can come about that Anselm's 'ontological argument' may have no impact on the thinking of an atheist, who merely *parasitically* refers to 'the God of the faithful', without himself believing that the specification of the sense of the term provided by Anselm actually applies to anything whether in the mind or in reality. For even if Anselm's description may validly imply that what is referred to in the mind as that than which nothing greater can be thought also has to exist in reality, and that it has to be one, omnipotent, omniscient and so forth, the atheist, not making constitutive reference to this object of thought in the first place, is not committed to any of these implications, and thus he may consistently describe that intended referent as 'that God of the faithful, that figment of their mind, which they mistakenly believe to be that than which nothing greater can be thought, whereas there is no such thing at all, since for any given object, whether in the mind or in reality, a greater than it can be thought'.[9]

Indeed, this type of reference is ubiquitous not only in communication across different belief-systems, but also in the more mundane, and thus perhaps better understood, conversations about make-believe characters. So, for instance, when the question is raised whether Othello killed Desdemona, it is certainly not on a par with the question whether O.J. killed Nicole Simpson. For the latter question concerns a matter of fact. But the former question only concerns facts about how Shakespeare shaped the plot of his play, of course, without himself believing that he was reporting any facts. Thus, whoever refers to the Moor of Venice, intending thereby to refer to Shakespeare's make-believe character, will certainly understand that the Bard's description of the character has such-and-such implications – say, that he was a man, and therefore he had to be extended in space, and he could not have been in two places at the same time and so on (which Shakespeare never explicitly detailed); still, no one in their right mind would take these implications to prove any facts (say, that Othello was in fact in historical Venice, etc.) besides facts about what Shakespeare invented.

---

9 Cf. '… nihil inconveniens accidit ponentibus Deum non esse: non enim inconveniens est quolibet dato vel in re vel in intellectu aliquid maius cogitari posse, nisi ei qui concedit esse aliquid quo maius cogitari non possit in rerum natura.' – '… no inconsistency arises for those who claim that God does not exist, since it is not inconsistent for anyone to be able to think, for any given thing, whether in reality or in the understanding, something greater than it, except for someone who concedes that there is something in reality than which a greater cannot be thought.' Aquinas, *Summa contra Gentiles* I, 11, 2. For further discussion, see the references of the previous note.

So, all descriptions and their implications concerning the make-believe characters of the play are understood with the usually tacit prefix 'in the play'.

But then, in a similar vein, whoever does not share, for example, the Greek poets' beliefs about their gods can refer without further ado to what the Greek poets believed to be gods, and even retell their stories, say, about how and how many times Zeus cheated on Hera etc., with the perhaps tacit understanding that all this is prefixed with 'according to the Greek poets' or 'in Greek mythology' or something to the same effect. Thus, the person not believing in the Greek gods is not committed to any of the implications of the Greek poets' beliefs about their gods. After all, he is just reporting the Greek poets' beliefs. But at the same time he may notice what those implications of the Greek poets' beliefs are, and he may also legitimately confront those implications with the implications of his own conception of God.

This is precisely what Xenophanes did when he expressed his disagreement with the poets' descriptions of their gods.

> 7. Homer and Hesiod attributed to the gods all things which are disreputable and worthy of blame when done by men; and they told of them many lawless deeds, stealing, adultery, and deception of each other.[10]

In contrast to this, Xenophanes provides what he takes to be a proper description of God in the following way:

> 1. God is one, supreme among gods and men, and not like mortals in body or in mind. 2. The whole [of god] sees, the whole perceives, the whole hears. 3. But without effort he sets in motion all things by mind and thought.[11]

Obviously, the God Xenophanes is talking about is, according to him, the only God properly so-called, in contrast to the imperfect gods of the poets. Xenophanes thus apparently uses the same word in the same sentence once in the proper and once in the putative sense, precisely in order to make the contrast between what he takes to be divine nature properly signified by this word and what the same word can merely putatively signify, in accordance with the false beliefs of the poets about this nature. The important point of the disagreement here is that it shows why, despite all their linguistic authority, the poets' claims concerning their gods cannot be taken as *regulative* of the *proper* usage of the term. For in its *proper* usage the term must signify true divine nature, but the poets' descriptions, Xenophanes would argue, are incompatible with what that sublime nature would have to be like.

Thus, although linguistic authority establishes proper usage, it is not just any usage that can be established as proper by a mere *fiat* of linguistic authority. For as long as the proper usage of the term requires that it should signify the true nature of a certain sort of thing, discoveries about the nature of the thing may go against

---

10 Xenophanes, "Fragments and Commentary", in Arthur Fairbanks (ed. and trans.), *The First Philosophers of Greece* (London: K. Paul, Trench, Trubner, 1898), 65–85, p. 69. Cf. Zeller, *Vorsokrastische Philosophie*, 525, n. 3. Diog Laer. ix. 18; Sext. Emp. *Pyrrh*. i. 224.

11 Xenophanes, "Fragments and Commentary", 67. Cf. Zeller, *Vorsokrastische Philosophie*, 530, n. 3.

linguistic authority, no matter how well established. Thus, the die-hard alchemist would insist in vain that gold has to be a mixture of the Aristotelian elements by virtue of the *meaning* of the term 'gold', given what has been discovered about the true nature of this element we properly call 'gold'. In the same way, the Greeks could not insist that a morally flawed 'god' is truly and properly God, as long as the word 'God' is to be used with the intention to refer to something that has truly divine nature, which as such has to be flawless. So, the proper usage of a term is not *only* a matter of recognized linguistic authority. For such linguistic authority has to be *earned*, as it were, by being able to provide *true* characterizations of the true natures of things intended to be signified by our terms. For only such authoritative claims can *solidify* as semantic rules for proper usage that 'pass the test of time', and even then their status may change, and their scope may become restricted to some specific usage. Take for instance the phrase 'straight line' as used in geometry. For centuries, the proper usage of this phrase (and of its equivalents in other languages) was regulated by the Euclidean postulates. However, the discovery of consistent systems denying Euclid's postulate of parallels resulted in a modified usage, restricting Euclid's authoritative usage only to what we now would have to designate properly as 'Euclidean straight lines'.

Therefore, authoritative usage, especially authoritative usage in sophisticated theoretical systems, can only be semantically regulative to the extent that it is embedded in a consistent, true, substantive theory that 'passes the test of time'. It is only when regulated by this type of theory that the strict technical usage of a term will be (or should be) regarded as properly capturing the original, intuitive sense of the term, imposed to signify the true nature of the thing to which it is properly taken to refer. Indeed, it is only in this case that the technical usage regulated by the authoritative claims of the theory can serve as the proper explication of the originally intended, simple pre-theoretical notion of the nature of the thing. Thus, Augustine's explication of the notion intending to reach up to the true nature of the God of gods can only be properly understood within the theoretical context in which his authoritative claims concerning the proper usage of the term gain their technical sense. Indeed, since Augustine's technical usage is only a part of a vast tradition he partly inherited, partly originated, we can have a proper grasp on and thus a proper evaluation of the ever more refined notion intended by the technical usage of the term in this tradition only if we properly engage the relevant substantive theories of this tradition. For we can have a proper understanding of Augustine's explication of the term 'God' as an integral part of this tradition only if we realize how it was further articulated, for example, by Anselm's formula in his *Proslogion*, which in turn is properly understood only if it is seen as consistently explicated, say, by Aquinas's notion of *esse purum* or *ipsum esse subsistens*.[12] In brief, we can have a proper understanding of the intended sense of the term as it functions in this tradition only if we understand its proper theoretical context: the premodern metaphysics of being and perfection.

---

12   And this, Aquinas would insist, is not to be confused with *esse commune*, or being as such, being *qua* being, in general (despite his modern commentators' tendency to do so). Cf. Aquinas, *Scriptum super Sententiis*, lib. 1, d.8, q.4, a.1 ad 1.

The Premodern Metaphysics of Being and Perfection

In this context it is important to emphasize why we have to add the qualification 'premodern' in dealing with the notions of being and perfection. The reason is provided by the radical conceptual differences between premodern and contemporary thinking on these issues that evolved with the disintegration of scholasticism and the emergence of modern philosophy (roughly, around the time of Descartes). In this paper it is impossible to trace even in outline the history of these conceptual developments. So, the best I can do here is simply point to some of the most important differences that usually hinder contemporary philosophers in properly engaging the premodern tradition.

Being as a Predicate, and the Predication of Being in All Predications

The first difficulty concerns the interpretation of the notion of being or existence. The analytic philosophers' *mantra*, according to which existence is not a predicate, even if recently it lost its grip on many minds, is still capable of influencing the judgment even of such eminent interpreters of Aquinas's thought as Anthony Kenny. As in a critical review of his recent book on Aquinas on being I pointed out, Kenny's insistence on trying to understand (or sometimes just to judge) Aquinas's claims concerning existence in terms of the modern quantifier analysis dooms his arguments to committing *ignoratio elenchi* in almost all his criticisms of Aquinas's position.[13]

Since words are used by convention, the claim that existence is not a predicate is either absolutely futile with regard to other people's usage who have every right to use it as a predicate, or it is meant to express a substantial claim regarding the logical impossibility of coherently using the words 'is' and 'exist' or their equivalents as predicates of individuals. But it can easily be shown that the only serious argument to this effect one usually finds in the literature is simply *unsound* in the framework of medieval logic. The argument tries to show that treating existence as a predicate would entail the obviously false conclusion that all negative existentials have to be false. The argument assumes that in a subject-predicate sentence the subject has to refer to something if it is to be true. But then, if the negative existential claim 'Santa Claus does not exist' is true, then its subject has to refer to something. However, this is precisely what the sentence denies, for saying that Santa does not exist is precisely the claim that the name 'Santa' does not refer to anything. So, the truth of the sentence entails its falsity, whence it cannot be true, whereas anybody over six should know it is true.

This argument is flawed in more than one ways, but here I just want to point out why it would be regarded as flawed by medieval logicians. In the first place, medievals attributed existential import to (non-'ampliative', that is, non-intensional)[14] affirmative propositions. Accordingly, they treated the contradictory

---

13 G. Klima, "On Kenny on Aquinas on Being: A Critical Review of *Aquinas on Being* by Anthony Kenny", *International Philosophical Quarterly*, 44 (2004): 568–80.

14 The point of this parenthetical qualification is to account for cases when the truth of an affirmative predication does not require the actual existence of the reference of its subject,

negations of these propositions as *not* involving existential import. The primary reason for this decision is their unrestricted adherence to the principle of bivalence, and their theory of predication. In accordance with the principle of bivalence, if a proposition is true, its contradictory negation must be false, and *vice versa*. But then, if on account of their theory of predication they attribute existential import to affirmatives, medieval logicians have to say that such a proposition is false if its subject refers to nothing, whence its contradictory negation must be true. But this is precisely the case with the affirmative 'Santa exists' and its contradictory negation 'Santa does not exist'. *Ergo*, the modern argument assumes something false when it claims that the truth of a predication, whether affirmative or negative, requires that its subject should refer to something. For the contradictory negation of an affirmative having existential import has to be true if its subject refers to nothing, precisely *because* its subject refers to nothing.

The theory of predication on account of which Aquinas and his contemporaries attributed existential import to affirmatives is what historians of medieval logic dubbed 'the inherence theory of predication'.[15] The theory can be summarized in a simple formula:

(ITP) the predication 'x is F' is true iff x is actual with respect to its F-ness, that is, the F-ness of x actually exists.

This simple formula, however, has far-reaching metaphysical consequences. For on this basis just *any* simple predication expresses an existence-predication: claiming that x is F amounts to the assertion of the existence of the F-ness of x.[16] But a further, metaphysically even more important feature of this theory, especially from the point of view of Aquinas's metaphysics of being, can be detected if we notice in this formulation that the absolute predication of existence of the F-ness of x is the same as the predication of existence-with-qualification of x, stating that x *is*-with-respect-to-its-F-ness.

Predication *Simpliciter* vs *Secundum Quid*

Medieval logicians primarily considered the logical connections between the absolute (*simpliciter*) and qualified (*secundum quid*) predication of common terms in connection with the fallacy of *simpliciter et secundum quid*. A typical case of the fallacy would be, for example, 'This shield is round with respect to its bottom;

---

as in 'Santa is believed to be nice'. Cases like this, which in modern logic would be treated in some system of intensional logic, were treated by medieval logicians in the framework of their theory of *ampliation*. Cf. G. Klima, "Existence and Reference in Medieval Logic", in A. Hieke and E. Morscher (eds), *New Essays in Free Logic* (Dordrecht: Kluwer Academic Publishers, 2001), 197–226.

15 For more discussion see the paper referred to in the previous note.

16 This *did not* have to yield the unjustifiable proliferation of unruly entities of which Ockham and his followers started to complain. Cf. G. Klima, "Ockham's Semantics and Ontology of the Categories", in P. V. Spade (ed.), *The Cambridge Companion to Ockham* (Cambridge: Cambridge University Press, 1999), 118–42.

therefore, this shield is round', or the not so trivial, theologically relevant case of 'Christ is created with respect to his human nature; therefore, Christ is created', leading to a heretical claim.[17]

In connection with this type of paralogism, medieval logicians observed that it is not always fallacious to move from a qualified predication to an absolute one. Take for instance, 'Socrates is blond with respect to his hair; therefore, Socrates is blond.' What makes the difference, according to these logicians, is that in this case the qualification added to the predicate is not 'diminishing' (*determinatio non diminuens*), whereas in the fallacious cases it is. The reason they call the qualification 'diminishing' in the fallacious cases is that in those cases the diminishing qualification weakens or diminishes the strict conditions of applicability of the absolute predicate: the predicate 'round' stated absolutely of a shield would imply that the shield is round all around, so strictly speaking it would only apply to circular shields, but the qualification 'with respect to its bottom', weakens this condition, so with the qualification added it can also apply to shields, say, with straight edges on the sides and on the top, but with a rounded bottom. A diminishing qualification, therefore, is some determination added to a predicate that is intensionally diminishing, but, precisely for this reason, extensionally enhancing. Thus, a diminishing qualification allows a predicate to be extended to things that without this qualification, in its strict, primary, absolute sense could not be applied, but in the weakened, secondary sense resulting from the addition of the qualification now it can.

But viewing the formula (ITP) above from this angle should immediately allow us to see the connection between this theory of predication and Aquinas's conception of the *analogy of being*.

The Inherence Theory of Predication and the Analogy of Being

If we look at all predications as variously qualified predications of being, then it will at once make sense to claim, as Aquinas does, that the different ways of predication distinguished by Aristotle that mark out the different Aristotelian categories determine different modes of being:

> being cannot be narrowed down to something definite in the way in which a genus is narrowed down to a species by means of differences. Since a difference does not participate in a genus, it lies outside the essence of a genus. But there could be nothing outside the essence of being which could constitute a particular species of being by adding to being; for what is outside of being is nothing and cannot be a difference. Hence in book III of this work (see n. 433) the Philosopher proved that being cannot be a genus. Being must therefore be narrowed down to diverse genera on the basis of a different mode of predication, which derives from a different mode of being; for 'being [*esse*] is signified,' i.e., something is signified to be, 'in just as many ways as something is said to be a being [*ens dicitur*]', that is, in as many ways as something is predicated. And for this reason the first divisions of being are called predicaments [i.e., categories], because

---

17 I deal with Aquinas's and others' treatment of this fallacy in my "Libellus pro Sapiente: A Criticism of Allan Bäck's Argument against St. Thomas Aquinas' Theory of the Incarnation", *The New Scholasticism*, 58 (1984): 207–19.

they are distinguished on the basis of different ways of predicating. Therefore, since some predicates signify *what something is*, i.e., substance; others *what something is like*, [i.e., quality]; and yet others *how much something is*, [i.e., quantity]; and so on; it is necessary that for each mode of predication, being should signify the same [mode of being]. For example, when it is said that a man is an animal, 'is' signifies [the being of] substance; and when it is said that a man is white, 'is' signifies [the being of] quality; and so on.[18]

So, for Aquinas, the Aristotelian division of being into the ten categories is not the division of a genus into its species. It is rather the division of an analogical term into its analogates, of which it applies only to one, the *primary analogate*, without qualification, while it applies to the *secondary analogates* only in a secondary, extended sense, with qualification:

> there are two ways in which something common can be divided into those that are under it, just as there are two ways in which something is common. There is the division of a univocal [term] into its species by differences on account of which the nature of the genus is equally participated in the species, as animal is divided into man and horse, and the like. Another division is that of something common by analogy, which is predicated according to its perfect concept [*ratio*] of one of those that divide it, and of the other[s] imperfectly and with qualification [*secundum quid*], as being is divided into substance and accident, and into being in actuality and in potentiality, and this sort of division is as it were midway between [the division of something] equivocal and [something] univocal.[19]

Thus it is no wonder that Aquinas characterizes the primary ontological distinction between substance and accident precisely in terms of these different ways of

---

18 'ens non potest hoc modo contrahi ad aliquid determinatum, sicut genus contrahitur ad species per differentias. Nam differentia, cum non participet genus, est extra essentiam generis. Nihil autem posset esse extra essentiam entis, quod per additionem ad ens aliquam speciem entis constituat: nam quod est extra ens, nihil est, et differentia esse non potest. Unde in tertio huius probavit philosophus, quod ens, genus esse non potest. Unde oportet, quod ens contrahatur ad diversa genera secundum diversum modum praedicandi, qui consequitur diversum modum essendi; quia quoties ens dicitur, idest quot modis aliquid praedicatur, toties esse significatur, idest tot modis significatur aliquid esse. Et propter hoc ea in quae dividitur ens primo, dicuntur esse praedicamenta, quia distinguuntur secundum diversum modum praedicandi. Quia igitur eorum quae praedicantur, quaedam significant quid, idest substantiam, quaedam quale, quaedam quantum, et sic de aliis; oportet quod unicuique modo praedicandi, esse significet idem; ut cum dicitur homo est animal, esse significat substantiam. Cum autem dicitur, homo est albus, significat qualitatem, et sic de aliis.' Aquinas, *In Metaphysicam* 5.9, n. 5

19 'est duplex modus dividendi commune in ea quae sub ipso sunt, sicut est duplex communitatis modus. Est enim quaedam divisio univoci in species per differentias quibus aequaliter natura generis in speciebus participatur, sicut animal dividitur in hominem et equum, et hujusmodi; alia vero divisio est ejus quod est commune per analogiam, quod quidem secundum perfectam rationem praedicatur de uno dividentium, et de altero imperfecte et secundum quid, sicut ens dividitur in substantiam et accidens, et in ens actu et in ens potentia: et haec divisio est quasi media inter aequivocum et univocum.' *In Secundum Sententiarum* 42.1.3, in corp. Cf. 'Unum enim eodem modo dicitur aliquid sicut et ens; unde sicut ipsum non ens, non quidem simpliciter, sed secundum quid, idest secundum rationem, ut patet in 4o Metaphysicae, ita etiam negatio est unum secundum quid, scilicet secundum rationem.' Aquinas, *In Perihermeneias* 2.2, n. 3.

predicating being, grounded by the different modes of being, namely, being absolutely speaking [*simpliciter*], which is the characteristic mode of being of substance, and being with qualification [*secundum quid*], which is characteristic of accidents:

> Again, since accidents do not seem to be beings insofar as they are signified in themselves, but only insofar as they are signified as inhering in a substance, it is clearly on account of substance that each of the other beings is a being. And from this it also appears that substance is 'the first kind of being and being in an unqualified sense and not just a being of some sort [*ens secundum aliquid*]', i.e., [a being] with some qualification [*secundum quid*], as is the case with accidents; for to be white is not to be without qualification [*simpliciter*], but with some qualification. This is clear from the fact that when a thing begins to be white we do not say that it begins *to be* without qualification [*simpliciter*], but that it begins *to be white*. For when Socrates begins to be a man, he is said to begin *to be*, absolutely speaking [*simpliciter*]. Hence it is obvious that being a man signifies being without qualification, but that being white signifies being with some qualification.[20]

However, even if being a substance of some sort is being *simpliciter*, we should notice here that in accordance with our general formula for the inherence theory of predication (ITP), even in the case of predicating being of a substance of some sort, the sort of the substance in question, that is, its nature or essence, does impose a certain determination on the sense in which the thing can be. Since for a man to be a man is for a man to be *simpliciter* (as opposed to for him to be wise or walking, which are cases of being *secundum quid*), the reverse also has to be true, namely, that for a man to be *simpliciter* is for a man to be a man. Therefore, for a man *to be simpliciter* is nothing but for him *to be-with-respect-to-his-humanity*, that is, to be in the way a human being has to be, living a human life, as opposed to the way in which, say, dogs are, living their canine lives. That these ways of being determined by these different natures have to be radically different is shown by the fact that it is not fitting for a human to live *like* a dog (that is, living a life *resembling* a dog's life), and that in fact it would be metaphysically impossible for a human to live *as* a dog (namely, living a life that literally *is* the life of a dog), which would have to involve, for example, the ability to pass down canine genes to canine progeny and so on.

So, even if substances are said to be beings without qualification as opposed to accidents, still, the being of substances also involves a certain determination or delimitation imposed upon it by their nature, at least, provided that this nature is distinct from their being. For consider the following formula (called PB, because

---

20 'Et quia accidentia non videntur entia prout secundum se significantur, sed solum prout significantur in concretione ad substantiam, palam est quod singula aliorum entium sunt entia propter substantiam. Et ex hoc ulterius apparet, quod substantia est *primum ens, et ens simpliciter, et non ens secundum aliquid*, idest secundum quid, sicut est in accidentibus. Esse enim album non est simpliciter esse, sed secundum quid. Quod ex hoc patet, quia cum incipit esse albus, non dicimus quod incipiat esse simpliciter, sed quia incipiat esse albus. Cum enim Socrates incipit esse homo, dicitur simpliciter quod incipit esse. Unde patet quod esse hominem significat esse simpliciter. Esse autem album significat esse secundum quid.' Aquinas, *In Metaphysicam* 7.1, n. 1256.

I believe it is the fundamental formula underlying Aquinas's conception of the *participation of being*):[21]

(PB)   An x of nature Y *is* iff x *is-with-respect-to-its-nature-Y*

As can be seen, the absolute predicate 'is' predicated of x, just by virtue of x being of nature Y, has to signify the same in x as the same predicate with a qualification referring to this nature. So the absolute predicate signifies being in some qualified sense, qualified by the nature of x. This is precisely why human life and canine life are radically different and necessarily determined by these different natures, even if they both are the *substantial* acts of being of humans and dogs, and thus make them *to be*, absolutely speaking, as opposed to making them *to be tall* or *to be heavy*, that is, actual in respect of some *accidental* being. Does this mean, then, that since anything that exists at all has to have some nature, *all* predications of being are predications with qualification? Is there nothing that just IS without any qualification or determination imposed upon its act of being by its nature? Indeed, can it be the case that anything can be said to be only *with* qualification and nothing *without* qualification?

Divine Essence, *Esse Purum*, and the Attributes of God

It is at this point that we have to notice that *if* the act of being signified by the predicate 'is' in x is the same as x's nature Y, *then* the qualification referring to the nature of x has to be *non-diminishing*, for, in general, if the qualification of a predicate refers to the significate of the predicate itself, then the qualification is non-diminishing. For example, if I say that x is white-with-respect-to-its-whiteness, then the qualification added to the predicate may be dropped without further ado, for whatever is white is of course white-with-respect-to-its-whiteness and *vice versa*. But then, in the same way, if x's nature Y is the same as x's being, then saying that x *is-with-respect-to-its-nature-Y* is the same as saying that x *is-with-respect-to-its-being*, which does not impose a limitation on the way x is, for nothing delimits itself. But in all other cases, the qualification referring to the nature of the thing, being distinct from the act of being of the thing, imposes a certain limitation or determination on the way the thing is, indeed, on the way the thing *can* be.

Accordingly, *if* there is a Being in which *esse* and *essence* are the same, *then* that Being, and *only* that Being, can be said to BE without any limitation whatsoever. But then that Being, which alone has unlimited, that is, non-participated existence will have to be God, and all other beings will have to be His creatures, which can only exist by participation, *secundum quid*, relative to the absolutely unlimited act of being of God. So, just as the being of accidents is being *secundum quid* relative to the absolute sense in which substances can be said to be, so also, proportionately, the being of created substances is just some limited form of being (limited in time, space, power,

---

21   Cf. G. Klima, "Thomas Sutton and Henry of Ghent on the Analogy of Being", *Proceedings of the Society for Medieval Logic and Metaphysics*, 2 (2002): 34–44. <http://www.fordham.edu/gsas/phil/klima/SMLM/PSMLM2/PSMLM2.pdf>.

perfection and so on) relative to the absolutely unlimited being of God (who, by reason of the meaning of His name has to be superior to all, and so cannot be limited):

> It is obvious that the first being, which is God, is infinite act, namely, having in Himself the whole plenitude of being not contracted to the nature of some genus or species. Therefore it is necessary that His being itself should not be an act of being that is, as it were, packed into a nature which is not its own being, for in that way it would be confined to that nature. Hence we say that God is His own being. But this cannot be said about anything else; just as it is impossible to think that there should be several separate whitenesses, but if a whiteness were separate from any subject and recipient, then it would be only one, so it is impossible that there should be a subsistent act of being, except only one. Therefore, everything else after the first being, since it is not its own being, has being received in something, by which its being is contracted; and thus in any created being the nature of the thing that participates being is other than the act of being itself that is participated.[22]

Thus, as far as the significance of the verb 'is' and of the corresponding participle 'being' is concerned, namely, the act of being of the thing of which they are truly predicated, their *only* pure, non-diminished significate is the divine being, namely, divine life. So, these terms in their pure, absolute, unlimited sense can only apply to God, just as the term 'gold' in the modern chemist's technical sense can only apply to a body that is a 100 per cent pure element consisting only of atoms of atomic number 79. It is only this subsistent *esse purum* that can properly be said to BE, in which there cannot be a distinction between the act of being and what receives it, for then the recipient would necessarily delimit the received act.

Therefore, it should be no surprise that in the medieval tradition we can repeatedly find the claim that, compared to God, nothing really exists[23] (just as compared to

---

22 'Oportet enim in substantia spirituali creata esse duo, quorum unum comparatur ad alterum ut potentia ad actum. Quod sic patet. Manifestum est enim quod primum ens, quod Deus est, est actus infinitus, utpote habens in se totam essendi plenitudinem non contractam ad aliquam naturam generis vel speciei. Unde oportet quod ipsum esse eius non sit esse quasi inditum alicui naturae quae non sit suum esse; quia sic finiretur ad illam naturam. Unde dicimus, quod Deus est ipsum suum esse. Hoc autem non potest dici de aliquo alio: sicut impossibile est intelligere quod sint plures albedines separatae; sed si esset albedo separata ab omni subiecto et recipiente, esset una tantum; ita impossibile est quod sit ipsum esse subsistens nisi unum tantum. Omne igitur quod est post primum ens, cum non sit suum esse, habet esse in aliquo receptum, per quod ipsum esse contrahitur; et sic in quolibet creato aliud est natura rei quae participat esse, et aliud ipsum esse participatum.' Aquinas, *De Spiritualibus Creaturis* q.1, a.1.

23 Thus, for example, Anselm writes: 'Quod vero sic simpliciter et omnimoda ratione solum est perfectum, simplex et absolutum, id nimium quodammodo jure dici potest solum esse: et econtra, quidquid per superiorem rationem, nec simpliciter, nec perfecte, nec absolute esse; sed vix esse, aut fere non esse cognoscitur; id utique aliquo modo recte, non esse dicitur. Secundum hanc igitur rationem ille solus creator Spiritus est, et omnia creata, non sunt; nec tamen omnino non sunt, quia per illum qui solus absolute est, de nihilo aliquid facta sunt.' – 'What is so absolutely and in every way is perfect, simple and absolute, that can in a sense rightly be said to be the only thing that exists. By contrast, whatever we recognize (as we did in our foregoing reasoning) to be neither fully, nor perfectly, nor absolutely, but rather scarcely to be or indeed almost not to be, that is in a sense correctly *not* to be. On the basis of this reasoning, therefore, only the Creating Spirit *is*, and all those that are created *are not*.

pure gold, no gold alloy is *really* gold).[24] So the *only* BEING, in the true, proper, absolutely unlimited sense is God, just as *only* pure gold is absolutely gold. And just as any gold alloy is "gold" only in an attenuated, qualified sense, as in "18-carat gold" or "14-carat gold", so any being other than God is only a being in an attenuated sense, namely, a being of this sort or that sort.

But then, with this conception of the relationship between the notions of being and divine nature in place, it is easy to see how the traditional divine attributes of simplicity, perfection, immutability, unity and so on should follow. For anything not absolutely simple has to be composed of distinct parts; but if the parts are distinct, then in respect of one part the thing has to be something that in respect of the other part it *is not*; but not-being in some respect is incompatible with being fully, in an absolutely unlimited sense; *ergo*, God has to be absolutely simple. Furthermore, anything that is not absolutely perfect in respect of all possible perfections[25] lacks perfection in some respect; but lacking perfection in some respect is not being actual in that respect, which is incompatible with being fully actual; so God has to be absolutely perfect. But given God's simplicity, his perfections cannot be distinct from Him or from one another. So God *is* all His perfections. Again, this excludes God's mutability. For changing is coming to be or ceasing to be actual in some respect. But God always has to be actual in respect of all possible perfections He is, so he can never come to be or cease to be in any of those respects, that is, can never change. Indeed, since coming to be or ceasing to be in respect of some perfection is becoming better or worse in some respect, change in God would entail that God could become better or worse, which goes against His absolute perfection. Finally, let me quote an argument from Aquinas for divine unity arguing from the same premise, namely, the identity of God's being and essence, because this will directly take us back to the original questions of 'Whose God?' in 'Which tradition?' we are talking about.

> If there are two Gods, then the name 'God' is predicated of each either univocally or equivocally. If equivocally, then this is not of our present concern, for nothing prevents anything from being

---

But they are not entirely non-existent, for they were, by that which alone absolutely exists, made into something out of nothing.' Anselm, *Monologion*, c. 28. Aquinas's early follower, Thomas Sutton, made the same point equally forcefully, backing his claim with the authority of Augustine: 'Respectu enim Dei alia sunt magis non-entia quam entia. Unde Augustinus dicit VII *De trinitate* c. 32: fortasse solum deum oportet dici essentiam. Est enim vere solus, quia incommutabilis est.' – 'Compared to God, others are rather non-beings than beings. This is why Augustine says in his "On the Trinity" that perhaps only God should be called an essence. For He alone truly *is*, as He is unchangeable.' Thomas of Sutton, *Quaestiones ordinariae*, ed. Johannes Schneider (Munich: Verlag der Bayerische Akademie der Wissenschaften, 1977), q.32, esp. pp. 882–3.

24 The jeweller's 18-carat "gold" actually contains only 75 per cent pure gold; the rest is silver and copper or other metals, such as nickel, palladium or zinc (24-carat gold, however, is pure gold, given that 'carat', as applied to gold, simply means 1/24.) Incidentally, I think I should mention here that I would find this logical-metaphysical framework the best interpretational framework for Parmenides's poem. His Being of *aletheia*, as opposed to the world of *doxa*, seems to exhibit exactly the same contrast. But exploring this suggestion would require a separate study.

25 For the relevant notion of perfection see n. 27.

named equivocally by any name, if the speakers [of the language] accept this usage. But if it is predicated of them univocally, then it has to be predicated of both in the same sense. And thus they would have to have the same nature in the same sense. But then this nature exists either by one act of being in both, or by one in each. If by one act of being [in both], then they will not be two things, but only one thing, for two things do not have one act of being if they are substantially distinct. [That is, if they are two distinct substances.] But if there is one act of being in each [distinct from the act of being of the other], then neither of them will have its essence the same as its being [for then their individual essences will have to distinguish their distinct acts of being by receiving and thus delimiting them]. But, as we have proved, this has to be the case with God. Therefore, neither of the two is what we understand by the name 'God'. Hence, it is impossible to posit two Gods.[26]

Different Metaphysics, Different Languages

Given that the name 'God' as intended by Aquinas, Anselm, Augustine and other authorities of this tradition can only refer to the one true God as they conceive of Him, the God of Aquinas, the God of Anselm and the God of Augustine has to be one and the same God, despite the variations in the individual conceptions of these authorities. Accordingly, anybody whose conception allows the multiplication of 'Gods' is not speaking properly according to this tradition. Therefore, he is either using the name equivocally, in which case he is just talking past this tradition, or he is talking parasitically about the same God, but without sharing the regulative beliefs of this tradition. But then, if he attributes to this God the implications of his own, clearly radically different 'technical' conception of what he takes to be God, then he is simply in error.

Now, for the sake of simple contrast, let us compare a hypothetical contemporary philosopher of religion, CPR, and a premodern, or contemporary 'premodernist' philosopher, PMP, with respect to some of their characteristic metaphysical positions.

Let us assume that CPR would subscribe to the following principles:

1. Predicates denote properties, abstract universal entities, instantiated by several particulars in different possible worlds.
2. The existence of a certain kind of thing, accordingly, is just the instantiation of such a property by an individual in some possible world, namely, in the distinguished possible world called the actual world.

---

26 'Adhuc. Si sunt duo dii, aut hoc nomen Deus de utroque praedicatur univoce, aut aequivoce. Si aequivoce, hoc est praeter intentionem praesentem: nam nihil prohibet rem quamlibet quolibet nomine aequivoce nominari, si usus loquentium admittat. Si autem dicatur univoce, oportet quod de utroque praedicetur secundum unam rationem. Et sic oportet quod in utroque sit una natura secundum rationem. Aut igitur haec natura est in utroque secundum unum esse, aut secundum aliud et aliud. Si secundum unum, ergo non erunt duo sed unum tantum: duorum enim non est unum esse si substantialiter distinguantur. Si autem est aliud et aliud esse in utroque, ergo neutri erit sua quidditas suum esse. Sed hoc oportet in Deo ponere, ut probatum est. Ergo neutrum illorum duorum est hoc quod intelligimus nomine Dei. Sic igitur impossibile est ponere duos deos.' Aquinas, *Summa contra Gentiles* I, 42, 10.

3. The existence of a particular, on the other hand, if this kind of talk is allowed at all (but nowadays increasingly it is), is simply the presence of that individual in the domain of a possible world, namely, in the domain of the actual world.
4. Necessary existence is just existence in all possible worlds.
5. Perfections are properties that make the thing instantiating them better.

By contrast, PMP would hold the following, roughly corresponding principles:

1. Predicates signify individualized forms or natures of individuals.
2. The existence of a certain kind of thing is the significate of the predicate 'is' or 'exists' or 'being' in that thing, which is also the actuality of the form or nature signified by the predicate naming this kind of thing.
3. The existence of a particular is again just the significate of 'is', 'exists' or 'being' in this thing.
4. Necessary existence is either the existence of naturally incorruptible substances, which nevertheless could be annihilated by God's ceasing to sustain them in His continuous creation, or the absolutely necessary existence of God, which can in no way be annihilated, for it is just Being itself.
5. Perfections, that is, absolute perfections, are the *significata* of such names that it is absolutely better to be named by than not.[27]

Even this very rough outline, which may not faithfully reflect the thought of any single actual thinker in either tradition, allows some important points of contrast concerning the respective conceptions of divine nature of these philosophers.

As we could see, premodern thinkers regarded the unity, simplicity and immutability of God as necessary conclusions, inevitably following from these principles along with what we are supposed to understand by the name 'God', no matter how we articulate this proper understanding, as long as it squares with the general intention of conceiving of a supreme being of utmost perfection. So, for PMP the classical divine attributes have to apply to God so conceived, and so he would claim that whoever denies these attributes of God is either mistaken, or he is talking about something else, using the name equivocally.

CPR's framework, however, does not seem to entail this as an inevitable conclusion. For even if he explicates the meaning of the name 'God' as the name of a necessary being that possesses all possible perfections, this would not entail the uniqueness of this being in CPR's framework. This is so because if we reject

---

27 'all those names which are imposed to signify some perfection absolutely are properly said of God, and they apply to Him primarily as far as the thing signified is concerned, although not as far as the mode of signifying is concerned, such as "wisdom", "goodness", "essence" and the like; and these are the ones of which Anselm says that [for any such name N] it is absolutely and entirely better to be [N] than not to be [N].' – 'omnia illa nomina quae imponuntur ad significandum perfectionem aliquam absolute, proprie dicuntur de Deo, et per prius sunt in ipso quantum ad rem significatam, licet non quantum ad modum significandi, ut sapientia, bonitas, essentia et omnia hujusmodi; et haec sunt de quibus dicit Anselmus, quod simpliciter et omnino melius est esse quam non esse.' Aquinas, *Scriptum super Sententiis*, lib. 1, d.22, q.1, a.2 co.

the logically not necessary principle of the identity of indiscernibles (the reverse of the logically necessary indiscernibility of identicals), then we have to say that no collection of properties uniquely determines a single individual. But then any number of individuals can have the collection of all properties that are regarded as perfections, and they can all be present in all possible worlds. Thus, for CPR it would not entail a contradiction to assume the existence of several supreme beings, that is, several 'Gods'. Also, for him it would not take away anything from the perfection of any of these 'Gods', if they turned out to be changeable. For they would still be present in all possible worlds and would still have all properties classified as perfections, if they also had some other (accidental) properties in some worlds that they would not have in others or if they had some such properties in some world at some time and would not have it at other times.

But then in this framework, an articulation of the meaning of the name 'God' that may be verbally similar to premodern articulations will obviously carry radically different implications. For CPR's changeable 'Gods' residing in all possible worlds would be nothing like the God of PMP. However, if it is PMP's articulation of the original intuitive idea of the God of gods that genuinely captures what all people understand by the name 'God' in the sense in which this term signifies true divine nature, then, CPR's 'God' or 'Gods' must be something else. This would have to be case, at least, *if* CPR were to insist on using the term 'God' according to his definition as a necessary, perfect being, *as interpreted in the framework of his metaphysical principles*.

However, in that case CPR's principles would serve *not* as *metaphysical principles*, but as *regulative semantic principles* to define a new sense of the term 'God'. But then his 'God' or 'Gods' will have nothing to do with the God of monotheistic religions, so he might as well just start a new religion, worshipping these 'lesser' gods, like the pagan Greeks and Romans did (except, maybe, with the difference that his gods will be more 'well-behaved' in all possible worlds).

On the other hand, CPR may choose to engage the premodern tradition, which, however, he finds in error in at least some of its claims concerning the one true God. He will, therefore, parasitically refer to the targeted referent of this tradition, without sharing the regulative beliefs of this tradition. In this case, however, if he genuinely contradicts this tradition in some of his claims concerning God, such as the mutability vs immutability of God, and the traditional arguments are sound, then CPR is simply wrong, as a consequence of his own misconception of divine perfection. But more likely, if he is proceeding by denying or just ignoring the premodern tradition's *regulative* principles, then he will again just talk past this tradition, for even if he now may refer to the same God, he may not properly understand the claims made about Him, and thus would still not properly be able to contradict this tradition.

For example, he might understand the traditional claim that God is all His perfections in terms of *his own* concept of perfections. So, the traditional claim *on his reading* will translate into the obviously absurd claim that God is identical with a number of distinct abstract entities. But this "translation" of the traditional thesis into CPR's own conceptual idiom yields absurdity only because it is in fact a *mistranslation*. So, while talking parasitically about the same God as the tradition, he still cannot properly engage this tradition, and thus his criticisms amount to *ignoratio elenchi*. To be sure, *some* such misunderstandings can relatively easily be dispelled by clarifying that 'perfection' in this tradition did not and could not refer to CPR's abstract entities. But for the proper understanding of what this tradition *did* mean by 'perfection' it is not enough just to give a formulaic definition of the term, for that definition can properly be grasped only if it is understood as it functioned in the entire conceptual system of this tradition. (Of course, it is useless to provide the mathematical definition of, say, the derivative of a function to someone who is unfamiliar with the theory of functions and set theory in the first place.)

So, finally, CPR can genuinely succeed in the task of properly engaging this tradition *only if* he clarifies not only the senses of this or that term or thesis in an *ad hoc* manner for the sake of some particular argument, but rather if he is willing to re-learn at least the basics of the entire conceptual framework without which the understanding of any particular term or thesis can only be partial. For picking up the meanings of some terms and phrases without an understanding of the conceptual system in which these properly function is pretty much like knowing some Latin words and proverbs, but without having at least the basics of Latin grammar and a decent vocabulary. But that would certainly not amount to competence in Latin.

Talking About the One True God

So, if CPR wants to talk competently about the God of Christianity, he has to be able to genuinely engage that tradition which is arguably the most reliable depository of the *authentic tradition* of Western Christianity, namely, the medieval theological tradition (although *that* argument is beyond the scope of the present discussion).[28] Therefore, if CPR's troubles with engaging the premodern theological tradition are like the troubles that speakers of different languages face in their communication, then the remedy should be obvious: he should *learn the language*. But learning a language does not consist in *translation*, for translation is a secondary activity *presupposing* mastery of both languages. And it does not consist in picking up single phrases like proverbs or the set phrases of travel guides either. What learning a language genuinely requires, as any bilingual person can tell, is the acquisition of *the ability to think in that language*. It is then, and *only then*, when a person has acquired this ability that he will be able to contrast, compare and argue about any thoughts formulated in either language. This can only be achieved, however, by *living* with that language for a considerable length of time.

But what does it mean to live with a different language? Well, what does it take to settle in a different country? It takes primarily openness, a willingness to learn and

---

28 I think it is also worth noting here that this tradition, precisely in its logical, semantical and metaphysical principles, was actually closer to the other great monotheistic traditions, namely, medieval Judaism and Islam, than it is to the Christianity of certain contemporary philosophers of religion. Aquinas never had any doubts that the God of Avicenna or Averroes, or the God of Rabbi Moyses, or for that matter the Prime Mover of Aristotle was the same God he worshipped. So, whoever wants to engage discourse not only about the Christian God, but also about the God of these great monotheistic religions in general, will have to have recourse to this tradition.

appreciate the customs and habits of its people before judging them, a willingness to learn the ways they think and talk. But the characteristic ways of thinking and talking are constituted precisely by those *regulative* beliefs the denial of which yields not simple disagreement, but a failure of understanding. It was in fact in this spirit that in a review of Anthony Kenny's book *Aquinas on Mind* I noted that the best parts of Kenny's discussion are those in which he notes that some of Aquinas's claims are to be taken as 'truisms'.[29] For recognizing such claims *as truisms* is precisely the recognition of their role as expressions of *regulative principles* that cannot be denied without failing to understand them properly, just as it is not possible to deny the English claim that bachelors are unmarried without failing to understand its terms properly.

Of course, accepting the regulative principles or grammatical rules of a language need not amount to accepting that whatever is said in that language is true. For not every claim of the language should be taken as an expression of a semantic rule. But understanding a language involves precisely the ability to tell apart those claims that express such rules from those claims that do not. And finding out about the truth of the latter can only follow upon the proper recognition of the former.[30]

---

29 G. Klima, Review of A. Kenny: *Aquinas on Mind* (New York: Routledge, 1995), in *Faith and Philosophy*, 15 (1998): 113–17.

30 Cf. G. Klima, "The Semantic Principles Underlying Saint Thomas Aquinas's Metaphysics of Being", *Medieval Philosophy and Theology*, 5 (1996): 87–141.

Voices in Discussion

D.Z. Phillips

G: There is an important difference between constitutive and regulative concepts. We could argue over what the nature of gold is. Here we could have a clash between two theories about the elements of gold. They genuinely contradict each other, but discussion can take the place or the basis of a shared rationality which is already in place. But what about a clash between chemistry and alchemy, where there seems to be regulative ideas separating the disputants over what is meant by 'gold'? What do we do here? What we need is to sit down and see what it is that we can agree on and start from there. That common meeting point will then be the starting point from which we can discuss the essential nature of God – as the most perfect being. We would then move from a pre-theoretical understanding of God to a more adequate theoretical understanding. After all, we are trying to understand the true divine nature.

K: One starts with the pre-theoretical language of course – the language of Scripture. That is to be respected. But questions are asked of it. What does it mean? What is the justification of it? The philosophers then fill things out, wondering what truth-conditions are involved, and so on.

C: Does the philosopher or the theologian know more about God than other people? Tolstoy's Father Sergius came to the conclusion that Pashenka, who cleaned the church while thinking that she was serving men, was in fact serving God, while he, thinking that he was serving God, was in fact serving men.

K: But there are these further questions to which theologians and philosophers address themselves.

C: But can it be done in the way G proposes? Take an example where there is a regulative conceptual difference between religious beliefs. Contrast a warrior religion, where the vision of eternity is a warrior's vision in which one goes out to battle, to return to feast with Odin and the gods, and the second person of the Trinity who is crucified as a common criminal. Any sense here of a common rationality which would lead to a resolution of the difference between these beliefs? Obviously not. But neither would it make sense, with this clash between regulative concepts, to come together to seek a common something on the basis of which eventual agreement can be reached.

A: I agree with C. An appeal to rationality alone will not do it. The argument that if there is a regulative conceptual difference between religious beliefs there must be different gods does not hold as a generality. For example, there is no doubt that the divinity of Christ is a regulative belief. It is not so for Jews or Muslims. Yet they believe in the same God. This is shown in the historical continuity of the tradition. Yet the Christian belief is truly regulative.

G: But the fact that a belief is necessary doesn't make it an analytic truth. One must remember here that Aquinas is operating with a conception of God as the sum of all perfections. As Anselm said, no greater can be conceived. So there can only be one God. So we can discuss what is involved in this notion of the sum of all perfections. It is a logically unique notion. It does not allow one to say of any other conception of God, 'That's God too'.

C: But here there would be a difference between 'use' and 'mention'. When I refer to the warrior God, I am mentioning the kind of belief it is. I am not saying myself, 'Thou art God'. That is a confession. That was my point in contrasting the Christian God with the warrior god – on looking at what the beliefs come to, one may be able to say 'Thou art God' of one, but not of the other. But one doesn't have to get behind the features of the god in question to explain why the confession goes one way rather than another. It is the mere fact that the one who confesses can give him/herself to one and not the other. He or she gives the status 'Thou are God' to one rather than the other.

A: And that is why in the case of Zeus, one is talking of a different god – different from anything Aquinas had in mind.

C: Even there, the appeal to 'perfections' by Aquinas can't take us very far, because regulative conceptions can themselves determine what talk of perfections amounts to. That talk is not given in abstraction. The perfections in question, in the case of a warrior god, would be perfections appropriate in that context.

L: I feel I must make a few remarks here. G appeals to a mode of argument that may flourish at Fordham. Well, it doesn't flourish at Claremont. It is an argument that belongs to a certain Thomistic tradition. But there are others' traditions. Luther thought that the influence of Aristotle's philosophy had distorted Christian belief.

G: Believe me, I couldn't agree more. I am talking within a tradition, one that includes Aristotle's hylomorphic metaphysics. Of course, in my paper, I am not discussing the difference between these traditions. I was arguing about what is made possible, and how argument proceeds if one accepts the general framework of Aquinas's thought. If the premises of that thought are not accepted, we can discuss that difference. My own conviction is that the difference between the traditions will not turn out to be as great as some have thought, but I do not claim to have discussed that here. But I do understand your point. My point is that questions of whether one is talking about 'the same God' are advanced by the kind of discussion I have talked about. There are differences between Christians and some of them go deep, but they are closer to each other than they are to Jews. On the other hand, when one goes outside monotheistic traditions altogether, one may not be able to talk of 'the same God'. That is why I prefer a discussion of comparisons with Maimonides or Avicenna.

C: But isn't that because you are already participating in a wider context that makes comparative discussions possible. The aim seems to be to arrive at conclusions about the true nature of God. But when we take wider examples such as the warrior god, one can still talk about 'the true' or 'the false' god, which goes back to my point about the confessional status of 'Thou art God'.

G: I am not saying that the fundamental articles of faith are capable of proof. I am talking about the scope of rational discussion within that context. That is why I prefer some examples rather than others. I am not talking about 'proof' in the abstract.

Chapter 5

Simplicity and the Talk About God

James F. Ross

Introduction

This discussion started from a commentary Brian Davies published in a 'Letter from America'[1] on a remarkable division among American, mainly, philosophers of religion in their suppositions about God. Here I bypass what Brian Davies and I consider the startling philosophical mistakes underlying the theories of the group who regard the divine being as 'a person like us', as temporal, not simple and, even some, as able to suffer, change and develop. Instead, I widen the question, as D.Z. Phillips does in his Introductory Invitation, to ask 'Whose God, whose tradition?', noting that, as Phillips comments, 'a tradition itself may be confused'. I am mainly concerned here with the historical origin of the divergence and with making some estimates of what will be the outcomes.

I think the division among the philosophers of religion originates in divergent traditions about what is to be said about God that trace back to a dispute about how to understand the Scriptures, especially after the Reformation. The philosophers of religion are usually, after all, arguing about certain claims they accept, or want to criticize, within some general religious framework.

The notions of God in those traditions may *appear* to originate in the philosophical explanation of the origin of all things, against which Brian Davies tests them. But the more powerful factor, I think, is the background *religious* conception in whose service the explanatory deity is adopted and employed. The explanation of why the differences are held does not rest primarily in the differing philosophy – even though it *seems* to – but in the differing religious traditions.

I further think that the two chief traditions in question here have a *common* problem about how to reconcile the mysteries of faith and its scriptural discourse with the cool but partial deliverances of reason about the divine ground and origin of all things. I make some suggestions in the last two sections and Appendix 3.

The Roots of Disagreement

1. The philosophers Davies and Phillips mention fall roughly into two groups. I'll call them 'reformers' – those temporalists and non-simplicists loosely within the protestant tradition of '*sola scriptura*' and '*analogia fidei*' [Appendix 1]; and the analogists, loosely, the 'catholics' – those in the tradition that there is *a unified Christian wisdom of mutually illuminating certainties of faith and secular knowledge* (philosophy, physical science and history), part of which, after the thirteenth century,

---

[1] *New Blackfriars*, 84/989–90(July/August 2003): 371–84.

is the *analogia entis et nominum* (or its current correlate) [Appendix 2]. That tradition of combining the resources of divine revelation with the accomplishments of secular reasoning is epitomized by Augustine (note his 'spoils of the Egyptians' doctrine in *De Doctrina Christiana*) and by 1,000 years of theology afterwards.

The first group, the 'reformers', come from a background where only Scripture and the faith determine what is to be said of God, and it is up to the philosophers to make their theories consistent with that. That's why they are trying to make the notion of a temporal and not simple deity coherent – that *seems* to be what Scripture presents. I am not suggesting, of course, that the current 'reform' philosophers are all purists like that, but rather that they are loose inheritors of 'plain meaning' talk about God that is based in Scripture. (Indeed some of them, like Plantinga, devise metaphysical analyses of religious discourse, like the free will defence, just as enthusiastically as the high scholastics.)

The latter, the 'catholics', think human certainties affect the understanding of the faith and of the Scripture both by determining that certain parts are *not* literal because Scripture cannot literally mean what science discloses not to be true (Aquinas, *Summa Theologiae* I.67.4; 68.3.) and because human philosophy and science can discern some theoretical truth conditions for the elements of the faith (like the identity of essence and being in God) and even, to a limited extent, for the mysteries (like Incarnation as involving two natures and one person, the Trinity involving subsistent *relata* but one being).[2]

Indeed the words of Scripture are sometimes explained *away* for reasons of science, even when they are not treated as merely figurative. For instance, interpreting Genesis, I.67.4, Aquinas says, Moses 'put before them only such things as are apparent to sense', rather than the scientific reality. And in q.70. a.1 he says 'Moses describes what is obvious to sense, out of condescension to popular ignorance, as we have already said', just as we would if we referred to the sun's rising in a context where people took that to be the same as the moon's rising by moving. (Interestingly, Aquinas took as science that, although we perceive planets and stars as moving, the movement is *really* of transparent spheres in which they are embedded like jewels in a plate, see Appendix 3).

Such differences of religious tradition show up in philosophy as opposed organizing certainties about the divine attributes and as simple refusal to take the opposed arguments as competent to be decisive. That is obvious in the discussion of whether God can be a being with successive states of consciousness – the apparent contradictions are simply ignored. (Philosophy is not such disinterested rationality and explicit justification as one might suppose, any more than science is. It has aesthetic and religious presuppositions, and even operative philosophical fashions (like modal metaphysics) and prejudices as well).

---

2   About which the scholastics, and even some of the Lutherans, Melanchthon, Stancar and Servetus, wrote. Cf. Emile Leonard, *A History of Protestantism*, trans. Joyce Reid (Indianapolis: Bobbs-Merrill, 1965); though, see p. 327, n. 1, 'the Trinity was not prominent with Calvin, *Institutes*, until after others had denied it'. See Claude Welch (ed.), *God and Incarnation in Mid-Nineteenth Century German Theology* (Oxford: Oxford University Press, 1965).

The two groups really do differ on what settles the sense of what is to be said of God, with the 'catholic' ones holding that independent philosophical analysis of the nature of divinity prompted, even provoked, by faith determines the divine attributes in a secular science of God, like that offered by Thomas Aquinas (*Summa contra Gentiles* [SCG] and *ST* I.2.26). The others deny or doubt that there is such an independent science of God, and hold to 'common pulpit talk' that derives from a different rule, *sola scriptura*, and *analogia fidei* (Appendix 1). That shows up among philosophers of religion as analysis aimed to accord with the 'plain meaning' of ordinary religious believing (the Gospels, and the talk of ordinary believers), and the denial of any 'replacement' analyses that make temporal talk of God's creation, say, to be merely (i) 'metaphorical' or (ii) 'according to appearances only' or even, as I propose below, 'according to resultant, but not the explanatory, reality'. [Notice, those are *different* kinds of accounts of the temporal talk in Scripture – of which I will make use in the last part, below.]

And it is true that religious believers do talk of and to God as *a* person, and talk of God's forgiving them, or calling them to service, as current *events* just as most people think of God's answering prayers in a response, like a telephone reply. Besides, it seems that reason would, absent revelation, commend and even command such talk: because an intelligent, free divine being would seem paradigmatically to be a person, even as Boethius defined the notion (*De Trinitate*) as a '*suppositum* – agent – of a rational nature'. So the 'reformers' need to reconcile talk of God as *a* person with the Christian commitment to a Trinity.

2. There's a further complication, too. Given that the present day 'catholic' group doesn't think of philosophy as a *demonstrative* science; they mainly rely, for their criticism, on two sorts of argument that Brian Davies actually uses: the first is to display an internal inconsistency between temporal notions of God and the explanatory role the divinity has to serve philosophically as origin of the being of all things. The second is to reject contemporary 'reformer's' assumptions about an infinite domain of possibility, properties and so on that are independent of the divine will that makes 'all things visible and invisible'. There is a third criticism, that regarding God as *a* person, that treats the name for a nature (like '*ipsum esse subsistens*', 'the thing that exists on its own') as a name for a person, when there are *three* persons in God.

Still, *absent* suppositions about the Divine Trinity, one *would* say, because of the divine freedom and intelligence, that the divine is *personal*, and as known to the philosopher alone, is *a* person (that is, is an unmultipliable 'suppositum – agent – of a rational nature' – Boethius). So is there a conflict of reason and revelation on the point?

3. I of course agree that talk of creation '*after* not creating', or of 'freedom' as requiring *alteration*, is inconsistent with the divine self-subsistence and, furthermore, that creation and free action do not, logically, involve the notion of change or succession. And I think we can be rationally certain about the divine nature and attributes (even though there are some remaining puzzles about omnipotence and

divine knowledge). Still, we don't have demonstrations (that eliminate all alternatives as impossible) as used to be supposed, because even the logic can be disputed.

Further, the 'catholics' need a story about the relation of the divine nature to the Divine Trinity that the 'reformers', the temporalists, don't have to attempt. For by positing a mutating divinity, they can allow for divine participation in human history, as the Gospel tells us; whereas with an immutable divinity, some special account of the Scripture is needed. So, think of the 'reformers' problem as one of making their changing God suitable for the explanation of all reality, and of the 'catholics' problem as one of reconciling the divine saving acts with the immutable divine nature, according to the plain meaning of Scripture and the Nicene Creed.[3]

So I conclude first that divergence among current philosophers about what is to be said literally about God has a long historical tail – long and springy like a kangaroo's, it can be twitching things a long way away.

4. **The resolution has three parts waiting and one part awe.** I predict, controversially, I know: (1) The philosophical positions of the 'reformers' will dry out and lose interest because of their internal conflicts and from the dying fashion of modal metaphysics (using interpreted quantified modal logic). (2) The *sola scriptura* (and *analogia fidei*) principle will also be gradually revised so that the 'rule of faith' (*analogia fidei*, Romans 12:4) part becomes less individual and 'local', as the desire for unity of faith gains force within Christianity.[That is illustrated by the recent unification of German Lutherans and Catholics.] (3) The rigid Aristotelian base of the thirteenth century will eventually be replaced with a new science-based philosophy that will function as Aristotle and the Islamic theorists did then, for a new mutual illumination of revelation and secular learning – a new theology. And (4) there will be a revived religious awareness of *mysterium tremendens*, that the divinity is certainly no other persons like us, but beyond all natural understanding and shown to us, even in the intimacy of the Incarnation.

Biblically governed discourse and discourse expounded with secular learning (for example philosophy) are partial, vantaged descriptions of one transcendent *deus absconditus*, the divine mystery hidden in the cloud of unknowing (just as Phillips conjectures, and Vatican I proclaimed, *caligine abvoluta* (*Const. Dei Filius* ch.4, Vat.I).

The idea of God as *mysterium tremendens* may uncover an additional division of the two groups of philosophers. For as Davies points out, some of the current 'reformers' think God is not mysterious but a person like us, not mysterious at all. (But that may be mainly in the context of conveying that God is manifest in Jesus, not as some general, metaphysical position.) The 'catholics', of course, say the hiddenness is fundamental: (i) that the nature of God exceeds the manifestive capacity of any finite effect, the way the vocabulary and imagery of a child's first reader that a child has to be able to read would limit the disclosure of an infinite intellect; and (ii) that the Divine Trinity is in principle indiscernible in the cosmos by unaided reason, the way a shimmering reflection in water is discernible only to those who already know the face.

---

3 Like 'descendit de coelo et natus est ex Maria virgine; Et Homo factus est', and 'et mortuus est, et tertia die resurrexit and ascendit in coelum', 'et itnerum venturus est'.

5. **Simplicity and immutability are negative** and logically consequent attributes of God that block certain comparisons to creatures. The nature of God, the unified, uncomplex and immutable reality, is disclosed under the light of human reason, like a strobe light presenting a perfect flywheel as one unchanging unity; whereas, under the daylight of revelation, we are shown the dynamic flywheel, the life, of the divine Trinity in knowing and loving. They are the same reality, differently disclosed, the one by limited human reasoning from creatures, the other by divine gift. And dynamism is not (necessarily) change; because change requires difference, whereas life that is love, knowledge and will can be unchanging, like contemplation. Thus, the same reality is presented diversely, with no real difference.

6. *So of course, the divine being is an indivisible unity and simple, insofar as denying that would entail God's incompleteness and dependence on things* ad extra, *and the Divine Trinity is forever in act in perfect understanding and love that we can only grasp as dynamic.* But the temporal discourse of the Nicene Creed is to be understood as true descriptions, like '*et iterim venturus est*' (contrasted with a few metaphors like '*sedet ad dexteram partris*'), of real divine consequent realities. The saving acts are the divine resulting *in* the finite, but not the divine's being finite.

7. **The explanatory reality and the consequent reality.** The 'catholics' can accommodate the temporal discourse of the Creeds and Scripture as describing divine *consequent* realities, that is, temporal finite realizations of transcendent explanatory reality [see Appendix 3]. It is not merely temporality from the vantage, the *appearance*, of the effects (like objectively *apparent* smallness of something at a distance, or the constellations), but real temporality of the consequences, like the sky where the explanatory reality (stars and galaxies) is organized quite differently from the real effects (constellations). The idea is that the effect, even of presence, can have features that belong properly to it as *effect*, and not to the cause as cause.

8. For, of course, we recognize the perceivable and apparent, indeed obvious, *reality* of the static mid-range world (tables, trains, cars, people), though we know the explanatory micro-reality (molecules, atoms, force fields and so on) has none of those perceivable features. Indeed the micro-causes, the photons and quanta, have no directly perceptible qualities at all. So, we should not be surprised that the real presence of the Logos in human history by Incarnation (Jesus) has its explanation in the transcendent Trinity that has none of the properties that belong to resultant reality at the human dimension. The same goes for the appearance of the Father (for example to Moses) and the presence of the Holy Spirit in history.

9. Thus, the reported events of Gospels and the statements of the Creed are the literal truth as descriptions of actual events, but the explanatory reality is the transcendent dynamic life of the Divine Trinity in dimensions unperceivable in finite creation and, of course, inexplicable by us. In fact, the divine reality so much overflows both human science and divine revelation as to be a *mysterium tremendens*, something that can only be imagined, like a mountain forever in a mist, and momentarily glimpsed by the few favoured with mystical encounters that they cannot literally express.

10. The relation of God, as revealed, to the world is in one respect the reverse of the relationship of the micro-constitution of things to the perceived things of our mid-range world. For the mid-range world is static and continuous, relatively, as fits our needs to be, whereas the micro-world is one of furious change and vast space among its items.

Some philosopher-theologians might want to 'save' the temporal discourse of the Creeds and Bible by saying those crucial passages that are not metaphorical are descriptions of the divine activity from the vantage of the *effects* but not from the vantage of the explanatory reality, the source. But that makes the difference merely one of perspectives of description (like the difference of seeking a car up close, or from a plane – a difference between appearances of a common objective reality, or a difference between mere appearances, say, constellations, and explanatory reality, the stars) (cf. *ST* I.67.4). I think there is a stronger way to make the distinction, as one between explanatory reality (the Trinitarian life of God) and consequent reality (salvation history), where the qualities of the latter, though real, are not the qualities of the former because they involve created elements as well.

The Divine Trinity is active in human history, not just as something that objectively appears that way and ought to *seem* that way (like constellations or stage sets), but as something that really *is* that way, like mid-range objects; though the explanatory realty, like atoms and force fields, is quite unlike it, and in the case of the Creed, is explanatorily entirely in the dynamic life of God that is unchanging. We, given our limited knowledge, cannot see *how* that is achieved, but we can know, by revelation, that it is.

So there are contexts of correct temporal discourse about God, just as the Gospels and the Creed present them. The 'reformers' are not mistaken to talk about God that way; they are just mistaken to describe the *nature* of God that way. I suggest they have taken discourse appropriate for the consequential reality of divine revelation (recorded in Scripture) and let it authorize talk about the divine nature for which it is not fitted. And so, D.Z. Phillips is right: there are 'traditions that are confused'.

Appendix 1. *Analogia Fidei*

Some theologians like Karl Barth say the meanings of 'God loves, forgives, redeems, commands' are determined by the *scriptural* context as understood by the Church: 'Language about God has the proper content, when it conforms to the essence of the Church, i.e., to Jesus Christ ... according to the analogy of faith' (Romans 12:6).[4] In accord with Luther and Calvin, he probably meant that nothing *more* than the *analogia fidei*, the faith as understood by the Church, determines what a faithful Christian is to believe and mean. And that far, the 'catholic' analogy theorist agrees. But if one means there can be *no further* truth-conditions at all, say, for 'Jesus is the Son of God', that would conflict with simple logic. So, sciences and philosophy might investigate such conditions. And whether extra-Scriptural theoretical content is sometimes required for faithful belief (say, Eucharistic consubstantiation vs

---

4   Karl Barth, *Church Dogmatics* (Edinburgh: T&T Clark, 1936), 1/1, 11–12.

transubstantiation vs mystical presence, or 'two natures' in Jesus to explain 'both God and man') is a matter of Church agreement not just philosophy.

There are *four* senses of '*analogia fidei*' that I quote from Walter C. Kaiser Jr:[5]:

Analogia fidei is a concept that has many advocates but few who carefully define it.

Henri Blocher {2} has carefully marked out four distinct meanings for the concept of the analogy of faith: 1) the traditional one as set forth by Georg Sohnius (c. 1585) 'the apostle prescribes that interpretation be analogous to faith (Rom 12:6), that is, that it should agree with the first axioms or principles, so to speak, of faith, as well as with the whole body of heavenly doctrine' {3}; 2) the 'perspicuity' of Scripture definition, as championed by Martin Luther, in which the sense of the text is to be drawn from the clear verses in the Bible and thus issue in the topically selective type of analogia fidei; 3) the thematically selective understanding of the analogy of faith, as defended by John Calvin: 'When Saint Paul decided that all prophecy should conform to the analogy and similitude of faith (Rom 12:6), he set a most certain rule to test every interpretation of Scripture'{4} and 4) the view held by the majority of Protestants, which may be described as a more formal definition, the analogia totius Scripturae. In this view all relevant Scriptures on any topic are brought to bear in order to establish a position that coheres with the whole of the [faith].

{2} Henri Blocher, 'The "Analogy of Faith" in the Study of Scripture,' Scottish Bulletin of Evangelical Theology, 5 (1987): 17-38; {3} De Verbo Dei, as quoted in Otto Ritschl, Dogmengeschichte des Protestantismus (4 vols, Leipzig: Hinrichs, 1908-27), 1.357; {4} Institutes, Prefatory Address to King Francis I of France. Calvin also refers in the Institutes themselves twice to the analogy of faith as a theological principle: 4.16.4; 4.17.32 (less clear).

Appendix 2. *Analogia Entis et Nominum* (A Brief Summary)

Aquinas combined the influences of Avicenna, Maimonides and Pseudo-Dionysius, along with his mastery of Aristotle and Plato, to hold that God infinitely transcends every true description achieved by human philosophical efforts, but that, nevertheless, a great deal can be known and positively established about God; in fact there can be both philosophical science of God and a *divine science* whose first principles are given by Revelation (*ST* I.1.2). Furthermore, he included Aristotle's notion of analogy of 'being' (*pros hen*) for the categories within his own wider theory of analogy between creatures and God by participation, saying (*Quod.* 2, q.2, 1.1) 'being can be essentially predicated of God alone, because to be divine is to be subsistent and absolute, whereas being is predicated of any creature by participation; for no creature *is* its own being, but is something having being', as the actuality of its potentiality, because creatures do not exist on account of *what* they are, but on account of God. Further, *what* God is, essentially, is not naturally knowable to humans, though it is disclosed to the blessed by divine gift (*ST* I.12.1).

So, Aquinas variously developed his account of things to be predicated of God, for example *Summa Theologiae* I.13.4-5; *Summa contra Gentiles* I, ch.34 and *Quaestiones Disputatae de Veritate* q.2, a.1, holding that our knowledge is not

---

5 'Hermeneutics and the Theological Task,' 1 *Trinity Journal*, 12/1 (Spring 1991): 3–14.

limited to what we can attribute negatively or only by metaphor, or by merely by *extrinsic* attribution that would make 'God is good' mean merely 'God is the *cause* of creaturely goodness' (*ST* I.13.6) (the way a person is called "captain' because of what he does). Rather, he says we can know that pure perfections apply intrinsically to God (that is, attributes not requiring imperfection in the subject, like 'well fed' or 'educated') by *explanatory priority* since the divine perfections are the cause and exemplar of all perfections in creatures (like being, life, knowledge, freedom and love). Nevertheless, the names and concepts are acquired only through our experience with creatures (*ST* I.13.6). Thus the words 'loves', 'knows', 'chooses' and so on used of God and of humans have similar definitions (marked by the differing conversational presuppositions), but the manner of being (or realization) in God and creatures is diverse, being prior and the same as God's being, and finite, received and really separable from other perfections in creatures.

So whatever is predicated positively of God is either by *attribution*, as God is called 'creator' on account of what is made, or 'happy' because of His perfect enjoyment, or by *proportionality* and priority, as God is said to be 'knowing, loving, wise, excellent and beautiful' and so on, but in a manner explanatorily prior to the imperfect manner, and derived being, of creatures. Aquinas acknowledged metaphorical predicates of God, too (*ST* I.19.11), many sanctioned by Scripture ('angry', 'Prince of Peace'), and many useful negative ones (God is not a body, nor in space, nor with parts or complexity, nor with a beginning or end).

The religiously and philosophically central attributes are predicated literally and intrinsically, adjusting their presuppositions both conversationally (for example 'God chooses' but does not deliberate) and theoretically (God's attributes are all really the same as the divine being, *esse*, differing from one another only in definition). They include 'knowing, loving, good, righteous, just, omnipotent, omniscient, immutable and present everywhere' – and every other unmixed perfection, too. They apply to God by proportionality to creatures, adjusted to the priority and perfection of divine being. So, God knows but does not find out; God loves but does not miss. The divine being is prior, as that of which all creation participates not as being in any way divine, but as being continuously *from and on account of* God, and thus, having being analogously. Created being is God's proper and continuous effect, the way setting alight is the proper effect of fire, and the illumination of the air is the continuous effect of the sun (*ST* I.8.1).

Aquinas thought the real analogy between divine subsistent being (*ipsum esse subsistens*) and creaturely participated being grounds unaided human inquiry into the existence and nature of God (the Divinity). He claimed that humans have demonstrative knowledge of the existence, and of many attributes of God by reasoning that he displayed *Summa contra Gentiles*.

Nevertheless, Aquinas emphasizes that what is received is received in the manner of the recipient (*quidquid recipitur recipitur modo recipientis*, *ST* I.75.5); so God is disclosed through nature only as far as nature is capable, with all creation falling infinitely short of the divine reality. And he holds that the divine Biblical revelation, though vastly exceeding anything humans could discover or even conceive on their own, is nevertheless proportioned to what is fitting for mankind, leaving the infinite divine mystery 'wrapped in a mist' (*caligine abvoluta, Const. Dei Filius* ch.4, Vat.I), with the essence of God beyond all natural understanding.

By the Reformation, the mid-sixteenth century, the technicalities of scholastic philosophy were rejected and the reformers held the faith to be in no need of fragile and contested support from philosophy. Biblical authority was said to stand on its own, to be understood by the 'analogy of faith' (*analogia fidei*, based in Romans 12:4-6 according to both Luther and Calvin – see Appendix 1, above. But *analogia* in that context means 'measure', RVS, or 'standard').

So the philosophers, both 'catholics' and 'reformers' historically and now, like Karl Barth, the evangelicals, and philosophers like Swinburne and Plantinga, hold that talk about God is neither empty of intelligible content (non-cognitivism) nor only metaphorical, poetic or symbolic (Tillich); nor only negative, except for God's existence, (Maimonides) nor positive only in superlatives (Pseudo-Denis – *via eminentiae*). And they reject the principle that what is not observationally verifiable or falsifiable is meaningless. They agree that the Scripture is the norm for what is to be said about God as revealed. But analogy theorists additionally maintain (i) that analogous predication is literal and perfectly common in discourse generally, and characteristic of discourse about God, and (ii) that the metaphysical exploration of the divine, even of what is revealed, discloses theoretical truth-conditions, not otherwise accessible, for claims that God exists and has the divine perfections, just as science discloses micro-conditions for water that are not contained on the surface of the ordinary vocabulary. It is the latter activity that 'reformers' find suspicious, but themselves take up when they start mapping religious discourse onto metaphysical modal discourse (the logical discourse of possibility and necessity), as in the 'free will defence', for example Plantinga).

Appendix 3. Truth According to Objective Consequences vs Truth According to the Explanatory Reality

Aquinas's Version

St Thomas (i) offered a negative test for the sense of Scripture, namely 'what is repugnant both to reason and common sense is *not* contained there'.[6] (ii) He distinguished common sense belief from scientific truth. (iii) He treated successful natural science and philosophy as co-certain with the Scripture, because science, he thought, is demonstrative. (iv) He also says (q.68): '… since Holy Scripture can be explained in a multiplicity of senses, *one should hold to a particular explanation only in such measure as to be ready to abandon it, if it be proved with certainty to be false.*'

---

6   Now that's a very peculiar rule, because so much of Revelation is of the miraculous and the supernatural, and especially, of things contrary to the known necessities of nature, like raising the dead. There is an implicit further extrinsic test of real possibility in the background, namely, that what is consistent to think is possible. (That does not work, as Duns Scotus pointed out: *Tractatus de Primo Principio*.4. 000).

After seeing the deficiencies of his relying so heavily upon the certainty of secular learning (where the science he relied on was wrong, *ST* I.68.3c; 70.1 ad 3; 67.4; and *De Potentia* q.4), we ask anew, 'How does the theologian rightly use science and philosophy in restating the truth-conditions of the common faith, without *replacing* it?'[7]

Science is unstable. It improves and is revised, with an expanding confident centre (for example basic mechanics). Aquinas mistakenly endorsed Aristotle's theory that there are heavenly spheres (like translucent plates in which the distant stars are fixed) that are the *really* moving heavens, though some 'stars *appear* to move' but don't. 'And yet our senses perceive the movement of the luminaries and not that of the spheres' (De Caelo. ii. text 43). He says, 'But Moses describes what is obvious to sense out of condescension to popular ignorance, as we have already said' (implying that Moses knew the correct account).

And in talking about when the firmament is created, Aquinas says there, 'Although to the senses there appears to be one firmament [there are two] … the lower [planetary] will be that made on the second day and on the fourth the stars were fixed in the higher firmament.' So the 'scientific' truth conflicts with what appears to the untutored to be so.

Thus, Aquinas thought Moses sometimes talked condescendingly to the unlettered and ignorant people who understood only the appearances of things, as *we* might to a person who really thinks the sun rises by moving (not the earth), just as the moon moves when it rises.

So he acknowledged that the explanatory scientific reality may differ from what the hicks believe. Indeed he, essentially, denies what they believe, for example that stars move, though the text of Scripture accords with what the commoners believe and is the objective appearance of things.[8]

That lets a wolf into the farmyard. Aquinas's very examples show that 'science' can trick the theologian. It is unstable just because it is not demonstrative (contrary to what Aquinas thought). For light does not move instantaneously, as Aquinas supposed, and it is indeed (loosely) a body, that he denied. And things supposedly 'proved by solid reasons', like Aristotle's heavenly sphere theory, were wrong. In a word: he expected too much from science, and inadvertently made elements of the faith seem to be refutable by human inquiry.[9] No wonder reformers wanted to separate

---

7 For instance, might it be that the resurrected Jesus is present wherever there is a distinctive physical phenomenon (bread and wine appearances) made to be by the reality of Jesus' body, somewhat the way a ship on the horizon is visibly present to everyone in seeing range, whether they see it or not? Buildings reflected in water are like that: the appearance is supported by the light reflections from the building whether anyone sees the reflected image or not. I sketch this to show that 'really present' has a variety of relevant analyses under which the 'real presence' is literally accommodated.

8 For the moving individual stars is an objective appearance of Aristotle's explanatory reality, just as the moving sun, as it travels upward in the sky, is the objective appearance caused by the turning earth.

9 Not in the innocent way that the necessarily true (for example, and revealed) is dependent logically on everything else that is necessary (including truths humans can discover).

the faith from disputes among scientists and philosophers. It never occurred to them that an Enlightenment would reverse the preference and result in 'scientism'.

Still Aquinas may have been close to something very important when he distinguished *the common sense, objective appearance of things* from the *scientific explanatory reality* that explains the appearance.[10] For that, besides its own merits, suggests a more fundamental relation between consequent reality and prior and explanatory reality – not the merely (but objectively) apparent (like the constellations or the rising sun) vs really explanatory (stars and moving earth), but between prior and posterior *realities*, like molecules and surfaces, and between force fields and atoms.

One needs an articulate connection to show the religious reality of the Gospels *ought* to seem the way it does because it *is* the way it seems, even though the explanatory, overflowing reality (the divine being) does not have the qualities – that is, the perceptible features – of the consequent reality.

A Resolution?

Perhaps the conflict of Biblical and philosophical descriptions of God is only *apparent* because they disclose the divine reality *diversely*, the one disclosing *the divine nature as exhibited* in the creation of all else, and the other by revelation of the divine Persons in the distinction of Persons from one another, as disclosed scripturally in the economy of salvation. And the whole unity of divine being infinitely overflows either, and is hidden in a cloud of unknowing.

That I think may be useful, with further details to be expressed in an account of the relationship of prior explanatory reality to consequent explained reality, where the properties of the latter are not properties of the former. We are now familiar with that sort of relationship and can use the notion to harmonize the God of the philosophers with the God of the Revelation.

---

10 Furthermore, Aquinas *distinguished* situations where the Moses' talk diverges from the reality because *things are left out* (spiritual creatures are omitted) and cases where the whole story is not told. Aquinas approves Chrysostom's explaining that Moses *did not tell the whole story* because the hearers would have misapplied it (idolatrously). [He said the same thing earlier in *De Pot*. q.4.]. Maimonides and Avicenna had made similar remarks.

Voices in Discussion

D.Z. Phillips

K: I'd like to say something about differences between philosophers. Despite these, however, we are all committed to reasoned discourse.

A tradition may be confused, but adherents to it won't admit this. The nature of the disputes differs in Christianity, Judaism and Islam. These are the background religions, and philosophy should serve them. In the end, I don't believe the fundamental differences are philosophical. I believe they come from features of the traditions themselves.

The group I have called reformers (with a small 'r') tend to emphasize the difference between the mysteries of faith and the cool results of reason (see Appendix 1). The analysts or catholics (with a small 'c') see different areas as mutually illuminating (see Appendix 2). Philosophy detaches itself from the plain meaning talk to consider its wider implications. Christians should be like the Israelites when they left Egypt – they took with them everything that could be of value. I expressed concern about the influence of Aristotle on Aquinas's thought. But that influence was only successful for a couple of hundred years. The point is that the intellectual partner with which religion cooperates is inherently unstable. I happen to think that the use to which modal logic is put in contemporary philosophy of religion is incoherent.

C: If you say the intellectual partner is inherently unstable, why have the marriage in the first place, since if one regrets an intellectual partner, on this argument its successor will be just as unstable?

A: There are also problems with what you say about the timelessness of God. It is certainly in Augustine; but by the time one reaches the second century Church Fathers, one couldn't say this. I have similar qualms about making general claims about God's simplicity.

F: The notion of creation is central here. The notion of incarnation is thought to conflict with it, especially the emphasis on God's suffering. But in conversations between Christianity, Judaism and Islam, the accusation was made that Christians are the greatest idolaters. But it takes four centuries to realize that God is One. So the revelation cannot be taken to contradict the unity of God.

B: I think K's reference to the instability of religion's intellectual partner can be misleading, and it may have misled C. When Aquinas contrasts 'science' with religion, he never wheels it out as the justification of religion. So if someone says intellectual arguments cannot be employed with respect to religion, it is important to remember that these arguments are not meant to function as proofs of religious truths.

K: Quite so, but I think we ought to be ready to admit that many of the ways in which Aquinas argues have ceased to be part of our experience of religion today.

G: I agree that aspects of medieval thought are gone, and they confirm K's remarks about instability. On the other hand, this cannot be said of all aspects of such thought. They remain a stable part of theology and philosophy so they are not out of date.

K: It is a mistake to think that science is demonstrative. In 2,000 years, much that we take as established now will be questioned.

G: One of the stable elements in the tradition is the notion of the simplicity of the soul. If A says that the soul is composite, what is the something that holds its parts together? That 'something' must be present in the soul.

A: I don't agree. Just because something is composite, it doesn't follow that it is dependent on anything else. So God can be one and composite.

L: I think the talk of 'the unstable partner' is a usual one, but I want to emphasize that the instability is also in the other religious partner. Scripture does not deliver its own interpretation. Faith does not depend on all aspects of the Bible.

The sixteenth-century reformers don't always say that 'Father' refers to the first person of the Trinity. They say that the incarnate Logos is that by which God brings himself to finite creatures. But if we look at what this has been taken to mean, we'll see instability in the realm of Faith itself.

K: I couldn't agree more. I didn't want to create even more trouble for the discussion, so I concentrated on the intellectual instability and not instability in the realm of Faith.

D: If you are correct about the instability of philosophy as an intellectual partner, doesn't that drive you into the arms of the reformers? Philosophers do not do justice to what? To the scriptures; that is, to the pre-theoretical level of religious faith?

K: But in the fifteenth century, science was thought of as demonstrative.

D: But in any event, it looks as though philosophy either collapses under its own weight, or never does a good job.

K: You may think that because you make the doctrines more positive than they are. For example, the doctrine of divine immutability is concerned to show us what God is not.

E: Are 'the religious' and 'the intellectual' two different parties on the same level? Is there not an internal relation between them? Theological change can itself rebound on faith itself. Paradigm shifts can affect faith. Hans Küng emphasized this in his *The Paradigm Change in Theology*. Thomists have not paid much attention to this argument.

K: It is true that a philosophical influence may enter into the realm of piety long after that influence has ceased in philosophical circles.

E: Things go both ways. The changes occur not only in theology and philosophy, but in liturgy and worship itself.

C: I think some caution is necessary when we speak of instability in science, and of paradigm shifts. I remember John Wisdom saying every few minutes in a discussion of these matters, 'They told me Faraday made progress.' His point is that when science changes, everything prior to the changes is not overthrown. When we find that Newton's law of gravity does not apply outside the earth's atmosphere, it does not cease to apply within it.

K: But there can be a change in our categories of thought.

C: It sounds as though the lesson for us in leaving Egypt is to be selective in our choice of treasures.

G: When use was made of Aristotle's philosophy in theology, it was not thought of as something incapable of change, but as something that opened up new possibilities.

K: I think it is a mistake to overlook the extent to which Aristotle's work was accepted uncritically. Furthermore, there was undoubtedly a tendency to accept Aquinas in the same way.

M: There are real problems to be tackled. For example, if God is an unchanging reality, how can he also be active in history, being born and dying amongst us? Christians won't want to call all that 'mere appearance'. So there is the task of explaining what is meant by 'the unchanging Logos'.

B: 'Explain' is a bad word. It is an attempt, rather, to 'understand it better'.

K: 'Understand better' or 'what accounts for us saying this'. We recognize what looks like a conflict, so that should bring us together to work on a common problem.

N: For whom is it a problem? Who is going to work it out?

K: Initially, the explanation may be for specialists, but it can enter popular faith. Take, for example, the popular assumption about God's foreknowledge, when it was taken to mean that God knows yesterday what I am going to do today. But this can't be right because God has no yesterdays. So again, the exposition has negative value.

O: What about Hartshorne's attempt to solve this problem? Since God can have experiences which belong to the past as the present, doesn't it make sense to deny perfection to these?

K: I haven't done it here, but my task would be to show that a notion like 'the perfectability of perfection' is incoherent.

A: Of course, the Christian philosophers criticized in this conference have also thought about these matters, and have answers to the criticisms.

P: If the intellectual's partner is unstable, the best policy would be a divorce and the conduct of an ad hoc liaison. Can't the grammar of a religious belief be articulated without recourse to a metaphysical system?

C: May I make an attempt to do just that with reference to the question of how an unchanging God can nevertheless be active in a temporal situation?

Think of an earthly father who argues with his son over some religious issue or other. The father dies. The son abides by his wishes. There is no question now of arguing with his father. The will of the father is fixed and unchanging. One either comes to terms with it or one does not. Yet if one does, the demand of the father's will appears in relation to the temporal details of the son's life.

According to Kierkegaard, the nearest thing to the will of God is the will of the dead. God's call to repent, Kierkegaard tells us in *Purity of Heart*, is an essential demand. It cannot be made subject to our temporal convenience without ceasing to be repentance. Kierkegaard says that when we really repent, the clock always shows the same time – 11 o'clock – it was getting late for us. And so the eternal call can come at any time – in youth, middle age or old age.

So, here is an example of showing how an eternal demand can enter the temporal detail of human lives. But the 'showing' has nothing to do with recourse to a metaphysical system. Rather, it is an attempt to elucidate the grammar of a religious relation between God and human beings.

Chapter 6

Is God a Moral Agent?

Brian Davies OP

I

I am very grateful to Dewi Phillips for focusing on my 'Letter from America' and for using it as a springboard for the present volume. But I want to say at the outset that I do not believe that there is any such thing as 'the grammar of God' (a phrase which recurs in Dewi's introductory section).[1] 'God' is a word which people understand in different ways. It is, you might say, analogical – a term which people use without always meaning exactly the same thing, though without always meaning something entirely different.[2] But they often do use it differently, and they thereby show that they have different concepts of God (which I take to indicate that there is no 'grammar of God' in the sense that I suspect Dewi to have in mind).

One might argue, as Dewi has against Gareth Moore, that noting that people say different things about God does not mean that they are not confused in what they say – that it does not mean that they are not confused when it comes to what it is to believe in God (confused about 'the grammar of God'). Moore insisted that, if one is seeking to explain what belief in God amounts to, then one must look at what those who say that they believe in God assert, and one might well find that they say vastly different things.[3] Dewi's line on this was that differences in what people say

---

1   There is obviously a straightforward sense in which there is a grammar of God – the sense in which it is true to say that the grammar of God prohibits us from, for example, using 'God' as a preposition, or as the name of a cat's internal organ. We cannot treat 'God' as a preposition since there is absolutely no precedent for doing so and since doing so would conflict with the way speakers of English (and, so far as I know, most other languages) employ the term God, whether as believers or not. To use 'God' as a preposition would simply result in nonsense. And we cannot treat 'God' as the name of a feline organ since there is absolutely no precedent for doing so and since there would be no linguistic justification for doing so (we could appeal to no current dictionaries). One could, of course, lay down arbitrary rules according to which 'God' is to be used as a preposition or as the name of a cat's internal organ. But these rules would indeed be arbitrary and there would be no reason for making them apply to the letters making up 'God'.

2   People do not commonly understand the word 'God' in *completely* different ways. We can usually trace threads of connection between distinguishable uses (and, therefore, distinguishable understandings) of the term. Hence, for example, we can even relate what St Augustine of Hippo meant by 'God' to what it meant in Roman religion (with which Augustine had little sympathy). Or we can connect what Professors Richard Swinburne and Dewi Phillips say about God (though they clearly differ in what they think should be said about God). For Swinburne and Phillips, see Stuart C. Brown (ed.), *Reason and Religion* (Ithaca, NY and London: Cornell University Press, 1977), 81–139.

3   Gareth Moore, 'Wittgenstein's English Parson: Some Reflections on the Reception of Wittgenstein in the Philosophy of Religion', in D.Z. Phillips and Mario von der Ruhr (eds),

about God can yet be viewed against ways of talking about God, ways with respect to which people can be challenged – not evaluatively (because the challenger does not happen to like what the people are saying), but conceptually (because the people in question are making mistakes – mistakes about 'the grammar of God').[4] And I sympathize with Dewi to some extent here.

Someone who claims to know about the New York subway system might tell me that trains sometimes vanish and reappear between stations. Most people who ride the New York subway would not tell me this. So a sociologist might subsequently observe that there are different concepts of what a New York subway train is. And a certain sort of philosopher might add that there *just are* these concepts, and that philosophers have done all that they can do when they have noted this fact. But, of course, the philosophical investigation can hardly end there. We should be asking questions like: 'How does Fred's belief in disappearing trains cohere with what he or we would say of trains in general?' 'How does it cohere with what he or we would say of physical objects in general?' 'What does Fred think is going to happen to him when he gets on a train that is about to disappear?' 'How does Fred use the word "disappear" when he is not talking about trains?' 'Have we any reason to suppose that trains literally disappear?' These are perfectly proper questions to ask, and Fred's answers to them might well lead us rightly to conclude that he is confused (that, if you like, he is making grammatical mistakes), albeit that his belief about disappearing trains can be registered, for sociological purposes, as one of the beliefs about trains that people just happen to have.

When it comes to different beliefs about God, however, the matter, I think, is more complicated. Fred's belief about disappearing trains would be an aberration. But lots of people share very different (albeit connectable) understandings when it comes to what God is, and it is far from clear (to me, at any rate) that there is anything like a common bar to which they can all be called to account on a charge of grammatical confusion. And since they often differ significantly in what they say, and in the *reasons* why they say what they say, I again conclude that there is no such thing as 'the grammar of God' to be articulated. We should not assume (or, at least, I see no reason for assuming) that there is some common concept of God in the background, or somehow running through what people say of God, something to be analysed, explored or unpacked – something to appeal to when pressing a charge of confusion when it comes to 'the grammar of God'.[5] Here, I think, we just have to recognize differences (albeit possibly explicable ones).[6]

Religion and Wittgenstein's Legacy (Aldershot and Burlington, VT: Ashgate, 2004).

4 D.Z. Phillips, 'Senses and Sensibilities', *New Blackfriars*, 84/989–90 (July/August 2003): 346–53.

5 In his introductory essay, Dewi says that I claim that certain philosophers are confused. But I never use the word 'confused' in my 'Letter from America'. I suspect that Dewi wants me to be saying that the philosophers I criticize in my letter are confused about 'the grammar of God'. But I do not want to say that since, as I am now saying, I have problems with the phrase 'the grammar of God'.

6 Margaret Urban Walker makes what seems to me the same point in a very intelligent review of Dewi's *Wittgenstein and Religion* (New York: St Martin's Press, 1993). She asks: '*Whose* religious beliefs and behavior give the grammar the philosopher must mirror?',

And I take this to mean that we should not assume that philosophical concern with belief in God should be confined to noting the meaning of 'God' insofar as we can figure it out from the way in which 'God' is used by different (which?) people (or in relation to something called 'the grammar of God'). We can hardly debate about God without paying attention to what people who talk about God have to say. But then there are questions to ask about truth, coherence, validity and so on – philosophical questions which might need to be answered without recourse to 'the grammar of God'.[7] When, for example, Professor Richard Swinburne or Professor William Alston tell me that people can perceive God, I can ask whether what they write squares with what at least some of those who say that they believe in God affirm.[8] But then I can wonder what is driving Swinburne and Alston to say what they do. And I might conclude (as indeed I have) that (a) they largely agree on what they mean by 'God', (b) that they share certain epistemological beliefs, (c) that, for various reasons, they reject accounts of God which would not allow them to say what they do about perceiving God and (d) that they are wrong when it comes to (b) and (c). In reaching these conclusions I am not just drawing on something we might grandly call 'the grammar of God'. I am starting with what two people say using a word (God) with which I am familiar. And I am reacting to philosophical arguments. And that, it seems to me, is at least part of what philosophers of religion should be doing as they examine what people say when they use the word 'God'. They should be asking questions like 'What do you mean?' and 'Is what you say true and argued for well?' Dewi might say that I am here raising questions of a kind that do not belong to philosophy of religion properly speaking. He might say that I should ask Swinburne and Alston to account for themselves with respect to 'the grammar of God'. But, as I have said, I do not believe that there is any such thing (and I sometimes wonder whether Dewi does either).

Anyway, the questions I've just mentioned were much in my mind when I wrote my 'Letter from America' for the issue of *New Blackfriars* published as a tribute

---

Philosophical Investigations, 18 (1995): 86. Cf. also Bede Rundle, *Why there is Something rather than Nothing* (Oxford: Clarendon Press, 2004), 103: 'With respect to "God", likewise, there is not the agreement in judgements which testifies to a coherent concept. Given the uncertainty of its usage, it is questionable whether there is a well-defined network of conceptual relationships which further reflection might bring to light and which might provide a firm basis for a conception of the divine essence or nature.'

7   Years ago, I asked Dewi if he thought that what Aquinas has to say in the first 26 questions of the first part of his *Summa Theologiae* counts as an expression of religious belief. Dewi said that he thought that it was just philosophy. That reply puzzled me, and it suggested to me that Dewi has a somewhat simplistic belief in the existence of something called 'religious belief', to be sharply contrasted from anything one might express by means, for example, of philosophical arguments such as (whether we agree with them or not) we find in *Summa Theologiae* I.1–26. But there is surely no single entity rightly to be characterized as religious belief as such. And there is surely nothing to which we can appeal as being, in and of itself, *the* grammar of God.

8   Cf. Richard Swinburne, *The Existence of God* (2nd edn, Oxford: Clarendon Press, 2004), Chapter 13, and William P. Alston, *Perceiving God* (Ithaca, NY and London: Cornell University Press, 1991).

to Gareth Moore. As Gareth I think did not, I hold that there are beliefs about God (on certain understandings of 'God') which can, as I would put it, be defended philosophically – that is, without presupposing that God exists at the outset of the discussion. I do not hold that those who believe in God always explicitly adhere to a specific set of propositions about God.[9] Nor do I claim that they have to be able to defend themselves philosophically in order to be rationally entitled to retain their belief that God exists or their belief that God is thus and so. Much that we take ourselves to know is what we get from what people tell us. And as Aristotle and Wittgenstein say, arguments have ultimately to begin with what goes unquestioned. Belief is not necessarily inferior to knowledge. It is often its basis. Justification always presupposes assent.[10] In my view, though, we do not automatically have to agree with what Tom, Dick or Harry have to say about God – with the propositions they give us with 'God' somewhere in them. We do not have to do this even if we can tolerate many of these propositions.

We can, to start with, talk to Tom, Dick and Harry so as to find out what they mean by 'God'. Then we can look at why they say what they do. It may be that they can give us nothing we might take to be philosophical reasons for what they say. They might offer us something like 'Well, that's what I've always said. Isn't that what you're supposed to say? That's what I was brought up to say. Fr Murphy would kill me if I didn't keep saying that.'[11] But Tom, Dick and Harry might be professional philosophers of religion. And, since they are using the word 'God', they might be interested in, and in defence of themselves they might appeal to, what 'God' is supposed to mean among the philosophically enlightened.

The odds are that by 'the philosophically enlightened' Tom, Dick and Harry will now mean (or, you would think, ought to mean) 'those who, while trying to do philosophy of religion, are also well read in the history of theology [talk of God]' – so that their philosophy of God is done with some serious attention to ways in which people have spoken of God (especially those who have evidently had an influence when it comes to ways in which many other people speak about God). In that case, however, one can now expect Tom, Dick and Harry to have done their homework. One can expect them not to be defending their belief in God without some serious

---

9   I mean that I do not take what belief in God means for people to be always easily reducible to a set of propositions to be trotted out by those who say that they believe in God. I presume that many of those who think of themselves as believing in God would find it very hard, if not impossible, to articulate what it is that they believe when it comes to God. On the other hand, though, those who believe in God surely do believe that there are certain true statements to be made with 'God' as their subject.

10   This point is brought out well by G.E.M. Anscombe in 'What Is It To Believe Someone?', in C.F. Delaney (ed.), *Rationality and Religious Belief* (Notre Dame, IN and London: University of Notre Dame Press, 1979). See also Norman Malcolm, 'The Groundlessness of Belief', in Stuart C. Brown (ed.), *Reason and Religion* (Ithaca, NY and London: Cornell University Press, 1977).

11   I suppose you could say that Tom, Dick and Harry would here indeed be giving reasons for what they say. For they are telling us why they speak as they do. But they would not, it seems to me, be focusing on the content of what they say. They would not be seeking to explain why what they say is true.

attention to ways in which God has been conceived in traditions leading to what they have to say – traditions to which they might appeal in defence of themselves. The three of them may have sophisticated philosophical arguments favouring ways in which God should be thought of when it comes to some understandings of 'God'. But should we buy into these understandings?[12]

Since, as I have said, I have no belief in 'the grammar of God' I can think of only two ways of answering this question. First, we might challenge the philosophical arguments that Tom, Dick and Harry give us for thinking of God as they say that we should. Then we might challenge what they have to say about God given the religious tradition or traditions from which they claim to be coming (or on behalf of which they claim to be speaking).

And this is what I was basically doing in my 'Letter from America' to Gareth Moore. In this I began with the notion of God as Creator – a thoroughly biblical notion (one you might therefore think to be a fairly safe reference point when it comes to the grammar of God in some circles).[13] Without claiming that people who believe that a Creator God exists have to be able to offer 'philosophical reasons'[14] in their defence (on pain of being intellectually and morally culpable, as, for example, William Clifford and Antony Flew have argued), I tried to explain why I believe that we have reason to think about God in certain traditional ways – taking 'traditional' as roughly signifying 'what we find in the Bible and in Jewish, Muslim and Christian authors writing from around AD 100 to the middle of the nineteenth century'.[15] I then suggested that certain contemporary philosophers of religion seem to have strayed

---

12 'God' is a word used by speakers of many languages. So it has a meaning. That meaning cannot be ascertained by introspection (here, of course, Wittgenstein's attack on private language is relevant). So there is always a background of God-talk against which to measure what anyone is saying about God, insofar as the person in question is claiming to communicate and not to be talking a 'private language'.

13 So, you see, I am not implacably opposed to the phrase 'the grammar of God'! But I think that it needs to be backed up with reference to something concrete – like the Bible, or the writings of people taken to be authorities in various theistic traditions. This, of course, leaves us with the question 'What are we to make of the theistic beliefs of those who are not considered authorities in traditions such as Judaism, Islam and Christianity – the average person who goes to the synagogue, the mosque, the chapel or the church?' I have no answer to this question. The beliefs of these people are surely many and various. I doubt that Wittgenstein himself would have been able to do much with them except to note them and be puzzled about them (though he would never, even had he wanted to, have had the time and ability to work through them all). However, I suspect that most current Jews, Muslims and Christians who call themselves 'orthodox' would, as they have in the past, say that they believe in what the 'authorities' in their traditions have to say. I suspect, for example, that the average and not especially intellectual Roman Catholic would say (pointing, perhaps, to the Pope or the *Catechism of the Catholic Church*) that he/she believes what the Catholic Church teaches (even though he/she would be hard pressed to explain what that amounts to in detail [as might some of their supposedly more sophisticated brethren]).

14 That phrase could mean different things, of course.

15 For Clifford and Flew see: (1) W.K. Clifford, 'The Ethics of Belief', in Leslie Stephen and Frederick Pollock (eds), W.K. Clifford, *Lectures and Essays* (2nd edn., London, 1886); (2) Antony Flew, *The Presumption of Atheism and Other Essays* (London: Elek/Pemberton,

far from these ways of thinking and talking about God – my aim being to paint a picture in broad strokes. Courtesy of Dewi, however, I now have a chance to elaborate with respect to one topic on which I touched in my 'Letter': that of God and moral agency – a topic which I find to be especially difficult, but one on which I think that many contemporary philosophers of religion are wrong both on philosophical grounds and with respect to what they say given the tradition in which they claim to be writing or on which they claim to be commenting.

II

In *The Coherence of Theism* Richard Swinburne (who takes himself to be speaking on behalf of Christianity) writes as follows:

> In claiming that God is by nature perfectly morally good, I suggest that the theist be interpreted as claiming that God is so constituted that he always does the morally best action (when there is one), and no morally bad action. For God, as for us, there is often no one best action, but a choice of equal best actions, only one of which can be done ... Perfect moral goodness includes doing both the obligatory and supererogatory and doing nothing wrong or bad in other ways ... Perfect moral goodness surely involves fulfilling one's moral obligations ... 'Morally' good actions are those which it is of overriding importance to do, which are over all better than other ones ... I suggest that in our sense of 'moral' all theists hold that God is perfectly good, and that this is a central claim of theism.[16]

Note what Swinburne seems to be assuming here. He appears to be taking it for granted that to commend God as good is to commend him for doing what he ought to do – implying that God has moral duties or obligations just as we do (note his phrase 'for God, as for us'). Swinburne evidently allows that we might think of God as good because he does what goes over and above the call of duty, and because he never does what he ought not to do. But his focus is clearly on the idea that the core of God's goodness is a matter of obedience (God's obedience to moral laws).[17] And Swinburne retains this focus in *Providence and the Problem of Evil*.[18] Quoting me as saying that 'theologians have taught that God is good without holding that his goodness is moral goodness', he replies: 'Western religion has always held that there is a deep problem about why there is pain and other suffering – which there would not be if God were not supposed to be morally good.'[19]

1976), 13–30. These texts of Clifford and Flew are reprinted in Brian Davies (ed.), *Philosophy of Religion: A Guide and Anthology* (Oxford: Oxford University Press, 2000).

16 Richard Swinburne, *The Coherence of Theism* (rev. edn, Oxford: Clarendon Press, 1993), 184–7.

17 Swinburne regards moral laws ('necessary moral truths' as he sometimes calls them) as akin to laws of logic. He thinks that they are analytic and that they hold entirely independently of God. See Richard Swinburne, 'Duty and the Will of God', *Canadian Journal of Philosophy*, IV (1974): 213–27.

18 Oxford: Clarendon Press, 1998.

19 Richard Swinburne, *Providence and the Problem of Evil*, 7.

Now, as I noted in my 'Letter from America', this idea (that God is morally good) is a commonplace among contemporary philosophers of religion.[20] Hence, for example, William Rowe writes:

> Since God is unsurpassably good, he has all the features that unsurpassable goodness implies. Among these is absolute *moral goodness* ... God's moral goodness has long been thought to be in some way the source or standard of what it is for human life to be moral ... Clearly, given his absolute moral perfection, what God commands us to do must be what is morally right for us to do. But are these things morally right because God commands them? ... The dominant answer in religious thinking concerning God and morality is that what God commands is morally right independently of his commands.[21]

From other things that he says, it is clear that Rowe believes that there must be more to God's goodness than moral goodness. But, equally clearly, Rowe takes God's goodness to include this, and he suggests that those who believe in God predominantly think of God's moral goodness as a matter of conformity to moral demands which are somehow independent of God (just as my moral goodness might be thought of in terms of my conformity to requirements over and above me). And there are many who line up with Rowe on this matter. According, for instance, to Stephen T. Davis, 'God is good' means 'God never does what is morally wrong; all his intentions and actions are morally right. If it is always morally wrong, say, needlessly to break a promise, this is something God never does. If it is always morally wrong to cause needless suffering, this too is something God never does.'[22] Davis goes on to add that God's goodness also consists in the fact that he could do what is morally bad but does not. He writes: 'God is also laudable for being morally good, and I cannot see how a being who is unable to do evil can be laudable for being good.'[23] The idea here seems to be that God is someone trying to be good (and succeeding) while confronted by moral claims of various kinds (not to mention various options for acting). The idea seems to be that God is good because he manages, in spite of alternatives open to him, to be *well behaved*.

This notion of divine good conduct comes most to the surface, perhaps, in contemporary discussions of the problem of evil. Does the occurrence of evil show that God is not good or even that there is no God? I am simplifying dramatically now, but the most common recent responses to this question (from Anglo-American philosophical authors at any rate) answer it affirmatively or negatively while agreeing that if God exists, and if God is good, then God is morally good. So God's friends explain how God is *morally justified* for allowing the occurrence of various evils.

---

20 It can be found in earlier writers, however. It is present, for example, in Ralph Cudworth's *Treatise Concerning Eternal and Immutable Morality* (1731), who, I believe, had an influence on Kant's early moral thinking.

21 William L. Rowe, *Philosophy of Religion: An Introduction* (3rd edn, Belmont, CA: Wadsworth, 2001), 9.

22 . Stephen T. Davis, *Logic and the Nature of God* (London: Macmillan, 1983), 86.

23 Davis, *Logic and the Nature of God*, 95. For a similar conclusion see Nelson Pike, 'Omnipotence and God's Ability to Sin', *American Philosophical Quarterly*, 6/3 (July 1969): 208–16.

And God's foes tell us why this is not so. They tell us that any impartial jury would find God morally guilty when confronted with evils that he has allowed to come to pass. And they therefore conclude that God is bad – though, in fact, they almost always conclude that there is no God (on the supposition that if God exists, then God is morally good). In this discussion, the issue, time and again, seems to turns on whether or not God acts morally, where 'to act morally' means to act as someone we commend morally does – someone confronted by, and acting in accordance with, moral duties, obligations or laws.

Hence, for example, friends of God will say things like (a) 'Much evil is a means to a good end which God cannot bring about without allowing (or risking) the evil in question', or (b) 'God might have good reasons for allowing the evils that exists, though we (perhaps because of our limited information) cannot know what those reasons are.'

When it comes to (a) the basic idea is that, just as one might morally exonerate surgeons for cutting people open in order to save their lives, one can morally exonerate God for permitting various evils. So it is, for example, commonly argued that evil actions freely engaged in by people are no indication of God's moral badness. Why? Because, so the argument usually goes: (i) it is good for people to have freedom of choice; (ii) God, being good, wants the good of human freedom; (iii) but this means that God cannot prevent all evil human choices (not to mention their consequences) since this would undermine their character as free; (iv) so God is morally justified in allowing people freely to act badly. Or, in the words of Alvin Plantinga:

> Of course, it is up to God whether or not to create free creatures at all; but if he aims to produce moral good, then he must create significantly free creatures upon whose cooperation he must depend. Thus is the power of an omnipotent God limited by the freedom he confers upon his creatures.[24]

With respect to (b) the basic idea is that, just as morally good parents might act in ways that baffle their children, so God, being very knowledgeable and very moral, might be morally justified in allowing the evils that exist – evils the moral justification of which are not now apparent to us. Or, as William Alston says:

> The fact that we cannot see what sufficient justifying reason an omniscient, omnipotent being might have for doing something [does not provide] strong support for the supposition that no such reason is available for that being ... Being unable to estimate the extent to which what we can discern exhausts the possibilities, we are in no position to suppose that our inability to find a justifying divine reason is a sufficient ground for supposing that there is none.[25]

---

24 Alvin Plantinga, *The Nature of Necessity* (Oxford: Clarendon Press, 1974), 190. Since it was published in 1974, *The Nature of Necessity* might not be deemed to represent contemporary philosophical perspectives on God's goodness. But I know of no reason to suppose that Plantinga has abandoned its line of thinking. And its take on how God might be morally justified with respect to the evils that people freely perpetrate still prevails in many circles – as should be clear from even a cursory glance at, for example, Daniel Howard-Snyder (ed.), *The Evidential Argument from Evil* (Bloomington and Indianapolis: Indiana University Press, 1996) and Richard Swinburne's *Providence and the Problem of Evil*.

25 William Alston, 'Some (Temporarily) Final Thoughts on Evidential Arguments from Evil', in Snyder, *Evidential Argument from Evil*, 317 and 321.

At face value, Alston seems here to be suggesting that God is morally good (by human standards) and that, though (by human standards) we might incline to fault him on moral grounds, we might yet end up exonerating him (by human standards) should we come to know as much as he does (presumably concerning the entire history of the universe and the ways in which bits of it connect with each other).

Responding to thinkers like Plantinga and Alston (and to others who attempt moral justifications of God given the evil that we know of) one might argue that the justifications do not succeed – that they do not give us reason to suppose that, given evil as we know of it, there is any God who can defend himself morally.[26] But why, in the first place, should we suppose that God's goodness is moral goodness?[27] My reading of the literature coming from those who think that we should suggests to me that they do so for one major reason. Their big idea seems to be that belief in God's moral goodness is traditional. More specifically, they tend to argue (or, more often, to imply or take for granted) that it is part and parcel of what we find said about God in the Bible and in the writings of (mostly Christian) post-biblical religious authorities. But is that really the case?

Before I tackle this question head on, let me make it clear that in taking issue with the proposition 'God is morally good' (as you will realize that I am), I am not denying that one can never truly say (albeit with suitable qualifications) that God is what morally good people are. What moral goodness amounts to in people is, of course, a big question, and not one for me to comment on here.[28] But many would, for example, say that we might morally commend someone for helping those in need, or for telling the truth. And I am not suggesting that it is remotely inappropriate (whether one believes in God or not) to say that God is good in that he (sometimes, at any rate, though *manifestly* not always) helps those in need, or in that he tells the truth (or even that he *cannot but* tell the truth).[29] Nor am I suggesting that

---

26 D.Z. Phillips argues along these lines in chapters 1–3 of *The Problem of Evil and the Problem of God* (London: SCM Press, 2004).

27 A question which Phillips also raises in *The Problem of Evil and the Problem of God*.

28 Perhaps I should have mentioned this before, but I am here presuming that sentences like 'X is morally good' and 'Y is morally bad' express true propositions and are not, for example, expressions of feeling. It certainly seems to be the case that those (whether believing in God or not) who take God's goodness to be moral goodness are adopting this position. A possible exception is J.L. Mackie. In his famous paper 'Evil and Omnipotence' (*Mind*, 64, 1955: 200–212), Mackie argues that there cannot be a good omnipotent God given the evils that exist. His argument in that paper seems to make little sense unless we read it as supposing that '___ is good' tells us (at least sometimes, and certainly when it comes to 'God is good') what something is in and of itself and regardless of our tastes or opinions. In other writings, however, Mackie seems to endorse what we might call a subjectivist approach to the notion of goodness. Cf. *Ethics: Inventing Right and Wrong* (Harmondsworth: Penguin Books, 1977). I should add that 'Evil and Omnipotence' in many ways set the stage for contemporary philosophical discussions of God and evil. It has been reprinted many times and is, for example, the first piece to be found in Marilyn McCord Adams and Robert Merrihew Adams (eds), *The Problem of Evil* (Oxford: Oxford University Press, 1990).

29 I do, however, wonder what someone might have in mind when saying that God tells the truth. What does 'tell' mean here?

(whether one believes in God or not) it is wrong to say that God ever does what might be held to be morally impermissible. I think most of us would say that it is morally impermissible to torture someone to death just for the fun of it. And I can see no reason to object to the claim that God does not (or does not have it in him to) torture people to death just for the fun of it. And, I might add, I am not denying that God (whether you believe in him or not) commands what is morally good. Indeed, the opposite seems true. At any rate, given what the Bible says God commands much that many would take to be morally good (think of what we find given out in God's name by Old Testament prophets like Amos and Micah). And he prohibits much that many would take to be morally bad (think of most, even if not all, of the Ten Commandments). People sometimes say that God's commands and prohibitions as depicted in the Bible express his moral character, and I have no objection to that way of talking if it means that many of God's commands and prohibitions as depicted in the Bible are commands and prohibitions which lots of people today would find morally congenial.

But to say all this is not really to say very much. And it does not endorse the claim that God is morally good. For it is all perfectly compatible with the view that God is not a moral agent subject to moral praise or censure. Yet why should one want to support that view? I want to do so on two grounds. The first has to do with the notion of God as Creator. The second has to do with things that are said of God in some primary theistic sources.

III

How shall we construe the assertion 'God is the Creator'? A Wittgensteinian-minded philosopher might reply to this question by saying 'Let's look and see how those who believe in a creator God talk about him.' I fear, though, that the look and see method is here going to produce no overall result. For there just do seem to be different (or, at least, possibly different) understandings of what is involved in God creating.

Take, for example, the familiar notion that God creates *ex nihilo* – that he makes things to be, though not out of anything. This notion of creation is classical, and you can find it expounded and defended by writers like Augustine and Aquinas. Is it biblical, however? There are certainly biblical texts which might be cited in its defence – Romans 4:17, for instance (in which God is said to 'call' into existence 'the things that do not exist'), or Isaiah 48:13 (in which God is described as saying that he 'laid the foundation of the earth'). But there are other biblical texts dealing with the topic of God as Creator which do not seem to express a belief in creation *ex nihilo*.[30] Genesis 1:1 is a famous case in point. Here, a 'formless void' covered by water seems to precede God's creative act.[31]

---

30 I am not suggesting that the two texts I just cited do this either. I just note them as ones which might reasonably be cited as biblical support for creation *ex nihilo*.

31 See John Barton and John Muddiman (eds), *The Oxford Bible Commentary* (Oxford: Oxford University Press, 2001), 42 ff. Some philosophers might say that to speak of a 'formless void' as preceding creation is as good as saying that God creates *ex nihilo*. And I can sympathize with that view. But it seems to me (as it also seems to many biblical commentators) risky to attribute that conclusion to the author of Genesis 1:1 – not to mention the authors of other

Then again, should we take God to be continuously creating, or should we think of him as having created only in the past? Here also we find conflicting (or possibly conflicting) understandings (or ways of talking). According to Aquinas, for example, there is a serious sense in which what God did by bringing it about that the universe began to exist is something he continues to do insofar as he makes things to be for as long as they exist. For Aquinas, the Genesis narrative of creation is an account of creation *ex nihilo*, and it prohibits us from saying that God makes 'new creatures'.[32] But Aquinas also holds (a) that for God to create is for God to make something to exist, and (b) that creatures need God in order to exist at any time.[33] As far as I can gather, however, the biblical scholars seem to agree that the account of creation in Genesis 1 views it as over and done with in a matter of days – even though other biblical passages seem to be supposing that God is continually creating.[34] And, so I suspect, many religious believers would find it odd to think of creating as an activity to be continuously attributable to God. Simply going by what I have heard a lot of them say, they often agree that God continues to 'sustain' his creation. But I do not think that they mean what, for example, Aquinas has in mind when he speaks of God making everything to exist for as long as it exists (this, for him, marking the first difference between God and creatures). I suspect that they mean that God props up (and sometimes tinkers with) things that he has somehow set up in advance – this not implying a total dependence on God as an efficient cause (something which Aquinas always has in mind when he writes about God as Creator). And, so I might add, there are contemporary Christian philosophers of religion who seem to think that something might exist which is not created by God. Hence, for example, explaining what it means to believe in God as Creator, Richard Swinburne tells us: 'The main claim is that God either himself brings about or makes or permits some other being to bring about (or permits to exist uncaused) the existence of all things that exist.'[35] What Swinburne says here arguably coheres with some biblical texts, but it is very far removed from anything we find in writers like Aquinas. Even a perfunctory reading of his writings should leave one concluding that Aquinas would never have spoken of anything other than God as existing uncaused.

Now my view is that writers like Aquinas can be credited with drawing out the drift of what biblical texts say about God as Creator. But I also think that they do so by rightly reading them with philosophical eyes. And, one might ask, how else can one read the Bible? The Bible does not interpret itself. People need to interpret the Bible, and they certainly cannot do so simply by citing biblical texts taken at their face value (or interpreted literally, as we might say). As far as I can work out, neither the Old nor New Testament ever comes out with a precise teaching to the effect

---

biblical passages such as Psalms 74:13–14 or Isaiah 51:9 in which there appear to be echoes of a notion of creation which sees it as following a conflict between God and other agents.

32   *Summa Theologiae* I.73.2 ad 2.

33   See *Summa Theologiae* I.44.1 and I.45.1 – but also many other places in Aquinas's writings.

34   See John L. McKenzie, 'Aspects of Old Testament Thought', in Raymond E. Brown, Joseph Fitzmyer and Roland E. Murphy, *The New Jerome Biblical Commentary* (London: Geoffrey Chapman, 1968). See especially p. 1293 ff.

35   Richard Swinburne, *The Coherence of Theism*, 131.

that God is incorporeal.[36] But both of them often seem strongly to want to distinguish between God and various creatures so as to suggest that God is no inhabitant of the physical world. In the Old Testament, for instance, God is frequently referred to as lacking certain needs and limitations found in human beings and other creatures.[37] But the Old Testament is also full of talk about God which depicts him in thoroughly human terms. The Old Testament God has hands, eyes, ears and a face.[38] He laughs, smells and whistles.[39] And he undergoes emotions such as hatred, anger, joy and regret.[40]

How are we to deal with these apparent discrepancies? If our interest in biblical texts merely extends to noting what they appear literally to say verse by verse, then we can do just that and have no problem of interpretation. But we might, as for example Aquinas did, think of the Bible as helping us to some understanding of God and ourselves – in which case we have to introduce what I can only call philosophical reasoning. Is God a body or not? There are biblical texts which can be cited on both sides here. So what if we say that God is a body? Then we presumably need non-biblical arguments (in my current terminology, 'philosophical arguments') for supposing that God is indeed corporeal and that anything in the Bible which suggests otherwise should be regarded as metaphor or something like that. Or again, what if we think that God is not a body? Then we presumably need non-biblical arguments (in my current terminology, 'philosophical arguments') for supposing that God is indeed incorporeal and that anything in the Bible which suggests otherwise should be regarded as metaphor or something like that.

With those thoughts in mind I now want to suggest that we have philosophical reason to deny that God is a moral agent. And the line I am going to take is what I believe to be that of Aquinas. So let me now focus on him for a while.

IV

Contrary to what many people seem to suppose, Aquinas does not maintain that belief in God stands in need of philosophical justification (that one is somehow unreasonable if one believes in God without being able to provide an argument, or a

---

36 Isaiah 31:3 says 'The Egyptians are men, and not God; their horses are flesh, and not spirit.' But I gather that Old Testament scholars commonly read this text as making a distinction between power and weakness, not immateriality and materiality. John 4:24 says 'God is spirit.' But this, in context, does not seem simply equivalent to 'God is incorporeal.' Taken in conjunction with the rest of John 4:24 ('and those who worship him must worship in spirit and truth') it seems to be an allusion to what God imparts to people, this being something to do with his very being (with echoes of Old Testament talk about the 'spirit of God', conceived of as life, force, power and so on). For more on the lack of Old Testament teaching on God's incorporeality, see Walther Eichrodt, *Theology of the Old Testament*, vol. 1 (Philadelphia: The Westminster Press, 1961), 210 ff.

37 See ibid., 213–20.

38 See 1 Samuel 5:11; Psalms 8:4; Isaiah 52:10; 2 Kings 19:16; Numbers 11:1; Genesis 3:8, 32:31.

39 See Psalms 2:4; Psalms 37:13; Genesis 8:21; Isaiah 7:18.

40 See Deuteronomy 16:22; Isaiah 61:8; Exodus 22:24; Genesis 9:5; Deuteronomy 32:35, 30:9; Isaiah 62:5; Genesis 6:6.

set of arguments, for God's existence). For Aquinas is clearly happy to note that many people believe that God exists as a matter of faith (which Aquinas contrasts with knowledge [*scientia*] obtained through philosophical or empirical investigation).[41] And, from what we know of his biography, Aquinas himself clearly did not embrace belief in God (did not start believing in God) on the basis of anything we might recognize as philosophical arguments.

But Aquinas also thinks that, without presupposing any belief in God, we have reason to say some of the things that Christians (not to mention Jews and Muslims) want to say about him.[42] He thinks, for example, that we have reason to say that God exists (*Deus est*). And, if we stand back and survey his work as a whole, we ought to conclude that he chiefly does so because he is struck by the question 'How come something rather than nothing?'

By 'something' here I mean 'anything one could identify as a member of the universe', 'anything one could regard as an instance of a kind, or anything we might name by a mass noun (for example water) as opposed to a count noun (for example a *blade* of grass)'. For Aquinas, our knowledge arises on the basis of what our senses put us in touch with (and by virtue of what Aquinas calls the *intellectus agens* – which, for him, enables us to proceed from, say, smelling a cat to understanding that what we have smelt is a cat). Then, so he thinks, we can begin to get a handle on the world by classifying, relating and, in general, trying to do what scientists take themselves to be doing when they seek to provide an account of what there is.

But why is there any world to be investigated scientifically? Aquinas is happy to endorse the asking (and answering) of scientific questions, but he also wants to press this one – a question that he often construes in terms of what he calls 'efficient causality', though he also construes it in other ways.[43] For him, it seems reasonable to ask what *produces* the world as we investigate and understand it. Or, as he puts it, it seems reasonable to ask why anything in the world, and by implication the world as a whole, has *esse* – this not being a question about what (if anything) got the world started (assuming that the universe had a beginning), and this also not being a question about what in the world produces what (a scientific question), but a (causal)

---

41 See *Summa Theologiae* I.2.2 ad 1.

42 Note that Aquinas consistently denies that all that Christians want to say about God can be defended (that is, proved) philosophically. In fact, he thinks that none of the central Christian doctrines, as contained in the Apostles' Creed, can be demonstrated (even though he thinks that they can be defended against charges of incoherence). See *Summa Theologiae* I.32.1 and I.1.8. I should here, perhaps, add that Aquinas does not take 'God exists' (*Deus est*) to be an article (his word) of Christian faith (*fides*) – not surprisingly, since he knows that Jews and Muslims believe that there is a God.

43 One might construe 'Why is there any world?' as asking what the world's purpose is, or whether there is a goal for all things, or something like that. So far as I know, Aquinas never asks what the world's purpose is (and perhaps that is a good thing, for the question is hardly a clear one). But he does speak of things having ends, goals or purposes of various kinds, both mundane and (in Aquinas's language) supernatural. But this aspect of his thinking is not what concerns me at this point in my discussion.

question about why there is any world containing producers of things occupying the same world as their products.[44]

It is not hard to see why Aquinas, considered as both a Christian and a philosopher, finds this question to be significant.[45] That our world is made by God, that everything that is not divine owes its existence to him, was very much part of Christian (as well as Jewish and Islamic) thinking by the time of Aquinas. And explicit belief in God as Creator *ex nihilo* well pre-dates Aquinas. But it is surely something that anyone can accept if they follow Aquinas in thinking that there is indeed a question (to do with efficient causality) to raise about the existence of the world – a question to be framed along the lines 'How come something rather than nothing?' Here, of course, I am not taking 'nothing' to be an alternative to 'something' (as you might take acquiring a black cat to be an alternative to acquiring a white one). I am assuming, as Aquinas did, that 'nothing' is not the name of anything. And, I might add, I am here taking no sides on the thorny question as to whether '___ exists' is (in Frege's terms) a genuine first-level predicate.[46] I am, however, suggesting, as Aquinas does, that one might well use the word 'God' to refer to whatever it is that accounts for there being any world at all. And, though I have not here developed an argument for this conclusion, I want to suggest that Aquinas is entitled to ask 'How come something rather than nothing?'[47]

What follows if I am right? What follows, I think, is at least part of what Aquinas argues for in defence of his claim that God is entirely simple.[48] If God accounts for there being any universe at all, says Aquinas, then God is (a) not something material, (b) not to be thought of as belonging to a class of which there could be more than one member and (c) not something dependent for its existence on something distinct from itself. Aquinas is saying here that God is not an existent among others, that, as Herbert McCabe once put it, 'it is not possible that God and the universe should add up to make two'.[49] Or as Aquinas himself says, the claim that God is the source

---

44 For a nice account of Aquinas on *esse* (one which makes interesting comparisons between Aquinas and Wittgenstein) see Herbert McCabe, 'The Logic of Mysticism', in Martin Warner (ed.), *Religion and Philosophy* (Royal Institute of Philosophy Supplement 31, Cambridge: Cambridge University Press, 1992). Aquinas's teaching on *esse* has been savagely attacked by Anthony Kenny in *Aquinas on Being* (Oxford: Clarendon Press, 2002). I discuss Kenny's critique in 'Kenny on Aquinas on Being', *The Modern Schoolman*, 82/2 (2005): 111.

45 There have been long debates concerning the correctness of describing Aquinas as a philosopher. For my views on this matter, see my *Aquinas* (London: Continuum, 2002), Chapter 2.

46 Some have suggested that what I am here reporting as Aquinas's philosophical approach to the question 'Can we know that God exists?' is flawed given things that Frege says. See, for example, C.J.F. Williams, 'Being', in Philip L. Quinn and Charles Taliaferro (eds), *A Companion to Philosophy of Religion* (Oxford: Blackwell, 1997). Kenny's *Aquinas on Being* takes a similar line to that offered by Williams.

47 I develop an argument for this conclusion in 'Why is there anything at all?' (*Think*, Royal Institute of Philosophy, 2003). McCabe develops a comparable argument in 'The Logic of Mysticism' (referred to above) and *God Matters* (London: Geoffrey Chapman, 1987), 2–9.

48 See *Summa Theologiae* I.3.

49 Herbert McCabe, *God Matters*, 6.

of the universe implies that 'God is to be thought of as existing outside the realm of existents, as a cause from which pours forth everything that exists in all its variant forms'.[50] And that, I think, is what we have to say if we take God to account for there being any universe at all. An existent among others is one of a kind, or something unique, occupying a world where things can be classified. But the source of the universe as a whole, the cause of its sheer existence, cannot be any such thing. Nor can its existence be derived. Since it accounts for the being of what we call the universe, it certainly cannot owe its existence to anything within the world. And since we are invoking it as accounting for what exists but might not, it cannot be something whose existence is distinguishable from its nature – as, for example, the existence of my (actual) cat is distinguishable from its nature (to know what felinity is, considered as a nature had by various cats, is not to know that there is any such thing as my actual cat).[51]

Notice that none of the above suggestions amount to an attempt to describe God. As I have stressed elsewhere, in his teaching on divine simplicity Aquinas is chiefly drawing attention to what God *cannot* be if he is indeed the Creator.[52] And that is all that I am trying to do now. So, like Aquinas, I am engaging in what is sometimes called 'negative theology'. But it is negative theology with what we might think of as positive results. For it puts up 'No Entry' signs (positive, you might say) at the beginning of certain roads down which one might be tempted to wander and explore the details. And one of these roads is called 'God is a moral agent'.

For how do we typically think of moral agents? Primarily, we think of them as people living in the world and capable of acting well or badly. Philosophers, of course, have disagreed about the key terms to invoke when it comes to good and bad action. Some focus on 'duty' and 'obligation'. Others make much of 'virtue' and 'vice'.[53] But they are all talking about people and what makes them to be (morally)

---

50 Thomas Aquinas, *In Peri Hermeneias* I, XIV, 22.

51 This, I think, is what Aquinas is arguing in *De Ente et Essentia* IV (though in other places also). I defend this reading of Aquinas against Anthony Kenny in 'Kenny on Aquinas on God', to which I have already referred. Note that neither Aquinas nor I take it to follow from 'God's nature is to be' that 'God does not exist' can be proved in some abstract sense to be logically contradictory. Our point is that, given the appropriateness of asking 'How come the universe as opposed to nothing?', one cannot reply by referring to something to which the same question equally applies. So neither of us is endorsing some of the most familiar versions of the so-called 'Ontological Argument' for God's existence (in various texts Aquinas rejects a version of this argument). All the same, though, both of us are noting what cannot be true of God given that there is a God (we are saying that God cannot be something the existence of which is derived) – which might be thought of as a 'grammatical' observation – see D.Z. Phillips, *The Concept of Prayer* (London: Routledge and Kegan Paul, 1968), Chapter 1.

52 See my *The Thought of Thomas Aquinas* (Oxford: Clarendon Press, 1992), Chapter 3. See also my 'Aquinas on What God is Not', *Revue International de Philosophie*, 52 (1998): 207–26. This text is reprinted in Brian Davies (ed.), *Thomas Aquinas: Contemporary Philosophical Perspectives* (New York: Oxford University Press, 2002).

53 I associate 'duty' and 'obligation' talk with writers working within a Kantian tradition, and with ethical intuitionists such as H.A. Prichard. I associate 'virtue' and 'vice' talk with writers working within a broadly Aristotelian tradition, recent exponents of which include Peter Geach, Alasdair MacIntyre and Philippa Foot. I am not assuming that reference to virtue

good or bad (and what it therefore is for them to be moral agents). But God is not a human being. And if what I have said above has anything to recommend it, we have to think of God as radically different from something created.[54]

We also have to think of him as radically incomprehensible. We can get our minds around Smokey, my cat. We can examine him, compare and contrast him with other things, note his progress and character, and even note how well or badly he is doing (considered as a cat). Can we do the same when it comes to God? Not if what I have been suggesting above is correct. There can be no laying hands on the source of the universe's being, and no way of comparing and contrasting it with other things on which hands can be laid (that is, God is not remotely subject to scientific analysis, as Smokey is). And if there is time only because there is a universe in which things change, God has no progress or character (taking character to be something displayed over time). And what sense can it make to talk of how well or badly God is doing? Such talk seems to suppose that God has a life-span in which he is now like this and now like that – one in which he changes from being better to worse or from worse to better. But how can one intelligibly conceive the Creator (my shorthand now for 'the source of the universe's being) as having a life-span or as lurching from one state to another? Something with a life-span has a beginning and end. But can we make sense of the claim that the Creator has a beginning and end? And can we make sense of the Creator as undergoing change? Let us suppose that X undergoes change. That means that X comes to be what it was not before. So a changing X acquires a way of existing that it did not have previously. If, however, it makes sense to ask 'How come the universe rather than nothing?' then the answer to the question (for me, now, God, the Creator) cannot be 'Something that acquires (or can come to acquire) a different way of being'. For something can do that only by being part of a world in which other things somehow modify it so as to make it different from what it essentially is. Or are we to suppose that there can be uncaused change in a God who exists independently of his creation? And if we do suppose that, what on earth could we be thinking of?

---

and vice has no place in Kantian and similar treatments of ethics. Nor am I assuming that Aristotelian-inspired moralists have no room for talk about duty and obligation (Aquinas, for example, though Aristotelian in his general philosophical approach to ethics, certainly allows for there being duties and obligations generated by contracts made between people).

54 R.F. Holland seems to be making much the same point as I am here in Chapter 15 ('On the Form of the Problem of Evil') of his *Against Empiricism* (Totowa, NJ: Barnes and Noble Books, 1980). He writes: 'It makes sense for *us* to have or fail to have moral reasons for our doings and refrainings because as human beings we are members of a moral community ... But God is not a member of a moral community or of any community. To be sure there are small "g" gods who have been conceived in that way, like those of the ancient Greeks: such gods are like fairies. To credit the one true God with having a moral reason for doing anything is to conceive Him in the manner of Greek popular religion as a being among beings instead of the absolute being who is the Creator of the world' (237 ff.).

IV

But, it may be said, there are moral laws which any decent God needs to take account of – this making him a moral agent. After all, is it not commonly said that God is a person? And are persons not subject to moral laws (or duties, or obligations)? And are not such laws (or duties, or obligations) binding on all persons – even divine ones? And does this not mean that God is a moral agent? And, focusing on moral goodness with an eye on virtues and vices, are not persons either virtuous or vicious? So is God (if he exists) not either virtuous or vicious?

The formula 'God is a person' is (given the history of theistic thinking and writing) a relatively recent one. I believe that its first occurrence in English comes in the report of a trial of someone called John Biddle (b.1615), who in 1644 was brought before the magistrates of Gloucester, England, on a charge of heresy. His 'heresy' was claiming that God is a person. Biddle was explicitly defending Unitarian beliefs about God, already in evidence among Socinians outside England.[55] Yet 'God is a person' is a formula which has stuck with many who take themselves to be expressing orthodox Christian belief.[56]

By 'person' they seem always to mean what Descartes thought that he was when ruminating on himself in his *Meditations*. They believe that a person is an incorporeal substance who reasons, believes and knows (in a private world, as if nothing else existed).[57] And they presume that God is just such a person. In doing so, they are, of course, taking sides on a series of philosophical debates that I can hardly begin to enter into here. So I am now just going to have to show my hand and move on – saying that the notion of person just mentioned (grounded as it is only on reflection about *people*) has been blown out of the water by philosophers such as Wittgenstein (not to mention Aristotle and Aquinas). And with this thought in mind, I suggest that 'God is a person' is not the best slogan to invoke in defence of the claim that God is a moral agent. It would not be a good one to invoke even on the supposition that Descartes's basic understanding of himself is right. For let us grant Descartes all that he says in the *Meditations*. It still remains that the incorporeal thing that he takes himself to be belongs to a world containing other such things (things of a kind, all of them members of a world). So Descartes, on his own admission (to which he seems to hold), is, on my count, a creature. And why should we suppose that God is a creature?

Note also that the formula 'God is a person' does not fit easily with biblical accounts of God. These, as I have said, vary. But while there is plenty of biblical

---

55 For more on this see Philip Dixon, *Nice and Hot Disputes: The Doctrine of the Trinity in the Seventeenth Century* (Edinburgh: T&T Clark, 2003).

56 I am here (I presume uncontroversially) assuming that Unitarian or Socinian teaching about God cannot be regarded as orthodox when it comes to the history of Christian thinking in general. It is certainly unorthodox by, for example, current Roman Catholic canons of orthodoxy.

57 Insofar as they do so they are, at any rate, subscribing to a position verbally at odds with Christian orthodoxy. This tells us that God is three persons in one substance, not that God is a person (or three persons in one person). And, of course, 'person' in classical Trinitarian discussions does not mean what Descartes took himself to be.

language suggesting that God is very like a human being,[58] the Bible also contains texts which discourage the supposition that God is really like anything we can conceive. It makes much, for example, of God's hiddenness.[59] And it makes much of his holiness – certainly not a moral category, but one used (in the Old Testament anyway) sharply to distinguish between (a) God as an awe-inspiring mystery distinct from creation, and (b) created things (familiar, understandable, manipulable and responsible to something or other).[60] And the Bible, of course, sometimes explicitly warns against comparing God with anything creaturely – as, for example, in Isaiah 40:18–26:

> To whom then will you liken God,
> or what likeness compare with him?
> ...
> To whom then will you compare me,
> or who is my equal? Says the Holy One.
> Lift up your eyes on high and see:
> Who created these?[61]

One might, of course, say that biblical texts implying a serious likeness between God and creatures (especially people) should be deemed to trump texts implying a radical difference between them. But whether or not this line of thinking is defensible on purely philosophical grounds, it seems to me that, taken as a whole, the Bible stresses the incomparability of God more than it does the similarity between God and any creature. I also think that the very concrete descriptive language it often uses when talking of God favours this conclusion. If you try to compose anything that we might call a picture of God from what the Bible says about him, you will fail precisely because of the diversity of its depictions of God. The Bible portrays God as a man who can walk in a garden, but also as surveying the created order and as being distinct from it.[62] It tells us that he is warrior and a king.[63] But it also tells us that he is a woman who cries out in childbirth, that he is various kinds of non-human animals, not to mention a case of dry rot.[64] And he *appears* in forms that *hide* him rather than show him forth. So Ezekiel sees only 'the appearance of the likeness of the glory of the Lord', and Moses sees only the 'glory' of God's backside.[65] Arguably, it is not an accident that the

---

58   I take it that when philosophers say that God is a person they are taking human beings as paradigm examples of persons – as, for example, Richard Swinburne does in Chapter 7 of *The Coherence of Theism*. (Swinburne does not take God to be all that human persons are; he believes that there are differences between them. Nevertheless, his defence of the coherence of 'God is a person' starts with an account of what he takes people to be.)

59   See Samuel Balentine, *The Hidden God: The Hiding of the Face of God in the Old Testament* (Oxford: Oxford University Press, 1983).

60   See Walther Eichrodt, *Theology of the Old Testament*, vol. 1, 270 ff.

61   I am quoting from the New Revised Standard Version of the Bible.

62   Genesis 3:8; Isaiah 40:28.

63   Psalms 24:8; Psalms 44:4.

64   Isaiah 42:14; Deuteronomy 32:11; Hosea 5:12.

65   Ezekiel 1:28; Exodus 33:18–23.

Bible does not settle for any clear image or picture of God. Arguably, also, many of its various authors are of Aquinas's mind when he says that crude imagery used when talking of God is appropriate since it conveys something to us in terms we can do something with, and since it obviously cannot be taken literally.[66]

V

Yet (and at this point I put the formula 'God is a person' behind me) it might still be said that Biblical texts present us with the notion of God as a moral agent. For does not the Bible continually speak of God as being righteous? And is it not thereby teaching (a) that God acts in accordance with the requirements of morality and that (b) God is therefore a *good* moral agent? And is this not the picture of God that comes to us in post-biblical Christian texts – ones which we might think of as embodying 'the Christian tradition' when it comes to God's moral status?

The Bible certainly says that God is righteous. So far as I can gather, however, it never conceives of God's righteousness along moral lines – by which I mean that it never takes God to be righteous because he does what is (morally) the right thing to do (as someone might commend me for doing what it is morally right for me to do).

In the Old Testament, God's righteousness seems to consist in his acting in accordance with his covenant with the people of Israel (all the terms of which are drawn up by him).[67] So it amounts to the notion that God can be relied upon to do what he has said he will do (with respect to Israel).[68] Righteousness, in this context, clearly does not mean 'moral goodness which accords with standards of goodness binding on all who seek to be morally good'.[69] And Old Testament texts *never* suggest that God is good because he conforms to some code or other (which I take to mean that they never suggest that God is good as a good moral agent is good).

The Old Testament notion of God's righteousness carries on into New Testament texts and is clearly displayed in, for example, what St Paul has to say in Romans 9. Here he is worried about his fellow Jews. They, he says, were given promises, the law and the covenant. And they were given the patriarchs and the assurance of a Messiah. But they do not seem to have turned to Christ (whom Paul takes to be the Messiah). So what shall we say about all this?

---

66 *Summa Theologiae* I.1.9.

67 See Walther Eichrodt, *Theology of the Old Testament*, vol. 1, 339 ff. See also Edmund Jacob, *Theology of the Old Testament* (New York: Harper and Brothers Publishers, 1958), 94 ff.

68 To say that one shall do such and such is, among people, to make a promise. And people able to make promises are, surely, moral agents. But when biblical authors talk of God's righteousness they are clearly not taking him to be a human being making a promise. They are obviously taking him to be one who has declared what he shall do and who acts in accordance with what he has said.

69 See K.L Onesti and M.T. Brauch in Gerald F. Hawthorne and Ralph P. Martin (eds), *Dictionary of Paul and his Letters* (Downers Grove, IL: InterVarsity Press, 1993), 829: 'Righteousness [sc. in the Old Testament] is not primarily an ethical quality; rather it characterizes the character or action of God who deals rightly within the covenant relationship and who established how others are to act within that relationship.'

We cannot, says Paul, claim that God's word has failed. For some Israelites are not *true* Israelites. And yet, Paul adds, some people are God's chosen regardless of what they have done in their lifetimes. For what about Jacob and Esau? Their fates, says Paul, were settled 'even before they had been born or had done anything good or bad'.[70] There is, says Paul, a matter of God's election to consider here. God, he adds, does not always deal with people on the basis of what they do. He deals with them as he sees fit. 'As it is written, "I have loved Jacob, but I have hated Esau".'

But, so Paul then asks, does this not mean that God is not just? His answer (emphatic in its Greek) is 'By no means'. But this answer is clearly not intended to stress that God is just by (say) Aristotelian views about what it is for people to be just. Paul's point seems to be that we have to deal with God as he does what he does – that God's justice is what God takes it to be (not something conforming to standards to which he ought to conform). Not surprisingly, therefore, Paul can add (in Romans 9:20) 'Who indeed are you, a human being, to argue with God?' (a question which strongly echoes what we find at the end of the book of Job, which is another good example of a biblical text refusing to think of God as an agent subject to moral requirements and, therefore, as intelligibly defensible or impugnable with reference to them).

At this point in his discussion Paul invokes some familiar Old Testament imagery – that of God being a potter making what he wants from the clay on which he works.[71] We might think that God ought to make things to be thus and so. But, says Paul, we should not do so. He writes: 'Has the potter no right over the clay to make out of the same lump one object for special use and another for ordinary use?' It should, I think, be obvious that St Paul is not here conceiving of God as an individual who needs to justify himself in the light of moral canons to which he is bound or obliged. And, so I might add, notions of God's righteousness in the Bible seem pretty much to accord with what St Paul says in Romans 9.[72]

Once again, therefore, I suggest that (whether or not we believe in God) we have reason for fighting shy of the formula 'God is a moral agent'. To do so seems to me to accord with biblical ways of thinking. And, so I have argued, it accords with what follows from the notion of God as Creator.[73] As I have noted, Richard Swinburne

---

70 Romans 9:11.

71 See Isaiah 29:16.

72 See the article 'Righteousness in the New Testament' in *The Interpreters Dictionary of the Bible* (New York and Nashville: Abingdon Press, 1962): 'If, as has been stated, righteousness is to be understood basically as a relational term, then it is also true that it cannot mean basically "conformity to a (moral) norm" ... Aside from the fact that righteousness as meaning conformity to a moral norm would mean that God too conforms to this norm, since God is called "righteous" (an idea incompatible with the NT view of God's sovereignty), such an understanding makes it difficult to see how the term "righteousness" can so often be applied to God's saving act on behalf of those who are supremely unrighteous and thus morally delinquent (Rom.5:8, among others) ... The clear statement of Paul than no man is counted righteous before God on the basis of works should be enough to eliminate moral conformity from consideration (Gal. 3:11 etc.).'

73 If we take a moral agent to be subject to duties, then it is, perhaps, worth noting that Immanuel Kant can be invoked as denying that God is a moral agent. In, for example,

thinks that mainstream religious traditions conceive of God's goodness in moral terms since they think of there being a problem as to why there should be pain and suffering. But his inference here is open to question. *Of course* religious people have asked why there is pain and suffering. But it is not obvious that they have always done so as posing a question about God's moral integrity. This is not, for example, how Old Testament writers proceed. They sometimes worry about what causes pain and suffering. And, when believing that it comes from God, they sometimes ask how *some* pain and suffering can be inflicted by a God who, in a covenant, has promised *some* people certain goods on condition that they act in accordance with his decrees.[74] But they never engage in a general moral defence or attack on God because of the existence of pain and suffering.[75] And this is especially so if we take 'pain and suffering' to mean 'pain and suffering as such, not just that of those who take themselves to be faithful to God's covenant with Israel'. Someone like Swinburne might say that morality requires that, all things being equal, everyone should be treated as equals. But this is clearly not a position ascribed to the biblical God. He is incredibly partisan, electing some and wreaking havoc on others without providing anything like a meticulous moral defence of himself for everything he brings about, and without being *required to* by any biblical authors.

Then again, consider the way in which Aquinas discusses pain and suffering. If Swinburne is right, you would expect his various treatments of these topics to home in at once on questions of the form 'Is God morally justified to ...?' But he never raises any such question. He asks whether God can be thought of as causing evil (his conclusion, grounded in metaphysical views about causation and privation of *esse* is always 'No', though he does say that God causes the act of sin).[76] He asks whether God can bring good out of evil (his answer being 'Yes'). But he never makes God's moral integrity something to consider given the existence of pain and suffering. And his silence here seems to me to be yet another reason for supposing that Swinburne is wrong in his inference concerning the 'problem' of pain and suffering to which he refers.[77]

'Toward Perpetual Peace' he explicitly asserts that God 'is the only being to whom the concept of duty is inapplicable'. See Immanuel Kant, *Practical Philosophy*, trans. and ed. Mary J. Gregor (Cambridge: Cambridge University Press, 1996), 323.

74 I stress 'some' here because Old Testament worries about people who suffer do not extend to non-Jews. In Old Testament texts there is no concern raised when it comes to suffering people overseas (so to speak).

75 For more on all this see James L. Crenshaw (ed.), *Theodicy in the Old Testament* (Philadelphia: Fortress Press, 1983). Pain and suffering is, of course, the major concern of the book of Job. As I have noted, however, that work is clearly not endorsing a view of God as subject to moral demands. Quite the contrary, as should be obvious even from a casual reading of it.

76 For Aquinas on God and the act of sin (*actus peccati*) see *Summa Theologiae* I-II.79.2: 'The act of sin not only belongs to the realm of being but it is also an act. And from both these points of view it somehow comes from God.' (I quote from volume 25 of the Blackfriars edition of the *Summa Theologiae*, London: Eyre and Spottiswoode/New York: McGraw-Hill Book Company, 1969.)

77 Aquinas has a commentary on the book of Job. As you will see if you read it, however, he does not there engage in the task of morally exonerating God. For more on this see Eleonore

VI

Notice, however, that this conclusion does not entail that one can in no sense speak of morality (that is, being moral) as somehow being in what it is to be God. And it does not entail that we cannot think of God as good.

I defended many of the points I am now advocating in a chapter called 'The Problem of Evil'.[78] Commenting on my claim that God is not a moral agent, Brian Shanley subsequently attacked me for not being faithful to the writings of Aquinas.[79] He has three main charges to level: (1) that my claim is not consonant with texts of Aquinas since 'Aquinas argues that the moral virtues can be attributed to God in the form of exemplar virtues'[80]; (2) that my claim conflicts with Aquinas's teaching on God's justice; and (3) that (so a Thomist might say) moral goodness (which Shanley calls a 'spiritual perfection') can be ascribed to God analogically. Elaborating on (3) Shanley says that goodness 'fundamentally means perfect actuality in being' and that 'that is precisely what the achievement of moral goodness is in a rational creature'.[81] Perhaps my position might become clearer if I respond to these criticisms.

To begin with, Shanley is right to say that Aquinas attributes moral virtues to God in some sense. Hence, for example, in *Summa Theologiae* I-II.61.5 we read: 'The exemplar of human virtue must needs pre-exist in God, just as in him exist the patterns of all things.'[82] Aquinas is here working on the principle that the effects of efficient causes resemble their causes (which must, somehow, have in them what they produce). So he is thinking that moral virtues in people somehow reflect what God is (just as he thinks that other human perfections – like being able to do a crossword puzzle in ten minutes – reflect what God is, and just as he thinks that what I am when drunk reflects what alcohol is, this being something the nature of which is shown forth in its effects on me because it is acting in me).[83]

But this line of thinking is far removed from what I am presently targeting (from what I am objecting to in the claim that God is a moral agent). Aquinas certainly does not think of God as an individual subject to duties and obligations, or as something displaying Aristotelian virtues as Aristotle took good people to do. If he takes moral virtue to exist in God, it is only because he thinks that nothing God produces can fail to have some grounding in God's nature. It is not because he takes God to be morally virtuous in any sense we can fathom and adjudicate on (or ought to try to fathom and adjudicate on). In the passage from Aquinas just quoted, his basic idea is: moral

---

Stump, 'Aquinas on the Sufferings of Job', in Eleonore Stump (ed.), *Reasoned Faith* (Ithaca and London: Cornell University Press, 1993).

78 In Brian Davies (ed.), *Philosophy of Religion: A Guide to the Subject* (London: Cassell, 1998).

79 Brian Shanley, *The Thomist Tradition* (Dordrecht/Boston/London: Kluwer Academic Publishers, 2002), Chapter 5.

80 Shanley, *The Thomist Tradition*, 115.

81 Shanley, *The Thomist Tradition*, 116.

82 I quote from volume 23 of the Blackfriars edition of the *Summa Theologiae* (London: Eyre and Spottiswoode/New York: McGraw-Hill Book Company, 1969).

83 Elementary, my dear Watson. You can always deduce something about causes from their effects.

goodness as it exists in people must derive from God and must therefore reflect what he is. I do not here want to quarrel with that conclusion. But it does not seem to me that the most perspicuous way of expressing it is to say that God is morally good. At any rate, given ways in which people commonly think of moral goodness, it is misleading to say that God is morally good if we are thinking of God along the lines that Aquinas does. Aquinas thinks that cats derive from God and therefore reflect what he is. But he never suggests that we should embrace the slogan 'God is feline' (albeit that he is committed to the conclusion that felinity is somehow in God).[84]

Again, Shanley is right to observe that Aquinas says that there is justice (*justitia*) in God. But consider what that claim amounts to – as elaborated in, for example, *Summa Theologiae* Ia, 21. Here Aquinas says: (1) God is in no sense anything's debtor, so we cannot associate (Aristotelian) commutative justice with him; (2) God can be said to indulge in distributive justice since he gives what is owed to various things. But notice how Aquinas explains what it is for God to give what is owed. He clearly does not think that God is (distributively) just because he provides for things what some moral law to which he is subject says that he should (and is, therefore, a good and just God). He says that God is distributively just by being the Creator who, by his providence, makes things to be what they deserve to be insofar as they are creatures fashioned by him (for example, he provides hands and feet for human beings). He also says that God gives what is owed to himself insofar as he brings about what is owed to him. Yet this is not the justice that people often have in mind when commending God for being just (or denying that he is just). It is not the justice of one who ought or needs to act in certain ways in order to be deemed to be morally respectable. And it is surely significant that in *Summa Theologiae* I.21, Aquinas can say:

> Since the object of will is an understood good, God can only will what falls under his wisdom. For his wisdom is, as it were, the law of justice by which his will is right and just. So he does justly what he does according to his will (as we do justly what we do according to law). But we, of course, do things according to the law of someone superior to us, while God is a law unto himself.[85]

With respect to analogical prediction, I agree with Shanley (but cannot here argue for the thesis) that goodness is a matter of actuality (that to say that X is good is to say that it has succeeded in being in some way – that, for example, a good cat is one which actually has what you look for in healthy cats).[86] But being good as a human being is not, for Aquinas, to be what God's goodness is (even though it is a reflection of that). Talking about analogical predication (defending the view that we can apply some terms to creatures and God analogically) Aquinas argues that terms signifying perfections (in creatures) can be applied both to creatures and God so long as we realize than nothing essentially creaturely can be literally attributed to God. Now we

---

84 See *Summa Theologiae* I.15.3.
85 *Summa Theologiae*, I.21 ad 2.
86 Here I am simply assuming that 'good' is an attributive adjective as applied to things in the world and that it can be used when talking of all sorts of things (not just moral agents). So I take it that there can be good meals, good washing machines and good cats – meaning healthy, fit, thriving ones. And so on.

might think that 'being morally good' (basically, being well behaved) is a perfection in a creature. So we might say that God is morally good. But I see no reason to think that Aquinas would have said so. His basic line seems to be that the moral goodness of creatures (the fact that there are creatures who are morally good) derives from God. But he never seems to suggest that their goodness (be it moral or otherwise) should be taken as a model for God's goodness (except in the sense that, for Aquinas, all goodness is a matter of actuality). I take him to be saying (or firmly implying) that being well behaved is not a perfection ascribable to God (just as being able to ride a bicycle is not).[87]

VII

Shanley attacks me on Thomistic grounds. What I am saying now is that he was not really engaging with that I was saying when claiming that God is not a moral agent (or not morally good). And, so I should add, what I am currently saying is not concerned to deny that God is good. For why not say that God is good? Isn't that a biblical teaching? And might it not even be defended without reference to biblical texts?

Actually, that God is good is not a teaching that the Bible emphasizes. Most biblical sentences directly ascribing goodness to God (and there are not very many of them) occur in the Psalms.[88] But, in these sentences, 'God is good' seems regularly to mean that God is faithful to the terms of the covenant he (freely and without any obligation) established with Israel (and *only* with Israel). In Jeremiah 33:11 we also have 'God is good'. But the meaning seems to be the same as that in the Psalms, as it also seems to be in Nahum 1:7 ('The Lord is good, a stronghold in a day of trouble; he protects those who take refuge in him'). In the New Testament we find 'God is good' only in two verses: Mark 10:18 and Luke 18:19 (in both of which Jesus says 'Why do you call me good? No one is good but God alone').[89] Of course, there is plenty of biblical talk about goodness. People are told to do good or are said to have done good; they receive good things (often from God); various kinds of human behaviour are said to be good in God's eyes; and so on. But, apart from the verses

---

87 Can God ride a bicycle? If we suppose that 'God is omnipotent' means that 'God can ___ ' might be filled in by any phrase which captures what can be done by people, then Aquinas would say 'No'. On his account, God is omnipotent since he can bring about the existence of anything of which it makes sense to say that it exists.

88 See Psalms 34:8; 54:6; 69:16; 86:5; 100:5; 106:1; 107:1; 118:1; 119:29; 135:3; 136:1.

89 What are these verses asserting? Nothing, so it seems to me, in defence of the proposition 'God is morally good' as I am construing it. And I find little to contradict this conclusion in what contemporary biblical critics have to say about them. Hence, for example, in *The Gospel of Luke* (Collegeville, MN: The Liturgical Press, 1991) Luke Timothy Johnson suggests that 'Jesus's response is the reflex deflection of human praise in favor of God as source of all being or goodness' (276). Suppose that Johnson's exegesis (a fairly common one) is right. We still do not have a clear statement to the effect that God is morally good (in my sense). On Johnson's reading, if I interpret it rightly, Jesus is effectively saying 'Stop flattering me; focus on God and start from there.' For a reading of 'No one is good but God alone' which compares with Johnson's, see I. Howard Marshall, *The Gospel of Luke* (Exeter: The Paternoster Press, 1979), 684.

just mentioned, the Bible does not push the idea that God is good. What it typically says is that he is holy, or righteous, or just, or faithful, or merciful or loving.[90] In doing so, however, it does not seem to be commending God for conforming to moral standards (or to what we might call 'universal moral standards'). There are, of course, the verses from Mark and Luke. But it is not obvious what they are driving at. Their main function seems to be to say that 'good' should only be predicated of God (not a typical biblical view). But in what sense is not explained. The notion that God is good really only comes into its own in post-biblical theological and philosophical reflection (maybe because of the influence of St Augustine, who, at one point in his life, had real problems with evil considered as a power alongside God). Notice, however, that until relatively recently, the notion that God is good has not been construed in moral terms.[91]

To illustrate the fact I shall again focus on Aquinas, who several times over asks whether God can be said to be good. His answer is 'Yes', but only (I repeat, *only*) because God is the source of the being of everything created. Or, as Aquinas writes in the *Summa Theologiae*:

> We should especially associate goodness with God. For something is good insofar as it is desirable. But everything desires its perfection, and an effect's perfection and form consists in resembling its efficient cause (since every efficient cause produces an effect like itself). So an efficient cause itself is desirable and good, what is desired from it being a share in resembling it. Clearly then, since God is the first efficient cause of everything, goodness and desirability belong to him. That is why Dionysius ascribes goodness to God as to the first efficient cause, saying that we call God good 'as the source of all subsistence'.[92]

Aquinas is here thinking in terms of Aristotle's claim that good is what everything desires.[93] He thinks that we would not call something good unless we took it to be desirable. He also thinks that effects of efficient causes reflect their causes' natures and that the good desired by an effect is first of all in its cause. So he reasons that all creatures desire (though not necessarily consciously) what is in the first cause of all (namely God) and that God is therefore good.

---

90 It is sometimes said that, for the Bible, God's love is an ethical attribute of him. But I cannot imagine why anyone should think that. Talking of God's love as recorded in Hosea (big on God loving), Walther Eichrodt (rightly to my mind) observes: 'This demonstration of the way in which the concept of love is worked out in history is far removed from any attempt to reduce the love of God to a rational principle, to turn it into some sort of "ethical law of the universe". This is ruled out first by *the strong emphasis on the inexplicable and paradoxical character of God's love*, which is portrayed in terms of the wooing of a wanton – an absolutely grotesque proceeding, flying in the face equally of morality and of justice' (*Theology of the Old Testament*, vol. 1, 252).

91 Maybe lots of religious believers from the time of the New Testament to the modern period have actually construed God's goodness in moral terms. And if that is the case, then I look forward to evidence supporting it. But I am not aware of any serious evidence to support it.

92 *Summa Theologiae* I.6.1 (my translation).

93 Aristotle, *Ethics*, I, 1.1094a3.

You may not like the argument. What you cannot say, though, is that it is an argument for God being morally good (that is, well behaved). And, quite generally, and in spite of what Brian Shanley says against me, Aquinas has no concept of God as being good in the sense implied by the philosophers of religion to whom I referred above when introducing the notion of God's moral goodness. He does not, of course, want to say that, for example, God can determine by fiat whether or not it is right to torture children (though there have been some who seem to have embraced this position). But neither does he want to say that God's law forbidding such a practice comes from one who has checked on what is right and wrong and decreed accordingly. His position is that God cannot effect (bring about) anything bad since for God to create is for him to bring about what is real, and therefore (at least to some extent) good. For Aquinas, it makes no sense to conceive of God as producing (and therefore as willing) evil. He also wants to say that being perfectly actual, God cannot be thought of as lacking in any way.

As philosophers know well, in debates about God's goodness it is often asked whether God wills something because it is good or whether something is good because God wills it. Aquinas, who never directly tackles this question (so far as I know) can, I think, be said to hold that the answer must be: (a) God wills us to do what is good because it is good, and (b) what is good for us to do depends on the way in which God has made creatures to be. In terms of this account, Aquinas would say that God could never command us to torture children because, in effect, that would involve him in contradicting himself, or going against his nature as the source of creaturely goodness (the nature of which Aquinas thinks that we can determine, at least to a large extent, independently of theological reflection). And this, of course, is not to suggest that God's goodness consists in him acting in accordance with moral norms to which he responds in any sense.

Is Aquinas right when it comes to ascribing goodness to God? I can hardly take this question on here. For the record, though, I think that what he says makes sense. If you can swallow the notion that the goodness of creatures reflects what is in God before it is in them, then you might be able to agree (as I do) that in seeking what is good for us we are seeking what lies in God – which gives us a reason for saying that there is goodness in God. Furthermore, if, like Aquinas, you take 'X is perfect' to mean 'X cannot be improved' (and if you are happy to take 'good' and 'perfect' as possibly interchangeable, in some contexts anyway), then, like Aquinas, you will think that God is good (perfect) since (being immutable – if you have time for divine immutability) he is not something of which it makes sense to say that it is capable of improvement (that to be God is to be all that it takes to be divine, with no possibility of improvement).[94] In agreeing with Aquinas on these matters, though, you will not (as I hope should seem obvious) be conceding that God is well behaved and, for that reason, is a moral agent or is morally good.[95]

---

94 See *Summa Theologiae* I.6.2–3. I have defended these ways of thinking in Brian Davies (ed.), *Philosophy of Religion: A Guide to the Subject*, 185 ff.

95 For comments on previous versions of the above I am grateful (with the usual disclaimer) to Christopher Arroyo, Michael Baur, Norris Clarke, Gyula Klima, Luke Timothy Johnson and Margaret Walker.

Voices in Discussion

D.Z. Phillips

B: I am still puzzled by the appeal to *the* grammar of 'God'. I have no clear idea of what is being described. There are lots of beliefs which can be described. There is no such one thing as 'belief in God'. We don't set the beliefs alongside the grammar. Rather, what we want to know is whether the beliefs are true. Do they square with what believing philosophers say – the ones I was concerned with. They call themselves Christian philosophers and, as such, they claim to be in accord with Christian tradition. Many of them try to make D.Z. Phillips a whipping boy. I think that some of what he says does not accord with the tradition, but he coheres far more with it than his critics.

The Christian philosophers I have in mind say that God is a moral agent. I claim that this conflicts with what we should say philosophically, and with Christianity. Why say that God's goodness is moral goodness? In the main, the answer lies in the way the problem of evil is discussed. God's friends and foes share common presuppositions. The friends try to justify him. The foes say that he can't be justified, and that this shows that he does not exist.

I am not saying that God is never what morally good people are. It is morally good to help people. God, sometimes at least, helps people. It is good to tell people the truth. Sometimes, God does that too (though there are difficulties about this). In denying that God is moral, I don't mean that he does what it is immoral. It is immoral to torture anyone for pleasure. God does not torture anyone for pleasure. God can command what may be morally good, for example, in the Ten Commandments.

I then try to sketch a positive case for not saying that God is a moral agent. I emphasize the essentiality of God as Creator in Christianity, Judaism and Islam. On that view, we live in a created order. There are a number of different views of creation. Sometimes it seems to be treated as a discrete event. From Augustine onwards, God is said to have brought the world into being and to have sustained it thereafter. That view is maintained up to the eighteenth century. Aquinas's view is that creation is 'making it to be' out of nothing. That coheres with biblical understanding. The Bible does not interpret itself – some verses suggest that God is corporeal, while others deny it. So we read the Bible and try to make sense of it. We ask, 'How comes it that there is anything at all?' The world is not self-explanatory. It raises the question, 'How come there is something rather than nothing?' What is the 'something' that accounts for it? The answer can't be an item we can put alongside other items. This is the beginning of the reference to 'divine simplicity'. God is not a member in the world. If we can say that, God cannot be called a moral agent. There is one tradition pointing that out which runs from Kierkegaard to D.Z. Phillips. If Aquinas is right in saying that God is the source of all goodness, there is a 'No Road' sign on the road which leads to calling him a moral agent. He is not a member of a moral community who can do well or badly. God as Creator is radically different from moral agents. We cannot speak of his progress. He has no life span. We can't say he is doing well or badly.

God is said to be a person. I am deeply troubled by this. It is never said in the Bible, in any patristic formula or even in Descartes. It occurs first in 1644 in the trial of one John Biddle who was tried for heresy. He was a Socinian and was said to contradict the Trinitarian view.

Christian philosophers think of God as a Cartesian ego, but better behaved, more powerful, better beloved. People like Swinburne argue for a strong dualism – a person is an incorporeal substance. He is an interactive dualist. The self acts on the world. It is a causal interaction. Descartes never gives this account of God. God is 'simple'. He is not like us only stronger. But the Bible speaks of God in a number of flamboyant images, but never as a Cartesian ego.

The Bible speaks of God's righteousness, but not of him acting well or badly. He abides by the terms of a covenant which is set up by him in the first place. Even when his promises seem to fail, God doesn't owe us an explanation. The problem of evil does not exist in the Bible. People wonder about evils; wonder why God doesn't do something about them. But this is never a question of God being well behaved, and there is not even a whiff of a suggestion that he should defend himself. That was the case for centuries. Aquinas never raises the traditional problem of evil.

I end with what I am not saying. It doesn't entail saying that morality is not in God or that God is not good. 'God make it so' – God as the fount of goodness. God is a cause which shows itself in what it brings out. When I'm drunk, I don't look like alcohol, but alcohol is working in me. Morality is in God in that it flows from him.

The Bible doesn't give much room to the notion that God is good. The Psalms have a covenantal concept, but not like Swinburne's . There are only two occurrences in Mark and Matthew, where Jesus rebukes the disciples for calling him good, because, he says, no one is good but God. I have no idea what that means.

For Aquinas, 'God is good' is not equivalent to 'God is morally good'. Rather, he means that we are drawn to him. He is the alpha and omega of goodness.

What about the *Euthyphro* dilemma? Does God will the good because it is good; or is it good because God wills it? God wills that we do good according to our natures. In that sense, goodness flows from the will of God.

A: What do you make of the belief that God created human beings in his own image? Many statements are true about God, but not in the same sense that they are true about us. God causes and God loves, but not in the same sense that we do. Can you make God sound like people but then say he is quite apart from them?

B: But that is precisely where divine simplicity comes in. God is strongly what we are not.

A: I think God has moral obligations to keep the covenant once he has made it, but the obligations are to himself, not to us. He cannot keep or break the covenant.

B: Breaking it will not happen.

A: I agree. That is ruled out for God. He cannot do that.

G: It does not make sense to think otherwise.

C: A comparison with induction, which may seem unlikely at first, may illustrate the sense of saying that God is the source of goodness for believers. In the problem of induction, people have asked why the fact that things have happened in such-and-such a way in the past gives one good reason to say that the same will occur in the future. Sometimes, such an expectation is false. But when an expectation is not realized, an explanation is sought; it is *due to* something or other. In other words, the divergence is itself explained in terms of inductive procedures. If someone asked for a proof of those procedures as such, one wouldn't know what it would mean to doubt them. One might say that, with respect to reasoning, we live and move and have our being within an inductive spirit of reasoning. For believers, God's faithfulness is that in which they live and move and have their being. Whatever comes along is met within the parameters of the context of God's faithfulness. It is the spirit in which things are met. *How* this is mediated in the particular case may prove arduous and difficult. It may lead to loss of faith even, but then it would be the loss of a whole spirit or light within which life's travails are met.

Having said that, I am speaking about God as the source of goodness for believers. There are other conceptions of goodness. How is the religious notion related to these? In other words, I missed any treatment of the heterogeneity of morals.

B: I would begin by emphasizing that God is the source of 'being' as such.

C: But I go back to my warrior example. The warrior, unlike the Good Samaritan, does not go to the aid of the sufferer. Like Callicles, he may say that suffering doesn't happen to a man.

B: For Aquinas, 'the good' is linked to desirability. It is something to which we are attracted by nature. It is what makes us happy.

C: But the way of Christ does not make the warrior happy. He may say that Christ 'has made the world grey with his breath'.

B: But the warrior will not want to suffer pain.

C: It depends. If he is caught, he doesn't want to be sent to a rehabilitation centre. He wants, maybe, to be tied to a tree, prodded with hot sticks to show how he can bear pain with courage. Not to do this would be to dishonour him. He dies happy if he dies with his sword in his hand. He dies happy if he dies as a warrior should.

K: But he isn't really happy, though he thinks he is.

C: I think that simply begs the question.

D: I think things are more ragged than B suggests. God is not a member of a moral community as we are, but is he not asked to keep his promises and seems to be rebuked sometimes for not doing so?

B: I do not deny that, but I'm thinking of philosophers who make God a moral agent in the way in which J.L. Mackie does, for example.

D: But people call on God to be faithful. There does at least seem to be some overlap with moral agency.

B: But I am not denying that it is possible to truly say of God what can be said of moral agents.

F: But isn't it paradoxical to call God virtuous, since virtues are dispositions in time?

E: Aquinas emphasizes that God is not situated in a moral community as one moral agent among others. On the other hand, God is the provider of the moral law, and is a moral agent in that sense. The analogical use of language is literal language as far as reference to God is concerned. It is the proper language in that context and, therefore, it was not metaphorical. Also, in stressing the way of negation, we should not forget the way of eminence.

B: What does it mean to say that God is just?

K: We might say that God's goodness is related to our moral ways as physics is related to our perception of physical objects – the underlying source beneath appearances.

B: If we are speaking of God, there are certain things we cannot say of him because he is other than us. So it is not a matter of spiritual otherness.

I: But don't we praise God, as when we say that his act of salvation is worthy of praise?

B: Not in the sense of praising him for acting well, for a job well done. It is more like saying, 'Blessed are you for your mercies. Grace is a gift – Praise God!'

O: If the traditional view you propose is correct doesn't it simply bail God out of moral responsibility?

B: What I am insisting on is that we cannot ask whether God is well behaved or not. That does not mean that we don't ask why in bewilderment in the face of evil. Causal explanations are known, yet the question is still asked. One may ask why God hasn't given one more grace to bear evils, but that is not questioning his motives.

O: Can God run amok?

B: No, God can have no regrets.

O: There seems to be examples of God regretting what he has done in the Bible.

C: It is true that the prophets seem to be saying to God, at times, 'You can't do that', where the implication seems to be 'You are that, and you should do better.' I wonder, however, whether this is a part of the struggle towards a worthy conception of God, so that 'You can't do that' is to be taken as 'You can't be that'.

B: Aquinas responded to the fact that the Bible uses a whole list of gross metaphors to speak of God. They are highly anthropomorphic. Aquinas said that the grosser they were the better, since no one would take them to be strict, let alone final applications. The danger is in refined uses of language where this will be thought. 'Person' is today's favourite. But it is just as gross as 'eagle' if it is thought to be an adequate application to 'the source of all things'.

Chapter 7
Anthropomorphism in Catholic Contexts

David B. Burrell CSC

As a confirmed Maimonidean, I am inclined to diagnose any trace of 'anthropomorphism' in philosophical theology as a failure to acknowledge the first principle of any theological inquiry: what Robert Sokolowski has identified as 'the distinction' of creator from creation.[1] For unless one pauses sufficiently to note the *sui generis* character of this relation, then 'god', it seems, will inevitably be treated as an item in the universe, indeed, as 'the biggest thing around'. And since such a god would fall short of the creator, one will have failed to take the initial step into the arena of theology. Many 'identity theologies' exhibit this impatience, as does the penchant towards one or another 'process theology', by endeavouring to map the 'interaction' between God and world. In fact, one can best trace the roots of anthropomorphism to an insouciance about, or 'fudging' of, the relation of creator to creatures. Put otherwise, if one fails to take care initially to identify the god in question as the 'beginning and end of all things, and especially of rational creatures' (*Summa Theologiae* I.2.Prol.), then one will quite unconsciously go on to speak of this god in categories tailored to the universe in which we live, thus treating it as an item in our world. Indeed, a theologian as uncompromising as Maimonides had to acknowledge the sole link of creation. Yet simply avowing a creator will hardly suffice; one must struggle to articulate what each of the Abrahamic traditions readily identified as *creatio ex nihilo*. For within that struggle lies the key to what Sokolowski identified as 'the distinction': attempting to articulate not merely origins, but the enduring relation whereby creatures are related to their creator as the source of their very being.

Moreover, while Sokolowski underscores 'the Christian distinction' (for reasons which he articulates), one can find analogous strategies in each of the Abrahamic faiths, and fruitful suggestions even beyond them.[2] Indeed, such encounters can open new dimensions in theology, as Sara Grant's Teape lectures show so eloquently.[3] By constructing a conversation between Aquinas and Shankara, she dramatizes how unique the relation between creation and its creator must be. Once we attend to the import of Aquinas's formula for creation as 'the emanation of being entire from the universal cause of all being' (*ST* I.45.1), we find that we cannot speak of creator and creation as two separate things. Sokolowski's way of identifying 'the distinction'

---

1   *God of Faith and Reason* (Washington DC: Catholic University of America Press, 1989).

2   See my 'The Christian Distinction Celebrated and Expanded', in John Drummond and James Hart (eds), *The Truthful and the Good* (Dordrecht: Kluwer Academic Publishers, 1996), 191–206.

3   Sara Grant, *Towards an Alternative Theology: Confessions of a Nondualist Christian* (Notre Dame, IN: University of Notre Dame Press, 2002).

of God from God's creation will effectively block any naive pantheistic images, certainly; yet we can hardly speak of two separate things, since the very being of creatures is a 'being-to' God (*ST* I.45.4). So the term adopted by Shankara and so redolent of Hindu thought – 'non-duality' – may turn out to render the elusive creator/creature distinction better than anything else. But it took a person whose study of Shankara's thought had been augmented by years actively participating in an *ashram* in Pune in India to bring to light the treasure latent in the Christian doctrine of creation. Read in conjunction with Rudi te Velde's *Substantiality and Participation in Aquinas*, Sara Grant's slim volume offers yet further perspective on Aquinas's recourse to this instrument of Neoplatonic thought – *participation* – to render coherent the radical introduction of a free creator into Hellenic metaphysics.[4] Yet in fact that was only accomplished in conjunction with Avicenna and Moses Maimonides: an Islamic philosopher who introduced a distinction which would prove key to Aquinas's elaboration of the creator as 'cause of being', and a Jewish thinker steeped in 'the Islamicate'.[5]

So what many regard as the classical Christian synthesis of philosophical theology, Aquinas's *Summa Theologiae*, proves in retrospect to have already been an intercultural, interfaith achievement, offering a constructive intellectual demonstration of the way that faith cannot be something which we grasp but which must grasp us; and even further, of the way those of other faiths can help us articulate our own. This retrospective should alert us to one more unintended consequence of anthropomorphism in religious thought: the more notions of the divinity tend towards idolatry, the more we will find them opposing one another like tribal gods. Yet as such 'theologies' also claim to be 'monotheistic', that opposition will be the more acrimonious in that each pretends to possess a complete account of reality: a posture academics call 'exclusivism'. And when that presumption of a complete account is reinforced by economic and political power, the opposition becomes deadly. Yet logically enough, one predictable response to such ersatz theology will inevitably be to deny such a god, resulting in cultural atheism. So the internal dialectic whereby anthropomorphic theologies lead inevitably to the demise of theology itself, as Maimonides warned, illustrates why the focus on creation, with attendant philosophical attempts to articulate the unique relation of creator to creatures, proves to be so crucial to the entire endeavour of philosophical theology.

In the operative sense, then, *anthropomorphism* need not be limited to crude human likenesses, or to naively simplistic analogies between divine and human action. Indeed, these latter are far more prevalent in those (largely Protestant) circles which often attempt to forge theological categories directly from scriptural language –

---

4   Leiden: Brill, 1996; for the crucial role of an Islamic text in this process, see my 'Aquinas' Appropriation of *Liber de causis* to Articulate the Creator as Cause-of-Being', in Fergus Kerr (ed.), *Contemplating Aquinas* (London: SCM Press, 2003), 55–74.

5   See my *Knowing the Unknowable God* (Notre Dame, IN: University of Notre Dame Press, 1986); the term 'Islamicate' was coined by Marshall Hodgson to convey the extensive cultural milieu: *Venture of Islam* (Chicago: University of Chicago Press, 1974).

a practice upon which our dual response exempts me from commenting.[6] Catholic 'anthropomorphism' is more subtle. It had rather to do with building complex conceptual apparatus whose logical outcome would be the God we worship. Indeed, it was that purported bridge between something so conceivable and something worshipful which elicited the scornful *nein* of Karl Barth. I insist on 'had', however, since that enterprise lasted little more than a half-century: from Leo XIII's rousing encyclical *Aeternae Patris* (1893) to the emergence of the *nouvelle theologie* in the 1950s, followed before long by the work of Barth's Catholic interlocutor, Han Urs von Balthasar. Crucially contributing to its demise was the penetrating historical work on Aquinas (of Chenu, Grabmann and others) under the rubric of *nouvelle theologie*, since that work followed the lineaments of *ressourcement,* refusing to content itself with conceptual elaboration alone. It was these contextual studies which informed the work of my mentor in Aquinas, Bernard Lonergan, whose 'search for understanding' revealed (by contrast) how much earlier responses to Leo XIII's call to return to Aquinas had been shaped by a Cartesian 'need for certitude'. Indeed, Lonergan's philosophical inspiration had been John Henry Newman – himself quite out of spirit with the early 'Thomism' he had encountered on becoming Catholic. Indeed, what has emerged in the best of Catholic thought has been a keen appreciation of the ways in which Aquinas himself can serve as a model for transforming inherited philosophical categories into subtle instruments for highlighting and elucidating the unique 'distinction' of creator from creatures. Awareness of this shift in focus, from a 'Thomism' which hardened traditional lines of delineation between 'philosophy' and 'theology' to one more sensitive to Aquinas's own practice of interpenetration, can be traced to the lapidary remark of Josef Pieper, that 'the hidden element in the *philosophy* of St. Thomas is creation' [emphasis added].[7] By which he meant free creation, itself an affirmation of faith; thereby subverting the simple bifurcation between 'philosophy' and 'theology' on which neoThomism had built its case.

Expositions of *analogy* can offer object lessons in this growing appreciation of Aquinas's subtlety, as treatments shifted from 'analogy of being' to 'analogy of "being"', under the aegis of Wittgenstein.[8] Benchmarks for these two phases can be found, respectively, in the work of James Klubertanz, and subsequently in that of

---

6 Though one cannot forbear taking note of one of the latest aberrations, collected under one cover as *The Openness of God: A Challenge to the Traditional Understanding of God*, by Clark Pinnock et al. (Downers Grove, IL: InterVarsity Press, 1994). A more recent attempt by William Hasker is *Providence, Evil and the Openness of God* (London/New York: Routledge, 2004).

7 Josef Pieper, *The Silence of St. Thomas: Three Essays* (New York: Pantheon, 1957): 'The Negative element in the Philosophy of St. Thomas', pp. 47–67; for a critical look at traditional lines of delineation between 'philosophy' and 'theology' issue, see my 'Theology and Philosophy', in Gareth Jones (ed.), *Blackwell Companion to Modern Theology* (Oxford: Blackwell, 2004), 34–46.

8 See my essay extending that title to the following phase: 'From the Analogy of "Being" to the Analogy of Being', in Thomas Hibbs and John O'Callaghan (eds), *Recovering Nature: Essays in Natural Philosophy, Ethics, and Metaphysics in Honor of Ralph McInerny* (Notre Dame, IN: University of Notre Dame Press, 1999), 236–49; reprinted in my *Faith and Freedom* (Oxford: Blackwell, 2004).

Ralph McInerny and James Ross.[9] My own early work on this fertile issue exploited the contrast between Joseph Owens and G.E.L. Owen's treatment of Aristotle, the latter displaying the celebrated sensitivity to language which Wittgenstein had introduced to Oxbridgean philosophical circles.[10] McInerny's signal contribution was to dethrone the sixteenth-century work of Cajetan as the canonical interpretation of Aquinas on the matter, which had undergirded standard Thomist expositions of analogy as a metaphysical issue, to remind us how consummately linguistic was Aquinas's treatment of the issue, focused on 'naming God'. As we shall see, that shift represents the penultimate word on the question, but it served to remind us that Aquinas had never offered a 'theory of analogy', but rather exploited the virtualities of our ordinary evaluative language to press it into service beyond our ken. For he responded explicitly to 'Rabbi Moses' objecting to our presuming to use any expression of human language to refer to God, by noting that we could only do so if we were acutely aware that such expressions could only 'imperfectly signify' divinity.[11] And the nub of that awareness would have to be our attention to the *sui generis* link of the free creator to all that is, such that whatever we recognize as perfections in creatures 'must pre-exist in God in a higher manner ... since God is the primary operative cause of all things' (*ST* I.4.2) – with the crucial caveat that a proper conception of that 'higher manner' will always escape us.[12] So Aquinas concurs with Maimonides' objection, but credits human beings, properly trained, with the semantic ability to 'intend to signify' something beyond their ken, so long as they realize that the One of whom they wish to speak is the creator.

So there is a set of terms available to be put to analogous use, which may be identified as *perfection* or *assessment* terms, and when used properly they will already be used analogously when used among various kinds of creatures, as well as when extended to the creator. Hence criteria will differ for assessing creditable performances, whether of dissertations or of concerts, yet those acquainted with these contexts know how to use them properly in each (and sometimes even in both).[13] That capacity, like the choice of an apposite metaphor, represents (as Aristotle remarked) a sign of human intelligence. The same term may be used properly in each case provided we acknowledge our ability to recognize similarity-cum-difference. Indeed, we find people who cannot do so unaccountably 'wooden', so there can be nothing recondite about analogous use of terms; they are essential to discerning human interaction. When these same perfection-terms are pressed into service to

---

9   Ralph McInerny, *The Logic of Analogy* (The Hague: Martinus Nijhoff, 1961) and *Studies in Analogy* (The Hague: Martinus Nijhoff, 1968) to *Aquinas and Analogy* (Washington DC: Catholic University of America Press, 1996); James Ross, *Portraying Analogy* (Cambridge: Cambridge University Press, 1982); Gregory Rocca, *Speaking the Incomprehensible God* (Washington DC: Catholic University of America Press, 2004).

10   *Analogy and Philosophical Language* (New Haven, CT: Yale University Press, 1973).

11   *Summa Theologiae* I.13.5, with an illuminating Appendix to the Blackfriars edition by Herbert McCabe on 'imperfect signification' (New York: McGraw-Hill, 1965).

12   See my 'Maimonides, Aquinas and Ghazali on Naming God', in Peter Ochs (ed.), *The Return to Scripture in Judaism and Christianity* (New York: Paulist Press, 1993), 233–55.

13   This is what James Ross calls 'Draft discourse' – see his *Portraying Analogy* (Cambridge/New York: Cambridge University Press, 1981).

denominate 'the primary operative cause of all things', however, we are introduced into what Denys Turner describes as 'a complex interplay, or dialectic, of affirmative and negative tensions'.[14] Turner's treatment of the activity of 'naming God', with the multiple strategies involved in properly doing so, culminates a series of salient accounts, including those of David Braine and four Dominicans (among others): Herbert McCabe, Fergus Kerr, Brian Davies and Gregory Rocca.[15] What distinguishes Turner's treatment is his sustained focus on the ineffable creator/creature relation, and the way this *difference*, differing as it does from any difference among creatures, demands a special set of strategies for properly affirming similarity-cum-difference. And what is more, these strategies of 'naming God' employed in Aquinas's 'natural theology reflect and replicate within reason the tensions between affirmative and negative moments which structure the inner nature of belief itself' (Turner, 51).

In fact, it is this internal parallel between the structures of reason and of faith which properly distinguishes Aquinas's philosophical theology from that of Scotus, and also (on Turner's incisive account) nullifies the standard objections (rooted in Scotus) to arguments employing analogous terms. As he puts it:

> Thomas and Scotus part company in that they cannot be said to have the same view of what the participation of human reason in the divine mind entails for reason's natural capacity in respect of its *destination*. For Thomas, reason so participates in the divine self-knowledge that it can, by the exercise of its distinctively natural capacity of reasoning – that is to say, of properly constructed inference – attain to a conclusion the meaning of which lies beyond any which could stand in a relation of univocity with the created order, which, of itself, is the ambit of reason's own, natural, objects. (51)

Here we have a preliminary response to the persistent query regarding to whom it is that Scotus is objecting in his insistence that 'being' (as used of creator and of creatures) must be used univocally. His obvious foil is Henry of Ghent's account of *analogy*, but the lingering suspicion has always remained that Aquinas is the hidden (and perhaps the real) target. But if their views so differ regarding the very capacity of reason, then Scotus's demand for univocity as the precondition for proper reasoning in theology would simply bypass Aquinas's presuppositions. Indeed, the move would be quite comprehensible in the terms in which Scotus poses it, as well as allow us to see why most philosophers of religion will spontaneously endorse it.[16] For the view of *reason* which Turner puts forth as that of Aquinas is decidedly other than the standard Enlightenment view which prevails in current philosophy of religion. Indeed, it is the burden of his work to develop such a view of reason, in defending the insistence

---

14 *Faith, Reason and the Existence of God* (Cambridge: Cambridge University Press, 2004), 51.

15 David Braine, *Reality of Time and the Existence of God* (Oxford: Clarendon Press, 1987); Herbert McCabe OP, *God Matters* (London: Geoffrey Chapman, 1987); Fergus Kerr OP, *After Aquinas: Versions of Thomism* (Oxford: Blackwell, 2002); Brian Davies, *Thought of Thomas Aquinas* (Oxford/New York: Oxford University Press, 1992), *Thomas Aquinas* (London/New York: Continuum, 2002); Gregory Rocca OP, *Speaking the Incomprehensible God: Thomas Aquinas on the Interplay of Positive and Negative Theology* (Washington DC: Catholic University of America Press, 2004).

16 Richard Cross, *John Duns Scotus* (Oxford: Oxford University Press, 2001).

of the First Vatican Council that Catholic believers must *believe* that the existence of God can be proved, notably against the salient objections of a Karl Barth.

For Barth's objections to this demand – adopted subsequently by many others, including myself – simply presume that anything which is a product of reason must be comprehensible to reason, so that whatever god might be so proven could hardly be the incomprehensible God of Abrahamic believers. Yet Turner's extended riposte delineates how the *reason* to which Aquinas introduces us 'reaches its limit not in some final question-stopping answer but rather in a final answer-stopping question. Proof comes into it on the one hand as the characteristically and centrally rational activity of demonstrating the necessity of the question [why is there something at all rather than nothing?], and on the other as the demonstration of the impossibility of taking full rational possession of what must count as its answer. For the answer could not have the form of a knowable "something".' Turner calls this exercise of reason '"kenotic", for as it were from "below" it completes itself in its self-emptying, apophatic, depletion in that which is "above" it' (232–3). Put more simply (perhaps): presuming that reason cannot negotiate the *difference* between creator and creatures without neutralizing it overlooks the sophisticated ways which reason itself has of delineating how this *difference* differs from differences between creatures. Echoing both Kathryn Tanner and Robert Sokolowski, he notes how 'Augustine's sense of the divine "otherness" is such as to place it, in point of transcendence, *closer* to my creaturehood than it is possible for any creatures to be to each other. For creatures are more distinct from each other than God can possibly be to any of them' (214).[17] And since 'the difference between God and creatures cannot stand on the same logical ground as differences between creatures stand on', he counters Scotus's insistence on univocity by insisting that 'no *a fortiori* case seems warranted that, since there are objections to arguments across genera [from Aristotle], even if successful, they must apply all the more to suppositious arguments for God. Hence it is a logically open question whether argument can get you 'across' the gap' (241–5).

And pulling the threads together to address this vexatious metaphor of the 'gap', he positively identifies this 'kenotic' exercise of reason as 'proto-sacramental', for it is in the *esse* or 'actuality' of creatures, 'their deepest reality, that creatures reveal the Creator who has brought them to be, *ex nihilo*, so that as the questioning gets closer and closer to God, it gets deeper and deeper into, not further distanced from, the creature' (256–7). Rational discourse of this sort becomes 'proto-sacramental' as it attempts to delineate the unique difference we have been circling around. For 'the difference between a created and an uncreated world is no difference at all in so far as concerns how you describe it. ... For Thomas, the logic of "... is created" is the same as the logic of "... exists": an uncreated x and a created x cannot differ in respect of what an x is, and so to say that the world is created makes not the least difference how you do your science, or your history, or read your literature; it does not make that kind of particular difference to anything. The only difference it makes is all the difference to everything' (257–8). Yet that peculiar *difference* is also the 'foundation of the very possibility of ... God's intimacy to the world as Creator, [which in turn] is the foundation of that other intimacy of God to creation

---

17 Kathryn Tanner, *God and the Doctrine of Creation* (Oxford: Blackwell, 1989).

which is the incarnation' (258). So a reason which keeps attempting to articulate this peculiar difference deserves to be called 'proto-sacramental' in the strongest sense. Moreover, in the other two Abrahamic faiths, al-Ghazali and Maimonides both argued that only a free creation could render possible the 'coming down' of the Qur'an to Muhammad or the giving of the Torah to Moses. Denys Turner has demonstrated that the deeper reason for this internal connection between the deliverances of faith and of reason lies in the capacity reason has to reason to a termination which shows itself to transcend the categories native to reason itself. Enlightenment reason, *ex professo*, was restricted (either on Kant's terms or the empiricists') to its categories, so its deliverances would be inherently 'categorial'. On the other hand, the exercise of reason most illustrative of this further reach lies in the judicious use of analogy. So a reason which professes not to be able to execute such a reach must also deny the propriety of analogous discourse. Could that be why the 'default position' of so much current 'philosophy of religion' demands univocity? In any case, since I have identified sophisticated 'anthropomorphism' with an unguarded reliance on *enlightenment* reason to articulate divinity, we are fortunate to find in Denys Turner's most recent work a diagnosis of this practice which offers a therapeutic alternative.

Chapter 8

Anthropomorphism Protestant Style

Paul Helm

Two Current Approaches

Current attitudes among Christians to philosophical reflection on God fall, at the extremes, into two camps. At one extreme, the basic assumption is that God is a person, or a trinity of persons, in a sense of 'person' which has strong affinities to the idea of a human person. Hence the frequent construction of thought experiments involving human persons used to throw light on the nature of the divine person or persons. Interestingly, this assumption is common both to this strand of current philosophy of religion and to popular Trinitarian theologies whose basic category is that of interpersonal relationality applying both within and without the godhead. At the other extreme is a position which is historically rooted in patristic and scholastic traditions though ultimately, of course, in the scriptural witness to the divine transcendence and 'otherness'. Here the philosophical tools more typically include negation and analogy, but not thought experiments with persons.

In what follows I wish to pursue the tendency to anthropomorphism in current philosophy of religion by focusing on two prominent contemporary philosophers of religion with a Protestant, or at least a non-Roman Catholic, allegiance, Richard Swinburne and Nicholas Wolterstorff. I shall attempt to sketch their respective approaches and, incidentally, to offer some criticisms of these. But the main purpose is not to critique their positions, but to show in how sharp a contrast their views stand to those who articulated classical Protestant theism, which is rooted in the patristic and scholastic traditions. So the focus of the paper is not on substantive philosophical differences over God and time, or divine simplicity, say, but on the philosophical approach which give rise to such differences.

Our two thinkers nicely complement each other. Swinburne's approach is firmly *a priori*, while Wolterstorff offers us a case-by-case approach in his endeavour to develop a biblically contoured idea of God freed from 'Hellenistic' influences, but one which at the same time passes philosophical muster. But whatever their differences what they have in common is the endorsing of a basically anthropomorphic approach to the concept of God.

Swinburne's Method

The examination of Swinburne's philosophical method is confined to his *The Coherence of Theism*,[1] the first of his many monographs on the philosophy of religion,

---

1   Oxford: Clarendon Press, 1977. A revised edition, substantially unchanged, was published in 1993 (Oxford: Oxford University Press). Page references and quotations are from

the one most indicative of his approach. In the opening lines of the book he sketches out a concept of God *ab initio*, according to which a theist is someone who believes that God is a person of an extraordinary kind, where 'person' is used in the modern sense, even though he thinks of himself as showing just what 'long traditions of theological thought would lead him (the theist) to expect' (305). In fact he develops a concept of God which is non-traditional in several important respects. It is significant that his sketching out of a concept of God is not regulated by any evidential constraints. He does not approach it by asking what must be true of the Creator of all that is as we might learn of this from natural theology or from supernatural revelation, though he makes frequent reference to writers in the Christian tradition. (The occasional references to the Bible, especially the Old Testament (182, 221, 224–5) are used to make one point, about God's interaction with his creation, and therefore to undergird Swinburne's endorsement of divine temporality, and his natural theology is logically subordinate to his concept of God.) He holds that it is only when we have a coherent theism that we are entitled to ask, is it reasonable to believe that there is actually something corresponding to the God thus sketched?

There are understandable historical reasons for this approach. Swinburne wrote the book in the twilight years of logical positivism. His primary concern was to show that sentences about God may be cognitive and coherent in order to rebut the standard charge of the positivists that such statements are cognitively meaningless. So the book is concerned with clearing enough space to revive the metaphysics of theism in a context fairly hostile to it. Yet it is not simply a case of logic before epistemology. Were it that then Swinburne could have contented himself with a rebuttal of logical positivism and with the provision of an account of coherence simply in terms of logical consistency and inconsistency between sets of statements whose logical subject is God or, more weakly, of arguing that the charge of logical inconsistency is not proven. (Let's call this the 'austere' approach to coherence.)

Although he gives himself the chance of resting content with the more austere approach, he does not take it. He offers instead what I shall call a more flamboyant account. This is how he explains what a coherent statement is:

> Among statements we must distinguish coherent from incoherent statements. A coherent statement is, I suggest, one which it makes sense to suppose is true; one such that we can conceive of or suppose it and any other statement entailed by it being true; one such that we can understand what it would be like for it and any statement entailed by it to be true. (12–13)

At first sight this seems pretty austere. But there is a hint of flamboyance in the reference to what we can conceive of and to the need to understand what it would be like for a set of statements to be true. But what then follows is a fairly standard discussion of the consistency of sets of statements in terms of what they entail and what is entailed by them. He goes on, ominously shifting between consistency and coherence,[2] to say the following

---

the revised edition.

2 Compare the approach of R.S. Heimbeck, written a little earlier, which understands coherence solely in terms of 'entailments and incompatibles' (*Theology and Meaning*, London: George Allen and Unwin, 1969).

Now a coherent statement, I am suggesting, is a statement such that we can conceive of it and any other statement entailed by it being true, in the sense that we can understand what it would be like for them to be true ... 'All men are mortal', 'the moon is made of green cheese', and 'I am now writing', are all coherent statements. It makes sense to suppose that they are true. We can conceive of them and anything entailed by them being true. In fact the first and third such statements are true. The second is false but we know what it would be like for it to be true; and we can conceive of it and statements entailed by it also being true. For instance, we can conceive of 'there is a moon' and 'the moon is made of cheese' and 'the colour of the cheese of which the moon is made is green' all being true. (13)

So a sufficient condition of the coherence of a set of statements is our ability to 'conceive' of their truth. Swinburne enlarges on this at several points in the book. To conceive of something is closely connected to us being able to tell a story. The argument for the coherence of the idea that there exists an omnipresent spirit who is free and the creator of the universe consists in 'telling a story of how the claim could be true, and in the process rebutting arguments to show incoherence' (129). And telling a story is in turn connected with picturing, as in this flamboyant passage:

Creating the universe *e nihilo* (not, that is, out of any pre-existing matter) would be a basic action of God. Human beings do not have the power to bring matter into existence (given that we construe 'matter' in a wide sense which includes energy). It is, however, fairly easy to picture what it would be like for them to have such a power. If I could just by so choosing produce a sixth finger or a new fountain-pen (not made out of pre-existing matter) I would have the power to bring matter into existence. Others could see that I had this power by asking me to perform the acts in question. It seems coherent to suppose that an omnipresent spirit have and exercise far more extensive such powers. (142–3)

Thought experiments are attempts at coherent thought about God based on how things might be for human persons. One of the characteristics of modern Christian philosophy is its frequent recourse to such ingenious thought experiments, as an examination of the pages of journals such as *Faith and Philosophy* and *Religious Studies* readily testifies. Conducting such experiments is warranted because of the central assumption that we noted earlier: God is a person much as we are. Thought experiments about ourselves are readily transferable to God. Perhaps the most notorious, the most flamboyant, of these thought experiments in *The Coherence of Theism* is the following hilarious example, which concerns omnipresence:

Imagine yourself, for example, gradually ceasing to be affected by alcohol or drugs, your thinking being equally coherent however men mess about with your brain. Imagine too that you cease to feel any pains, aches, and thrills ... You gradually find yourself aware of what is going on in bodies other than your own and other material objects at any place in space ... You also come to see things from any point of view which you choose ... You also find yourself able to utter words which can be heard anywhere, without moving any material objects. However, although you find yourself gaining these strange powers, you remain otherwise the same ... Surely anyone can thus conceive of himself becoming an omnipresent spirit. (106–7)[3]

---

3 Compare the comments of Peter van Inwagen: 'Well, *I* can't. *I* can't even imagine myself ceasing to be affected by alcohol, in any sense that will help Swinburne ... I can't

Imagining what it is like to enjoy a divine property may not be closed under entailment. But there seems to be nothing to stop imagining what it is like to possess any divine property if it is possible to imagine what it is like to be omnipresent. It follows that it is possible for any of us to imagine what it is like to be God. I said earlier that Swinburne offers such disciplines in order to provide a sufficient condition for coherence. But perhaps this is not so clear. Perhaps these procedures are also necessary. This is suggested by the central place that storytelling has in Swinburne's overall procedure, which in turn suggests that he is not altogether free of the influence of logical positivism, for the pictures in question look like imaginative extensions of empirically verifiable states of affairs.

But what is of more importance for our purposes is that how divine attributes such as omnipresence, omniscience, eternity and omnipotence are to be understood is to be governed by the earlier discussion about the nature of coherence and how it is to be established. Establishing the coherence of theism is assured because we have adopted a principle according to which the differences between ourselves, local spirits and an omnipresent spirit must be one of degree, never one of kind, and the differences may be bridged in our imagination. More on this later.

Only at the very end of his treatment of the coherence of theism does Swinburne resort to analogy, when considering the idea that God, up to that point understood to be a person in a literal sense, necessarily exists. This requires him to modify the sense in which God is a person, since human persons do not necessarily exist. God is necessarily omnipotent for he is necessarily the kind of being that he is. So it turns out after all that God is a person in a rather stretched sense of that term. Swinburne is forced to play the analogical card. But this does not affect his earlier discussion of the concept of God.

So in virtue of his belief that God is a necessary being, that he has certain non-temporally indexed properties essentially, it is necessary to think of God as a person in only an analogical sense.

Coupled with this flamboyant account of the coherence of statements about God are negative remarks on negative theology. This is what he says about the *via negativa*:

> To say that God is 'good' is, on this view, just to say that he is 'not evil' (in the ordinary sense). But this view failed lamentably to give an adequate account of what theists have wished to say about God. Sticks and stones are 'not evil'; but to say of God that he is good is clearly to say more of him than that he is, like sticks and stones, not evil. (82)

As an account of the *via negativa* this is, of course, a travesty. It fails to recognize that its distinctiveness lies in the precise character of the *set* of negative terms applied to God, and that it is linked with other ways of thinking about God, notably the *via eminentia*. It also fails to see that the *via negativa* has to do largely if not exclusively with what some later theologians have called the incommunicable attributes of God.

---

and I am sure that anyone who thinks he *can* "imagine" these things has just not thought the matter through ... I believe that they constitute a cogent argument for the conclusion that Swinburne's attempt to demonstrate the coherence of theism fails – although, of course, I think that theism is coherent.' *God, Knowledge and Mystery* (Ithaca, NY: Cornell University Press, 1995), 19–21.

To say of God that he is infinite is to say that he is not finite; invisible, that he is not visible; eternal, that he is not temporal; and immeasurable, that he is not measurable. None of this applies to sticks and stones. It is precisely in the cumulative impact of what is said of God negatively that the cognitive pay-off of the *via negativa* lies.

Rather than treat *aseitas*, for example, as a negative term Swinburne approaches it etymologically and shows that God cannot have existence from himself because nothing can cause itself (268)! Swinburne's reluctance to depart from literalness by invoking some aspect of the *via negativa* is vividly seen in his approach to divine eternality. One argument for God's sempiternity is that things that God is said to do – forgive or punish or warn – are all actions about which it makes sense to ask when they occurred. 'So, superficially, the supposition that God could bring things about, forgive, punish, warn, etc. etc. without his doing these things at times before or after other times ... seems incoherent' (229).[4] He accepts the use of 'person' in a metaphorical or stretched sense in the case of God's necessity but not in the case of divine atemporalism (which he rejects). Both require the stretching of terms. Why does Swinburne prefer to stretch 'person' by accepting a temporalist objection to his account, and not rather accept eternalism? The answer is because of the centrality of the libertarianism (both human and divine) in his account, of which more later.

What sets off Swinburne's approach from the tradition (even though, as we have seen, he thinks of himself as engaged in the practice of showing the coherence of traditional theism, is that in the tradition negative and analogical ways of thinking about God are intrinsic to any coherent thought about God. They are built in from the beginning, on account of the *sui generis* character of God and of his ways, founded on the distinction between God the creator and any creature, a distinction blurred by regarding God as a person in a sense rather like that in which you and I are persons.

Wolterstorff's Method

Nicholas Wolterstorff is engaged in the project of what he calls the 'dehellenization' of Christian theology because he believes that the patterns of classical Greek thought are incompatible with those of biblical thought. Two years before the publication of Swinburne's *The Coherence of Theism* he expressed the view that these Hellenistic patterns are especially dominant and pivotal in the case of God's eternality, 'the eternal God tradition'.

> Indeed, I am persuaded that unless the tradition of God eternal is renounced, fundamental dehellenizing will perpetually occupy itself in the suburbs, never advancing to the city center. Every attempt to purge Christian theology of the traces of incompatible Hellenic

---

4 Peter Geach is sometimes cited as one who stands apart from modern Christian philosophy (see Brian Davies, 'Letter from America', *New Blackfriars*, 84/989–90 (July/August 2003): 371–84) and there may be something in this. But like Swinburne and Wolterstorff, Geach is adamant that God is in time, and that the future is 'open'. (See *Providence and Evil* (Cambridge: Cambridge University Press, 1977), Chapter 3, 'Omniscience and the Future'. Perhaps at this point he was under the influence of Arthur Prior's Ciceronian metaphysics. See A.N. Prior, *Papers on Time and Tense* (Oxford: Clarendon Press, 1968).

patterns of thought must fail unless it removes the roadblock of the God eternal tradition. Around this barricade there are no detours.[5]

He has followed this up with a number of papers which bear on our topic, most notably 'Suffering Love'[6] and 'Divine Simplicity',[7] to which I shall refer shortly.

Naturally, if we are able to remove the roadblock of the eternal God tradition this results in a God who is much more anthropomorphic, someone much more like ourselves, than is a timelessly eternal God. For together we occupy the same temporal universe, and he, like us, changes in time; he has memories, hopes, regrets, expectations and much else, as Wolterstorff recognizes. He, like us, has a 'time strand' (193). So, as with Swinburne, Wolterstorff's emphasis is one which stresses the elements of continuity between God and ourselves, stressing that we are all in time.

Removing the roadblock of God's impassibility, as he does in 'Suffering Love', results in a God who can emote as we do. Here his argument has two phases: objections to the idea of divine simplicity, but also to the very idea of God as incapable of emoting. He says, in objection to divine simplicity, for example, that it requires not only that God's knowing is single but that what he knows is single (222). But this problem, which is certainly discussed in contemporary literature, seems to be of recent vintage. It is not found in Aquinas, for example.[8] It may come as a surprise to students of modern discussions of divine simplicity that Aquinas readily recognizes what might be called 'consequent complexity' in God, complexity in God which does not depend on something other than himself. So in discussing the question 'Does God know things other than himself?'[9] Aquinas asserts that God's essence contains the likeness of things other than himself, and since there are many kinds of things other than himself there are presumably many likenesses of things contained in the divine essence. However, Aquinas wishes to deny that God knows things other than himself by learning about them, since for such knowledge he would depend on others than himself. As he says, 'It is not contrary to the simplicity of the divine intellect to know many things; but it would be contrary to its simplicity were the divine intellect informed by a plurality of knowledge likenesses'[10] because then the divine intellect would depend on them, and (Aquinas thinks) God's sovereignty or aseity or Creatorhood would be compromised.

---

5 'God Everlasting', in C. Orlebeke and L Smedes (eds), *God and the Good* (Grand Rapids, MI: Eerdmans, 1975), 183.

6 In Thomas V. Morris (ed.), *Philosophy and the Christian Faith* (Notre Dame, IN: University of Notre Dame Press, 1988).

7 In James E. Tomberlin (ed.), *Philosophical Perspectives, 5: Philosophy of Religion* (Atascadero, CA: Ridgeview, 1991).

8 So, in discussing the question of whether justice and mercy are found in all his works (I.21.4), Aquinas never once refers to divine simplicity which would offer him an easy one-line answer. In I.13.4 he discusses how it is that our words for God are not synonymous even though God is simple. In *Summa Contra Gentiles* I.31 he discusses how the plurality of divine names is not incompatible with divine simplicity, but it's not the same problem as Wolterstorff identifies.

9 *Summa Theologiae*, trans. Thomas Gilby (New York: Image Books, 1969), I.14.5.

10 *Summa Theologiae*, I.15.2.

Wolterstorff's argument then is: Since God (because he is simple) cannot know things other than himself, he cannot know suffering, and if he does not know suffering then he does not sufferingly know it (223). So God does not suffer, but at the price of maintaining that God has no knowledge of the particular things in the world. But what if one does not have to pay that price? Suppose one can hold, consistently with the simplicity doctrine, that God knows and loves his creation. Here emerges the second objection: given divine simplicity God can only love and find delight in himself, and for Wolterstorff this is both repugnant (225) and in deep conflict with Scripture (226).

At this point Wolterstorff's argument against divine simplicity and what it implies takes the form of offering counter examples or thought experiments derived from human life. If there was a human being, such as a doctor, who did not care for her patients but only took delight in the deploying of her own skills, that would be repugnant (224–5). The limitations of such an argument are obvious. At other times his arguments are based on misunderstanding, as when he characterizes divine goodness as bliss (for example, 209–10, 211) and unperturbed serenity (211), as if God is carefree. He appears to think of divine impassibility as a kind of impassivity and not as supreme and unalloyed goodness which in order to be in exercise does not need to experience twinges of unhappiness or flickers of delight (227).

In his later paper, 'Divine Simplicity', he is somewhat more sympathetic to the doctrine, regarding it not as radically incoherent, as some do, at least when it is understood in its own terms, but nevertheless as getting in the way of both a philosophically responsible and a biblically faithful articulation of the idea of God. Discussing it by means of the three divine identity claims characteristic of the medieval simplicity doctrine (namely, that God is not distinct from God's essence; that God's existence is not distinct from God's essence; and God has no property distinct from God's essence), he argues that all these claims, which seem incoherent to many modern analytic philosophers, can be defended in terms of the medievals' own ontology (which he calls constituent ontology), according to which God does not *have* a nature – as in a modern, relational ontology (as Wolterstorff calls it), he must – but *is* a nature. But though he thinks that the medieval doctrine of divine simplicity is defensible in its own terms, it gives rise to tensions or perplexities when married to Christian theological concerns, particularly to the freedom and the triunity of God, and to adequately accounting 'for the multiplicity of distinct things that we find ourselves required to affirm of this simple being which is God. We say that God is wise, and that God is good, and that God is powerful. In speaking thus, we are not simply repeating ourselves'.[11] Despite this, he avers that the simplicity doctrine was retained because of its fecundity, for from it the medievals cascaded immutability, eternality and impassibility, notwithstanding the fact that they were, like Wolterstorff himself, bothered by the bearing of simplicity doctrine on the many different things that we wish to say about God.

---

11 'Divine Simplicity', 549–50. It is odd that someone concerned to do justice to Scripture does not consider whether one might hesitate to be dogmatic over the question of whether God is a property, or whether there might be warrant for constituent ontology, by reflecting on such sentences as 'God is love', 'God is light' and 'God is spirit'.

But there is some misunderstanding here, or perhaps miscalculation, of the procedure of Thomas Aquinas to whom Wolterstorff refers. Aquinas does not place divine simplicity at the head of other divine characteristics in order to deduce these from it. Rather, it is one of a set of ways in which God does not exist, ways which rule out compositiveness, change and the like. Simplicity is discussed quite independently of the others in the set, even though it implies them and is perhaps implied by them.

Wolterstorff fails to see that the root of the idea of divine simplicity is the Creator–creature distinction, and especially the Creator's aseity and sovereignty over anything that is not himself. This point runs like a thread through Thomas's treatment of divine simplicity. Because God is the first existent thing, there can be no potentiality in him.[12] Because he is first cause, his existence cannot differ from his nature, or be other than his nature, since if it did his existence would be a dependent existence.[13] In God nothing is derivative, but all derivation starts from him, so nothing exists in him by accident.[14] Since God is the first of all beings he cannot be composite, since everything composite is subsequent to its components and depends on them. And composite beings must be caused to be, but God is the first cause.[15]

The assertion of the three identity conditions – each of them a negative statement – is not made to lessen the perplexity we experience over the idea of divine simplicity; rather, it intensifies it. You get no sense of this from Wolterstorff's account. And invoking constituent ontology does not lessen our perplexity over what, if they are not to be taken purely negatively, the three identity principles could possibly mean.

The doctrine of divine simplicity is a negative doctrine, as Wolterstorff recognizes, but it is a case of what we may call antecedent negativity, not of consequent negativity. Antecedent negativity is affirmed precisely to defend divine aseity, necessity and Creatorhood. It is perfectly compatible with complexity in the godhead provided that this complexity is consequent, having its source only in God himself.

So in Wolterstorff as in Swinburne the anthropomorphic turn is helped along by some misunderstandings of the tradition.

Wolterstorff's project of dehellenization does not call for grounding the idea of God in some other, non-Hellenic, philosophy – say the philosophy of A.N. Whitehead. Rather, Wolterstorff wishes to ground his doctrine of God less in philosophy of any kind and more securely in Scripture. He proposes the following principle: 'An implication of one's accepting Scripture as canonical is that one will affirm as literally true scriptural representations of God unless one has good reason not to do so.'[16] For in Scripture God is presented as one who acts within human history, centrally and decisively in the life, death and resurrection of Jesus Christ. (It is not, incidentally, true that if one did not think of God's agency as occurring within human history 'one would have to regard the biblical speech about God as at best

---

12 *Summa Theologiae* I.3.1
13 *Summa Theologiae* I.3.4.
14 *Summa Theologiae* I.3.6.
15 *Summa Theologiae* I.3.7.
16 Nicholas Wolterstorff, 'Unqualified Divine Temporality', in *Four Views of God and Time*, ed. Gregory Ganssle (Downer's Grove, IL: InterVarsity Press, 2001), 188.

one long sequence of metaphors pointing to a reality for which they are singularly inept, and as at worst one long sequence of falsehoods').[17]

Suppose we try out this hermeneutical principle, even though it is not self-evidently true. It is not easy to see how such an apparently simple principle applies. Take some expressions in Psalm 102, where we are told the Lord 'looked down from his holy height; from heaven the Lord looked at the earth' (v. 19, English Standard Version [ESV]), and then later 'Of old you laid the foundation of the earth, and the heavens are the work of your hands. They will perish, but you will remain, they will all wear out like a garment. You will change them like a robe, and they will pass away, but you are the same and your years have no end' (vv. 25–7). Presumably given his stated position in relation to God's relation to time and space Wolterstorff will want to say something like the following: verse 19 ought to be interpreted figuratively, since we have good reason drawn from literally interpreted statements of Scripture elsewhere to think that God is non-spatial. But we have no good reason from elsewhere in Scripture to think that God is non-temporal, so verses 25–7 are to be interpreted literally.

But the arbitrariness of this procedure is apparent. Are there in Scripture statements about God's relation to space that are of such exactness that they entail the non-literalness of Psalm 102:19, and statements about God's relation to time of such exactness that they entail the literalness of Psalm 102:25–7? Naturally, we can only answer this question by looking and seeing, but it does not seem likely. It is going to be extremely difficult to formulate a hermeneutical principle which discriminates with sufficient plausibility between scriptural statements about God's relation to time and those about God's relation to space so as to ensure that at least some of the first are non-figurative while all of the second are figurative, and also (a separate point) that those which are non-figurative ought to 'control' those which aren't.[18]

Libertarian Freedom

There is a final element in the picture. Both Swinburne and Wolterstorff are strongly committed to human libertarian freedom. This commitment influences them in different ways. In the case of Swinburne, it leads him to tailor his idea of divine omniscience so that God limits himself with regard to what he knows about the future, both in order to safeguard the reality of his own libertarian freedom, and also that of his human creatures.

> If the theist is to maintain that there is a 'perfectly free' person, omnipresent, omnipotent, creator of the universe, who is also 'omniscient', he has to understand either 'perfectly free' or 'omnipotent' or 'omniscient' in yet more restricted ways than those which I have outlined. It seems to me clear that he would prefer a restriction on 'omniscient' ... I suggest finally, therefore, the following understanding of omniscience. A person P is

---

17 'God Everlasting', 181. Behind this remark is Wolterstorff's assumption that God must be in time to act in time, an assumption that it would take us too far away from our topic to discuss. I have discussed it briefly in my contribution to *Four Views of God and Time*, 52 ff.

18 It also assumes that there are no scriptural statements affirming divine eternality.

omniscient at a time *t* if and only if he knows of every true proposition about *t* or an earlier time and every true proposition about a time later than *t* which is true of logical necessity or which he had overriding reason to make true, which it is logically possible that he entertains then. (180–81)

Why this restricted sense of 'omniscience' is not analogical is presumably because all of its terms are literal. But analogical or not it is clearly unorthodox and manufactured[19] solely in the interests of maintaining libertarianism without tears. But it is not necessary for Swinburne to take this approach. He could have wrestled, as many have, with the question of the harmony of God's prescience and human libertarian freedom. Or he could have played the joker again, allowing that God's knowledge is beyond our ken.

Wolterstorff is also explicit that God must be in time in order to be able to interact with free human actions, though less explicit than Swinburne that God's actions must also be indeterministically free. He says:

Some of God's actions must be understood as a response to the free actions of human beings – that what God does he sometimes does in response to what some human being does. I think this is in fact the case. And I think it follows, given that all human actions are temporal, that those actions of God which are 'response' actions are temporal as well.[20]

In both Swinburne's and Wolterstorff's view God's free interactivity with human creatures possessed with libertarian freedom is a core value which is to be preserved at all costs in our efforts to think biblically and with philosophical responsibility about the idea of God.

The Tradition

In sketching the views of Swinburne and Wolterstorff it has not been my intention to offer a sustained critique of their views, but simply to provide a stark contrast between their approach and that of traditional Protestantism. Here a word or two of explanation is needed. It is obvious that Swinburne and Wolterstorff don't offer their views as Protestant, or non-Roman Catholic; nevertheless I use them as non-Roman Catholic representatives of what one might call 'modern Christian philosophy'. That's one word of explanation. Another is that as we juxtapose the 'Protestant tradition' with such modern Christian philosophy we should note that that tradition was in part sharpened and developed after the Reformation in controversy with Socinianism. And as a matter of historical fact Socinianism was, or is, a part of the 'Protestant tradition', broadly understood. But it is not Socinianism that could provide a point of contrast with Swinburne and Wolterstorff. In fact, what is remarkable is that many of the philosophical positions espoused by such as Swinburne and Wolterstorff are coincident with Socinian views. So in what follows the comparator will not be Protestantism in the sense of whatever is non-Roman Catholic, but the 'mainstream' of Protestantism, and especially of Calvin and the

---

19 At one point Swinburne writes of knocking theism into a coherent shape (165).
20 'God Everlasting', 197.

Reformed tradition, with which I am most familiar. (I suspect a similar project could be followed for Anglicanism using evidence from such writers as Richard Hooker (1553–1600), John Pearson (1612–86) and many others.) The third point is that what we find in these representative Reformed theologians that we shall discuss is not a novel doctrine of divine simplicity, but a restatement, or simply an acceptance, of divine simplicity, eternality and immutability – let's call these the Traditional Triad – as we find it exemplified in, for example, Aquinas and in Augustine.

John Calvin

Divine simplicity was not an issue at the Reformation and Calvin simply adopts the traditional view, derived from Augustine through the scholastics. Because it was not in the focus of his attention he gives us little detail about his views. Nevertheless

> [W]hen we profess to believe in one God, under the name of God is understood a single, simple essence, in which we comprehend three persons, or hypostases. Therefore, whenever the name of God is mentioned without particularization, there are designated no less the Son and the Spirit than the Father; but where the Son is joined to the Father, then the relation of the two enters in; and so we distinguish among the persons.[21]

For Calvin, God's essence – God himself – is simple and incomprehensible, 'simple and undivided'.[22] In discussing the divine simplicity as part of his very restrained Trinitarianism,[23] Calvin says:

> Here, indeed, if anywhere in the secret mysteries of Scripture, we ought to play the philosopher soberly and with great moderation; let us use great caution that neither our thoughts nor our speech go beyond the limits to which the Word of God itself extends. For how can the human mind measure off the measureless essence of God according to its own little measure, a mind as yet unable to establish for certain the nature of the sun's body, though men's eyes daily gaze upon it? Indeed, how can the mind by its own leading come to search out God's essence when it cannot even get to its own? Let us then willingly leave to God the knowledge of himself. For, as Hilary says, he is the one fit witness to himself, and is not known except through himself. But we shall be 'leaving it to him' if we conceive him to be as he reveals himself to us.[24]

---

21 *Institutes of the Christian Religion* [hereafter *Inst.*], I.13.20, trans. F.L. Battles (London: SCM Press, 1966).

22 *Inst.* I.13.2. This recognition of divine incomprehensibility is sometimes approvingly referred to as 'agnosticism' (Brian Davies, 'Letter from America'). But this is misleading, at least as far as Calvin (and I suspect, the entire tradition) is concerned. Agnosticism is a thesis about the degree of evidence for and against a proposition warranting a suspense of belief in it. But Calvin did not suspend belief in God's simplicity or eternity or immutability. He firmly believed in them. But he permanently suspended the endeavour to 'comprehend' these realities, to grasp them in their fullness and entirety.

23 Calvin's restrained Trinitarianism is in stark contrast to the confident social Trinitarianism characteristic of modern Christian philosophers, including Swinburne.

24 *Inst.* I.13.21.

That is to say, only God can know God in a full and comprehensive fashion; and if we try to know God as he knows himself, then we are attempting to overturn the Creator/creature distinction.

This distinction, considered alone, may strongly suggest that Calvin has a very unitary conception of God. He is certainly an undeviating monotheist, committed to the idea of divine simplicity, although he is committed to a version of it that is consistent with distinctions (though not divisions) in the godhead.

> Indeed the words 'Father,' 'Son,' and 'Spirit' imply a real distinction – let no one think that these titles, whereby God is variously designated from his works, are empty – but a distinction, not a division. The passages that we have already cited (e.g. Zech. 13:7) show that the Son has a character distinct from the Father because the Word would not have been with God unless he were another than the Father, nor would he have had his glory with the Father were he not distinct from the Father.[25]

We can make distinctions about God – between his attributes or among the persons of the Trinity, say – but these distinctions do not correspond to divisions in God. Presumably Calvin's reasoning here goes like this: only what has parts is divided (or divisible); God is without parts; therefore, God is undivided. But *distinctions* in God are not *divisions* of him. Distinctions are compatible with simplicity but divisions are not compatible. Even if we can distinguish between God's wisdom and his power, these are characteristics of one and the same God, just as distinguishing between Father, Son and Spirit does not imply that there are three gods, or three parts to God.[26]

Calvin not only adheres to a version of the idea of divine simplicity, he is an eternalist; that is, he holds that God exists beyond or outside time. Perhaps the idea of divine simplicity entails eternalism, although Calvin does not say as much. Nonetheless, he clearly affirms both positions.

> When we attribute foreknowledge to God, we mean that all things always were, and perpetually remain, under his eyes, so that to his knowledge there is nothing future or past, but all things are present. And they are present in such a way that he not only conceives them through ideas, as we have before us those things which our minds remember, but he truly looks upon them and discerns them as things placed before him. And this foreknowledge is extended throughout the universe to every creature.[27]

The same view is expressed in connection with the Trinity. Writing of the 'order' of the persons in the Trinity, he says:

---

25 *Inst.* I.13.17.

26 Calvin explicitly draws the contrast between distinction and division in connection with the Trinity in *Inst.* I.13.17. Of course there is a potential difficulty here. Although the persons of the Trinity are distinct from each other, and yet God is not divided, nevertheless the persons are not merely modes of God, or merely ways of thinking about God imposed by human finitude, in the way in which the distinctions between the divine attributes are.

27 *Inst.* III.21.5.

Indeed, although the eternity of the Father is also the eternity of the Son and the Spirit, since God could never exist apart from his wisdom and power, and we must not seek in eternity a *before* or an *after*, nevertheless the observance of an order is not meaningless or superfluous, when the Father is thought of as first, then from him the Son, and finally from both the Spirit.[28]

Francis Turretin

Francis Turretin[29] was a prominent representative of what is nowadays referred to as 'Reformed Scholasticism' which developed in the Reformed tradition in the face of the need to mount sustained arguments against the Counter-Reformation and Socinianism in particular. This tradition inherits much of the conceptuality of medieval scholasticism, but in its Protestant version it is much exercised with the exegetical and hermeneutical basis of the doctrine of God in Scripture. Notwithstanding these differences, there is a noteworthy coincidence of view between Turretin and the medieval scholastic outlook, not surprisingly given the fact that he makes explicit appeals to that tradition.

Here I shall look briefly at Turretin's attitude to the Traditional Triad in connection with what Reformed theologians came to call the 'incommunicable' attributes of God. These are 'attributes' of God which one might roughly call structural attributes,[30] called incommunicable because they are not shareable with any creature. The Socinians denied such incommunicability. And as we have seen Swinburne's procedure can be said to carry the implication that every one of divine attributes is communicable since our understanding of them is derived from our own powers and properties, qualified only by the consideration that God is a necessary being.

For Turretin the incommunicable attributes are essential attributes of God indicating 'perfections essential to the divine nature conceived by us as properties',[31] and in view of the divine simplicity, inadequately so conceived. The incommunicable attributes of God, likewise inadequately grasped, are to be distinguished from those attributes which God produces analogous effects in the creature – goodness, justice, wisdom and the like.[32]

The Socinians hold that the attributes of God are really distinct from his essence,[33] and from each other, and so see the divine essence as something like a *substratum*, but Turretin counters that they are only distinguished intellectually, but not merely nominally, since the distinctions are grounded in God's perfection. So for Turretin it

---

28 *Inst.* I.13.18. For a fuller discussion of these features of Calvin's theology see Paul Helm, *John Calvin's Ideas* (Oxford: Oxford University Press, 2004).

29 Francis Turretin (1623–87) was Professor of Theology at Geneva from 1653 until his death. Page references in the main text are to his *Institutes of Elenctic Theology*, trans. G.M. Giger, ed. J.T. Dennison Jr (Phillipsburg, NJ: P&R Publishing, 1992–97), vol. 1.

30 David Burrell refers to these as 'formal' features. See his 'Divine Eternity', forthcoming in *Creation, Time and Eternity*, ed. Paul Helm.

31 *Institutes of Elenctic Theology*, vol. 1, 187.

32 *Institutes of Elenctic Theology*, vol. 1, 190.

33 *Institutes of Elenctic Theology*, vol. 1, 188.

makes no sense to ask questions such as: 'What is God composed of? Does God have parts? Can anything be added to or taken away from God?'

As we have seen Turretin's procedure is markedly different from that of modern Christian philosophy where we are encouraged to build up an idea of God by starting with ourselves and, by thought experiments, to conceive of God as an Omnipresent Spirit. We knock the concept of God into a coherent shape by starting from ourselves. By contrast to Swinburne, Turretin starts from God, from the simplicity of God which is the key idea in the Traditional Triad, as we shall see.

> those attributes can properly be called incommunicable strictly and in every way, which are so proper to God that nothing similar of analogous, or any image or trace can be found in creatures. Such are the negative attributes which remove from him whatever is imperfect in creatures (such as infinity, immensity, eternity, which are such that every creature is either without them or has their contraries).[34]

So in terms of the three 'ways' of speaking about God the incommunicable attributes are the negative attributes, the communicable are 'the affirmative attributes which are attributed to God by way of eminence and causation'.[35]

The simplicity of God is expressed by his infinity, his immensity, his eternity and his immutability. These four features are therefore in turn closely allied: we can say of any of them that the possession of one of these entails the possession of the others because they are nothing more than legitimate intellectual distinctions drawn about one simple essence. Let us look, briefly, at Turretin's treatment of divine immensity and divine eternity.

Divine omnipresence is divine infinity with respect to created place, an aspect of God's immensity.[36] God is everywhere not only by power and operation and by his knowledge, but by essence.[37] He completely fills all places, though not in the same sense in which water may fill all places of the bucket. The Socinians (and of course Swinburne) agree that God is present everywhere 'as to virtue and operation',[38] but deny that God is all-present by his essence. But those who affirm God's omnipresence by his essence 'think the mode of it should neither be curiously inquired into, nor be rashly defined',[39] an example, perhaps, of Turretin's Calvin-like anti-speculative temper. Besides citing scriptural support for this view Turretin offers several arguments.[40]

So for Turretin, as for Calvin, it makes no sense to ask, How far away is God? Has he gone away? Where is God today? Is God located in heaven? Why isn't God acting, is someone getting in the way? Does his presence among the sick and needy mean that he might become infected? Has he arrived?

---

34 *Institutes of Elenctic Theology*, vol. 1, 190.
35 *Institutes of Elenctic Theology*, vol. 1, 190.
36 *Institutes of Elenctic Theology*, vol. 1, 196.
37 *Institutes of Elenctic Theology*, vol. 1, 197. For scriptural support he cites Jeremiah 23:24; Palms 139; 1 Kings 8:27.
38 *Institutes of Elenctic Theology*, vol. 1, 198.
39 *Institutes of Elenctic Theology*, vol. 1, 198.
40 *Institutes of Elenctic Theology*, vol. 1, 199.

Divine eternity is God's infinity with respect to time. God's life has no succession

> because his essence, with which it is really identified, admits none. This is so both because it is perfectly simple and immutable (and therefore rejects the change of former into latter, of past into present, of present into future, which succession involves), and because it is unmeasurable, as being the first and independent. (203)[41]

Turretin accepts the Boethian definition as a commonplace, 'the eternal duration of God embraces indeed all time – the past, present and future; but nothing in him can be past or future because his life remains always the same and immutable.'[42] He also has an argument against the *reductio* of the idea of divine eternity recently employed by Swinburne and Anthony Kenny, that if God's knowledge of A and B is simultaneous with A occurring in 1066 and with B occurring in 1789, then A and B must be occurring at the same time.[43] He argues that each temporal occurrence coexists with the whole of eternity, but the whole of eternity does not coexist with them taken together, but dividedly.[44]

> God is called 'the ancient of days' not as stricken with old age and sated with years (as the Saturn of the heathen), but as before and more ancient than days themselves and the birth of time. Therefore days and years are not ascribed to him properly, but after the manner of men. For we who live in time can conceive nothing unless by a relation to time, in which we are.[45]

So it makes no sense to ask how long has God existed? What was God doing yesterday? Where will he spend the summer? Isn't God getting on in years? How long will it take God to redeem Israel from the bondage of Egypt?

---

41 *Institutes of Elenctic Theology*, vol. 1, 203. Scriptural support is found in Genesis 21:33; Isaiah 57:15; 1 Timothy 1:17; Psalms 90:1, 2, 102:26–8, 102:25. As Richard Muller has recently shown, the use of such references by Reformed scholastic thinkers such as Turretin are not instances of naive 'proof-texting' but the outcome of elaborate hermeneutical procedures appealing (in the case of divine eternity) to five separate kinds of scriptural expression, involving an overall appeal to the 'scope' of Scripture. The five are: 1. The affirmation of divine eternity. 2. The dental of time and succession to God. 3. The affirmation of eternal powers and operations to God. 4. When time is attributed to God this is in a radically distinct way from which it is attributed to the creature. 5. The affirmation of divine eternity derived from other scriptural statements about God. To these might be added a sixth, the implications of the second Commandment for thought and speech about God. Richard A. Muller, *Post-Reformation Reformed Dogmatics* (Grand Rapids, MI: Baker Academic, 2003), vol. 3, ch. 4.

42 *Institutes of Elenctic Theology*, vol. 1, 203.

43 Richard Swinburne, *The Coherence of Theism*, ch. 12. Anthony Kenny, *The God of the Philosophers* (Oxford: Clarendon Press, 1979), 38–9.

44 *Institutes of Elenctic Theology*, vol. 1, 204.

45 *Institutes of Elenctic Theology*, vol. 1, 204.

Jonathan Edwards

The third example is Jonathan Edwards, whom I have picked because although in the tradition of Puritanism and Reformed Scholasticism there were strong elements of individuality about his thought; of idealism and occasionalism and even, it is said, of panentheism,[46] and certainly the influence of John Locke. Edwards developed an account of the Trinity, and indeed offered an *a priori* proof of the Trinitarian character of God, in Lockean terms. Nonetheless, for all his individuality there is a strong affinity between his thought about the character of God and the Reformed Scholastic tradition in which Edwards was steeped. For ease I shall refer only to his *Freedom of the Will*.[47]

> The eternal duration which was before the world, being only the eternity of God's existence; which is nothing else but his immediate, perfect and invariable possession of the whole of his unlimited life, together and at once; *vitae interminabilis, tota, simul et perfecta possessio*. Which is so generally allowed, that I need not stand to demonstrate it ... 'Tis as improper, to imagine that the immensity and omnipresence of God is distinguished by a series of miles and leagues, one beyond another; as that the infinite duration of God is distinguished by months and years, one after another. A diversity and order of distinct parts, limited by certain periods, is as conceivable, and does as naturally obtrude upon our imagination, in one case as the other; and there is equal reason in each case, to suppose that our imagination deceives us. 'Tis equally improper, to talk of months and years of the divine existence, and mile-squares of divinity ...[48]

In view of what we have noted about Richard Swinburne's procedure it is somewhat ironic that when Edwards considers the sort of conceiving and imagining that is at the heart of Swinburne's project he regards it as an instance of self-deception!

Of course Edwards does not think that thoughts involving such concepts as the eternity and immensity of God are easy to grasp.

> And it may be noted particularly, that though we are obliged to conceive of some things in God as consequent and dependent on others, and of some things pertaining to the divine nature and will as the foundation of others, and so before others in the order of nature: as, we must conceive of the knowledge and holiness of God as prior in the order of nature to his happiness; the perfection of his understanding, as the foundation of his wise purposes and decrees; the holiness of his nature, as the cause and reason of his holy determinations. And yet when we speak of cause and effect, antecedent and consequent, fundamental and dependent, determining and determined, in the first Being, who is self existent, independent, of perfect and absolute simplicity and immutability, and the first cause of all things; doubtless there must be less propriety in such representations, than

---

46 For Edwards's occasionalism see Oliver Crisp, 'How "Occasional" was Edwards's Occasionalism?', in *Jonathan Edwards, Philosophical Theologian*, ed. Paul Helm and Oliver Crisp (Aldershot: Ashgate, 2003).

47 Jonathan Edwards, *A Careful and Strict Inquiry into the prevailing notions of the freedom of the will which is supposed to be essential to moral agency, virtue and vice, reward and punishment, praise and blame*, ed. Paul Ramsey (New Haven, CT: Yale University Press, 1957). All page references in the main text are to this edition.

48 *Freedom of the Will*, 385–7.

when we speak of derived dependent beings, who are compounded, and liable to perpetual mutation and succession.[49]

Here the Traditional Triad of simplicity, eternity and immutability are closely linked.

On divine omniscience Edwards has this to say,

> Though it be true, that there is no succession in God's knowledge, and the manner of his knowledge is to us inconceivable, yet thus much we know concerning it, that there is no event, past, present, or to come, that God is ever uncertain of; he never is, never was, and never will be without infallible knowledge of it; he always sees the existence of it to be certain and infallible. And he always sees things just as they are in truth ... God's viewing things so perfectly and unchangeably as that there is no succession in his ideas or judgment, don't hinder but that there is properly now, in the mind of God, a certain and perfect knowledge of the moral actions of men, which to us are an hundred years hence.[50]

Herman Bavinck

With Herman Bavinck[51] we come into the twentieth century, and to the end of this brief survey. The reason for referring to him is not only to show the continuity of the tradition in Protestantism well beyond the Enlightenment, but to do so by using a thinker to which a prominent contemporary Christian philosopher of religion, Alvin Plantinga, also occasionally refers with approval.[52] There is another reason for using Bavinck. Two of the three thinkers that we have referred to, Turretin and Edwards, are favourably disposed to the necessity of natural theology; Calvin is more ambivalent on the question. But Bavinck is definitely hostile.[53] So it cannot be said of Bavinck that his theism is derived by implication from the results of cosmological arguments for God's existence. He draws conclusions about the nature of God from special revelation, and particularly from scriptural representations of the Creator–creature distinction. This, at least, is what he would claim. It is this suspicion of or rejection of natural theology that makes Bavinck attractive to Plantinga and in this respect Bavinck and Plantinga are in the same tradition. But there are also marked differences between them, as we shall see.

---

49 *Freedom of the Will*, 376–7. A recent commentator on Edwards, Amy Plantinga Pauw, has suggested that Edwards is somewhat ambivalent towards divine simplicity. See *The Supreme Harmony of All: The Trinitarian Theology of Jonathan Edwards* (Grand Rapids, MI: Eerdmans, 2002), 69 ff. But Edwards is pretty definite in the passage quoted here.

50 *Freedom of the Will*, 266–7.

51 Herman Bavinck (1845–1921) was Professor of Dogmatic Theology at the Free University of Amsterdam from 1902. The evidence cited here is from part of his *Reformed Dogmatics*, translated by William Hendriksen and published as *The Doctrine of God* (Grand Rapids, MI: Eerdmans, 1951).

52 Alvin Plantinga, 'Reason and Belief in God', in *Faith and Rationality*, ed. Alvin Plantinga and Nicholas Wolterstorff (Notre Dame, IN: University of Notre Dame Press, 1983), 64–5, 71–3.

53 Bavinck, *The Doctrine of God*, 78. He thinks that the standard proofs are weak as proofs but strong as testimonies to God's existence.

For Bavinck it is through God's revelation that we learn that 'there is one only God, personal yet highly exalted above nature, the Infinite, the Absolute, the All-powerful, and Omnipresent One'.[54] So that his doctrine of God is derived a posteriori from Scripture. It is from these data of Scripture (data respecting 'God's distinctness from and absolute exaltation above every creature')[55] that we also derive the theologically fundamental idea of God's independence:

> The first thing Scripture teaches us concerning God is that he has a distinct, free, and independent existence and life. He has a distinct being, a distinct 'nature, substance, essence', not apart from his virtues, but revealed in all his virtues and perfections. He has proper names that do not pertain to any creature.[56]

After briefly surveying the thought of those who in the tradition have separated the being of God from his attributes, including Gilbert of Pourçain and the Socinians (he would also have included Wolterstorff had he possessed the gift of precognition), he concludes that 'It is wrong to distinguish between determinations which are implied in the idea of God and attributes which are viewed as super-added.'[57] So he objects to the method of distinguishing being and attributes, to Wolterstorff's relational ontology. Apart from the fact that different theologians who have thought along these lines have made different and incompatible proposals,

> it results in an impoverished rather than an enriched conception of the Deity, inasmuch as it easily leads to the conclusion that the attributes, e.g. divine love, are not present in God in as absolute a manner as, e.g. infinitude, and that they merely result from the outward influence of the creation upon God.[58]

Bavinck defends the idea of divine simplicity in standard, familiar ways. Simplicity in God does not indicate a contentless essence but the absolute fullness of life. God's essence is infinitely rich, and so it cannot be taken in at a glance, and while God remains eternally and immutably the same he assumes different relations to his creatures and they enter into various relations with respect to him:

> For, although in God knowing and willing, justice and grace are one, and although they are always identical with his full and complete essence; yet in these excellencies God so reveals to our eyes that one and only, rich essence that these virtues appear to lie alongside of each and seem to follow each other.[59]

---

54 *The Doctrine of God*, 15.
55 Bavinck cites Genesis 1:1; Psalms 33:6; John 5:26; Acts 17:24 ff. and many more texts (*The Doctrine of God*, 126).
56 *The Doctrine of God*, 142. He offers a stout defence of the idea of divine simplicity and eternality. 'Whatever God is he is completely and simultaneously' (121). Note also Plantinga has this to say about God and time in 'On Ockham's Way Out': 'I am inclined to believe that this thesis – the thesis that God is both atemporal and such that everything is present for him – is incoherent' (in *The Concept of God*, ed. T.V. Morris (Oxford: Oxford University Press, 1987), 176).
57 *The Doctrine of God*, 122.
58 *The Doctrine of God*, 123.
59 *The Doctrine of God*, 131.

Along lines made familiar to us from Augustine onwards Bavinck is vehemently against the idea that God's essence is an abstraction, a kind of *substratum*, 'something I know not what'. He says

> It is immediately evident, however, that this concept of being or essence, which is the result of a process of continued abstraction or elimination, is nothing else and nothing more than an empty concept. It lacks all content and has no objective, independent, reality. On the other hand, when *theology* speaks of God as essence, it arrives at this concept not by ways of subtraction or elimination but by the opposite process, namely by addition i.e., by ascribing to God all creaturely perfections in an absolute sense and by viewing him as absolute reality, the sum-total of all essence, 'most pure and simple actuality'. The essence which theology ascribes to God is at once the richest, most complete, and most intensive essence and the most determined and concrete, the absolute, only, and simple essence.[60]

Seen in the light of the purpose of this paper it is ironic that Bavinck abjures an approach to theism in terms of 'person' or 'personality' on the grounds that it leads to confusion in that the term 'person' is used in a technical sense in Trinitarian theology, and that 'there is in the abstract, modern and formal conception of personality nothing that distinguishes God, as such, from man'.[61]

According to Bavinck it is part of the theological task in harmony with Scripture to bestow equal honour upon each divine attribute. And the way that the Church has fulfilled this task is to affirm that

> God is simple, exalted above all composition, and that there is no real distinction between his being and his attributes. Every attribute is identical with God's being He *is* what he *has*. When we speak about creatures, we distinguish variously between what they are and what they have ... But when we speak about God, we must maintain that each of his attributes is identical with his being. God is all light, all mind, all wisdom, all logos, all spirit etc. ... Whatever God is he is completely and simultaneously.[62]

Accommodation – Its Place and Significance

Earlier we saw that a part of Swinburne's and Wolterstorff's motivation for developing a theism in the way that they do is to safeguard human libertarian freedom. Those in the classical Protestant tradition whose views we have sketched had the resources, through the idea of divine accommodation, to show how we are to understand cases of divine–human dialogue as these are recorded in the narrative passages of Scripture.

---

60 *The Doctrine of God*, 123–4.
61 *The Doctrine of God*, 125.
62 *The Doctrine of God*, 121. For a discussion of Plantinga's arguments against divine simplicity, see Brian Davies's 'Classical Theism and the Doctrine of Divine Simplicity', in *Language, Meaning and God*, ed. Brian Davies (London: Geoffrey Chapman, 1987); reprinted as 'A Modern Defence of Divine Simplicity' in *Philosophy of Religion: A Guide and Anthology*, ed. Brian Davies (Oxford: Oxford University Press, 2000). Davies's argument, that divine simplicity is a piece of apophatic theology and not a description of the divine nature, is noted by Richard Muller in connection with Plantinga's views and their difference from the tradition of Reformed Scholasticism, *Post-Reformation Reformed Dogmatics*, vol. 3, 212.

The *locus classicus* of their treatment is the idea of divine repentance, or divine relenting, as we find it, for example, in narratives involving Moses, and Jonah and Hezekiah.

Thus Calvin

> What, therefore, does the word 'repentance' mean? Surely its meaning is like that of all other modes of speaking that describe God to us in human terms. For because our weakness does not attain to his exalted state, the description of him that is given to us must be accommodated to our capacity (*ad captum*) so that we may understand it. Now the mode of accommodation is for him to represent himself to us not as he is in himself, but as he seems to us. Although he is beyond all disturbance of mind, yet he testifies that he is angry towards sinners. Therefore whenever we hear that God is angered, we ought not to imagine any emotion in him but rather to consider that this expression has been taken from our own human experience; because God, whenever he is exercising judgment, exhibits the appearance of one kindled and angered. So we ought not to understand anything else under the word 'repentance' than change of action, because men are wont by changing their action to testify that they are displeased with themselves. Therefore, since every change among men is a correction of what displeases them, but that correction arises out of repentance, then by the word 'repentance' is meant the fact that God changes with respect to his actions. Meanwhile neither God's plan nor his will is reversed, nor his volition altered; but what he had from eternity foreseen, approved and decreed, he pursues in uninterrupted tenor, however sudden the variation may appear in men's eyes.[63]

And Edwards, who rejects the idea that God is ignorant of 'future volitions of free agents' because it would follow

> that God must in many cases truly repent what he has done, so as properly to wish he had done otherwise; by reason that the event of things, in those affairs which are most important, viz. the affairs of his moral kingdom, being uncertain and contingent, often happens quite otherwise than he was aware beforehand ... Yea, from this notion it would follow, that God is liable to repent and be grieved at his heart, in a literal sense, continually; and is always exposed to an infinite number of real disappointments, in his governing the world; and to manifold, constant, great perplexity and vexation; but this is not very consistent with his title of 'God over all, blessed for evermore'; which represents him as possessed of perfect, constant and uninterrupted tranquility and felicity, as God over the universe, and in his management of the affairs of the world, as supreme and universal ruler.[64]

In this they were echoing medieval approaches. Thus Aquinas, in commenting on the unchangeableness of God's will, and on Genesis 6:7, says

> These words of the Lord have a metaphorical turn accord to a human figure of speech. When we regret what we have made we throw it away. Yet this does not always argue second thoughts or a change of will, for we may intend in the first place to make a thing and scrap it afterwards. By similitude with such a procedure we refer to God having regrets, for instance in the account of the Flood, when he washed away from the face of the earth the men whom he had made.[65]

---

63 *Inst.* I.17.13.
64 *Freedom of the Will*, 253.
65 *Summa Theologiae* I.19.7.

And Turretin

> Repentance is attributed to God after the manner of men (*anthropopathos*) must be understood after the manner of God (*theoprepos*): not with respect to his counsel, but to the event; not in reference to his will, but to the thing willed; not to affection and internal grief, but to the effect and external work because he does what a penitent man usually does.[66]

And Bavinck

> Similarly, the people of God experience at one time God's wrath, then again his love; at one time his absence, then again his closeness; at one time they are burdened with the consciousness of their guilt, at other times they rejoice because of forgiveness of sins. Notwithstanding all this, Scripture testifies that in all these various relations and experiences God remains ever the same.[67]

Coherence

Swinburne, as we saw, is concerned with the coherence of theism, seeing it in terms of the consistency of a story when checked against certain thought experiments. But it should be noted that the classical theistic tradition sees the coherence of the idea of God in much tighter fashion. Although Wolterstorff is mistaken in thinking that in Aquinas from divine simplicity a number of other divine characteristics are derived, nonetheless simplicity entails aseity, infinity, eternality, immutability and impassibility.

These features may be said to provide a grammar[68] arising from the nature of God and his distinctness from his creation – a grammar founded on and bequeathed to us by the divine reality itself.[69]

---

66 *Institutes of Elenctic Theology*, vol. 1, 206.

67 *The Doctrine of God*, 146.

68 When one thinks of the parallel between theology and grammar the gnomic remark of Wittgenstein at *Philosophical Investigations* 373 – 'Grammar tells what kind of an object anything is. (Theology as grammar)' – comes to mind. In fact the parallel between theology and grammar goes back a long way. Cf. Lewis Ayres, 'The Fundamental Grammar of Augustine's Trinitarian Theology', in *Augustine and His Critics*, ed. R. Dodaro and G. Lawless (London: Routledge, 2000). Ayres writes of Augustine's theological grammar as 'the most fundamental rules for speech about God, if we are to speak appropriately, and run as little risk of speaking unworthily as possible'. He goes on, 'Using the term "grammar" in this context is particularly warranted because of Augustine's insistence that God is ultimately incomprehensible; the task for Christians attempting to set out appropriate terms in which to talk of God is not best described as one of learning how to describe God, but as one of learning how to articulate appropriate rules for human talk of God' (52).

69 Thanks to David Hoffner for all kinds of help.

Voices in Discussion

D.Z. Phillips

G: To say that you can adequately describe the source of all things would be like someone who counted 1, 2, 3, 5, 7, marking the prime numbers, and who then says that he didn't come across another one, so he had discovered the greatest prime number.

D: We'd say it wasn't a coherent story.

A: And if he said he could imagine it, we'd say he only thought he could imagine it.

B: We'd see the logical contradiction straight off.

G: Someone who understood mathematics would know it was incoherent. It is built into our understanding. Given this, someone may ask why we should believe stories about the greatest being called God.

B: But we could say that we arrive at this notion by asking why there is something rather than nothing at all.

F: Of course, we have to be careful, because in speaking of 'all things' we may assume that we are talking of a single class. We cannot answer the question 'How many things?' unless we specify what things we are talking about. So how many things there are in a room, for example, is dependent on this. The difference between one thing and another is not a simple 'given'.

C: What about the use of 'nothing' in 'something rather than nothing?' You say that 'thing' is used relatively. Why isn't this true of the use of 'nothing' too, as when I say 'There is nothing in the drawer' or 'There is nothing in my pocket'? But when we say there might have been nothing, it seems to mean 'nothing at all'. 'Nothing' is being used in an absolute sense. 'Nothing' seems to be talked of as a state that might have existed – 'might have *been* nothing at all', whereas the normal use is to deny the existence of something particular in contexts where something else does exist, such as the empty drawer or the empty pocket.

F: I think the use is counterfactual. For any thing you mention, God might not have created it.

C: But that means that something else would have existed. My difficulty is with the absolute sense which does not have a contrast.

D: But what about the contrast with God? 'Nothing except God might have existed.

C: The trouble with that in the context of the present discussion is that it leads, or seems to lead, to treating God as a particular existent, an item which could be alongside others, where the others do not exist as yet. But, that is the very conception of God in the tradition in question that it wants to deny, is invoking divine simplicity. If God is thought of as an 'existent', I think that implies the existence of other existents from which it can be distinguished.

L: I don't know whether this will help C's difficulties. Augustine had difficulty in thinking of 'nothing' as an ontological state, since thought presupposes being. But in the doctrine of '*creatio ex nihilo*' he thought that affirmation grows out of a double negation. On the one hand, creation is not an extension or emanation of God himself. On the other hand, creation is not the working on a stuff which is already formed. And so he wanted to express sheer origination in the doctrine of *creatio ex nihilo*.

E: Here we have the tension I referred to earlier, when we try to translate analogical language. We see anthropomorphism running rampant in the attempt. Wolterstorff and others get into trouble by equating 'the analogical' with 'the literal'. Analogical language is literal language when it is the proper language for its context. Thus, 'God is Father' is analogical and literal, while 'God is rock' is metaphorical.

D: Maybe we should speak of what is 'unqualified' in this context. Things are true of God without qualification. Thus 'literal' means 'unqualified'.

F: I agree that the use of 'literal' is confusing. Poetic language can be literal.

I: What is the relation of analogical talk to revelation? 'God is Father' is said to be not literal, or literal as in analogical. How do I know the analogical language is working or appropriate, though the analogy works in practice?

F: You've answered your own question. It is seen in practice. You don't have to draw philosophy into it.

D: I find a real tension here between what is called 'pulpit talk' and the contrast with philosophical language. There seems to be a suggestion that philosophy is a high road to religious truth, to which the pulpit language must be accommodated. Locke, for example, said one could work out one's moral philosophy privately, but that the ploughman needs pictures to help him in his moral endeavours.

P: It seems that throughout this whole discussion 'anthropomorphism' is being used as a pejorative term from the outset. It is something bad, something to be avoided at all costs. This is an attempt to affect a maximum distance between the Creator and the creature. So temporality, it seems, must be denied. This may be true in the Western tradition from Augustine on, but in the Eastern tradition temporality is emphasized.

G: If God is the creator of time, he cannot be in time. 'Time' is not 'God'.

P: Why?

G: If you think of the Trinity, how you think of it will be very different if you assume that there was a time when the Son was not.

F: Activity as a temporal process means that there is no such thing as a pure discrete act. Actions have their place in ongoing processes.

A: I cannot go into it now, but we do have answers to these difficulties from the point of view you are criticizing. We do put God on the temporal side. We say God is everlasting, not eternal. I don't believe in 'eternity'.

C: I did try to give an example of the eternal will of the dead and the eternal will of God, where, though eternal, indeed, precisely by virtue of that, they can have a distinctive effect on the lives of human beings.

A: I am not convinced. God, in his dealings with our changing state, has a nature in 1951 which, in certain respects, is different from his nature in 1950.

G: But in notions of sempiternity, one thing succeeds another, and that cannot be said of God.

D: For example, are you prepared to say that the life of Christ, the second person of the Trinity, is over?

R: These questions may be considered further in the light of certain theories about persons. According to one, a person is a reality over time through successive stages. According to another, however, the person is wholly present at each stage. So objections to successive stages in God's reality would apply to the first theory, but not to the second.

G: It still remains that in God's case we are dealing with an analogy of 'being'. If God is the cause of the entire class of existing beings, he cannot himself be a member of that class. So we have good reason for saying that he is a being as the cause of all things, but also good reason for denying that he is a being alongside others. And so the way of analogy is a middle way.

B: We cannot understand God's essence. If I am told that I have a brain tumour, what makes that true is not something linguistic, but something in my skull. But we cannot produce a science of God. We have reason to suppose that God is, if something is. But in asking *what* God is, we speak analogically, not literally, in our replies. What grounds do we have for doing so? We can only answer by exploring the reasons in our lives for applying such terms; the kind of explorations we have been undertaking in this conference.

Chapter 9

Is God Timeless, Immutable, Simple and Impassible? Some Brief Comments

Stephen T. Davis

I

To a surprising degree, the papers in this book converge around a common theme. The theme is that the view of God held by 'most Christian analytic philosophers of religion' these days is defective and that it ought to be replaced by the view of God found in such classic theologians as Augustine, Aquinas and Calvin. I say it is surprising because it had frankly never occurred to me that there could emerge this sort of *rapprochement* between Wittgensteinian, Thomist and strongly Calvinist philosophers of religion. Since I am widely regarded as holding to the defective view of God just noted, and indeed am mentioned in one or two of the book's essays, I should try to say something in response.

Before turning to substantive matters, let me first make a rather boring personal point. It is probably still correct to align me with the view of God against which most of the contributors to this volume argue. But I need to say that I no longer own many of the things that I wrote 22 years ago in my *Logic and the Nature of God*. I am not quite ready to ask all owners of that book to burn it, but I do now largely regret that I wrote it. For one thing, I should have kept it on my desk for a year longer before having it published. That would have given me a chance to read and think further.[1] For another, in the intervening years I have thought and read a great deal about God (including writings by contributors to this book), and have concluded that much that I wrote in my 1983 book is untenable. (Obviously, there is also much there that I continue to hold.)

II

I will make four main points.

First, it seems to me that Christian theology, and specifically its understanding of God, must be done, so to speak, in tension between two opposite poles. God is *transcendent* and God is *immanent*. Both claims are true, and the neglect of one in favour of the other leads to error. God as creator is infinitely greater than we are;

---

1   London: Macmillan, 1983. Frankly, I let go of the manuscript early under some pressure from the then dean of the college. He assured me that my upcoming promotion was pretty much a sure thing if the book appeared before the crucial decision. I have no resentment against him whatsoever – it was my decision, not his – but I should not have listened to him.

we are quite unable to understand God or God's ways;[2] God is not like a powerful and grand human being. But, equally, we were made in God's image; God reveals himself to us; in the incarnation God becomes one of us. Indeed, God is a person – not, of course, in the same sense in which we are persons, but at least in the sense of having a mental life that includes desires and intentions, as well as having the ability to bring them to fruition.[3]

Let me contrast (very roughly and incompletely) two different ways of understanding the Christian God. I will call them 'theories of God'.

> *Theory A*: God is the unique, omnipotent, omniscient and perfectly good creator of the heavens and the earth; God cannot fail to exist; and God is timeless, strongly immutable, impassable and metaphysically simple.
>
> *Theory B*: God is the unique, omnipotent, omniscient and perfectly good creator of the heavens and the earth; God cannot fail to exist, and God is temporal, weakly immutable,[4] passable and not metaphysically simple.

Theory A, then, is meant roughly to correspond to the view of God held by most of the contributors to this book, and Theory B to the view of God held by 'most contemporary Christian analytic philosophers of religion'.

My own opinion is that both theories are acceptable Christian theories of God, can be defended philosophically and can be commended to the faithful. (I recognize that a motion to that effect would probably fail for lack of a second among the contributors to this volume.) Yet as soon as we move too far in either the transcendence direction or the immanence direction we fall into error. Anthropomorphism is indeed the danger of going too far in the second direction. In my opinion, Process Theology and 'Openness Theology', both of which I have argued against in print, are guilty of going too far toward immanence. I disassociate myself entirely from theologies of this sort.[5] However, it is possible to go too far in the transcendence direction too. Think, for example, of the gods of the ancient Epicureans: they were ideal models of *ataraxia*, but they resided far away from the earth and had nothing to do with human affairs. Think also of seventeenth- and eighteenth-century deism, where God created the heavens and the earth and set its natural laws in motion but never interferes thereafter. Think also of

---

2 I completely agree with Paul Helm, against Swinburne, that we are unable to imagine what it is like to be God.

3 Paul Helm asks whether God is a person 'much as we are'. Put that way, the answer is clearly no. But God is a person in at least some of the ways in which we are persons.

4 Let's say that a person is 'strongly immutable' if it is never true that at one point she has a certain property and at another point does not have it (except for purely relational changes like, 'Is not believed in by Augustine'). A person is 'weakly immutable' if she always retains her nature, is true to her word, keeps her promises, never wavers in her purposes, is not fickle, mercurial, or moody, can be entirely relied on and so forth.

5 I include this last point because I have occasionally been accused or suspected of holding such views. I do not now, and never have held them, and that includes in *Logic and the Nature of God*. So far as I can tell, the suspicion is largely due to the fact that (1) I do not accept Theory A and (2) I live and teach in Claremont, California, which happens to be world centre of Process Thought.

extreme Christian apophatism, where it is said that human categories are not capable of conceptualizing God; accordingly, we can only know what God is not, never what God is. So the danger of going too far in this direction is that we arrive at a God who has little to do with us and about whom we can know little.

III

Second, why are so many contemporary Christian analytic philosophers of religion attracted to Theory B? I think there are four central reasons (the first two of which are recognized in other essays in this book): scripture, human freedom, apologetic issues and pastoral considerations.

Scripture

There is no doubt that many Christian philosophers have a hard time – as I do – reconciling the God depicted in the Bible with a God who is timeless, immutable, simple and impassable. Defenders of Theory B know, of course, that there is anthropomorphism, as well as very many literary genres, in play in the Bible. And we are aware of the exceedingly clever and nuanced attempts by medieval philosophers (especially Aquinas) and a few of our contemporaries to achieve such a reconciliation.[6] Still, many of us are dubious that it can be done. Especially for Protestants, but also for some Catholic philosophers of religion, this point constitutes a major impediment to accepting Theory A.

Human Freedom

Those who accept Theory A are inevitably drawn to compatibilist views of human freedom, a theory that is unacceptable to many contemporary philosophers of region, including me. That human beings are sometimes free in a libertarian sense is one of our deepest phenomenological convictions, and we do not find plausible the various efforts to reconcile compatibilist freedom with moral responsibility. And that human beings are morally responsible for their sins is one of the deepest principles of biblical religion. Again, we are aware of the thoughtful attempts in the tradition to reconcile compatibilist freedom and human moral responsibility, but we remain unconvinced.

Apologetic Issues

People who are committed to Theory A often insist that it makes no sense for Christians to try to argue that God is 'morally good', in some sense similar to the way in which respected and honoured human beings are morally good. Now I have no wish to deny that God's goodness far transcends even the best of human goodness. Still, apologetic issues come into play here whenever we try to answer Mackie-like objections on the

---

6   As well as some who are contributing to the present volume, this would include Brian Leftow, Ralph McInerny and Eleonore Stump.

problem of evil. Atheists do pose questions about God's moral integrity. I once met a man – a veteran of World War II – who told me, 'I have seen things with my own eyes that God would never permit if God existed.' In answer to people who say things like that (more frequent, perhaps, are comments like, 'I will not believe in a God who allows x, y and z'), Christian philosophers have felt constrained to argue that God can still be perfectly morally good despite the occurrence of events like x, y and z. I regard that as a perfectly understandable reaction. Does God need our apologetic interventions? Certainly not. But some people apparently do. They need to be told where their thinking has led them astray.

Pastoral Considerations

When I was a young assistant pastor just out of Princeton Theological Seminary, a member of my parish was diagnosed with lupus, a disease of which there was then (and so far as I know, still is) no known cure. I spoke with him, and with his wife, on many occasions. A metalworker without much education, he nevertheless in effect asked me the question, 'Why did this happen to me?' His wife was even more deeply troubled. Contrary to the intuitions of Brian Davies, I was faced with a pastoral situation where a believer, that is, the wife, was calling into question God's moral integrity. I saw it as my pastoral duty to let her express her pain and anger, to suffer with her (usually in silence) and occasionally to try to get her to see that God was good and could be praised for his goodness despite what had happened to her husband.

IV

Third, in various ways, the contributors to this book raise questions designed to increase the distance between God and human beings. David Burrell, for example, asks whether God is 'an item in the universe'. In my view, the answer to that question depends on what is meant by 'the universe'. Perhaps the term refers to the huge aggregate of all creatures, that is, to all the contingent things that have ever existed, now exist or will ever exist. On that understanding of the term, God is not an item in the universe. God is not a contingent thing. But if by the term 'the universe' we mean the set of all real or existing things, then – or so I would hold – God is indeed an item in the universe. Does it necessarily demean God's transcendence and sovereignty to affirm as much? I do not see why. One can still be quite clear about all the ways in which God differs from the creatures.

Is God a moral agent? Brian Davies says no. And I agree that God is not a moral agent in the same sense in which we are moral agents (namely, morally responsible to a higher agent). But I would have thought that God becomes a moral agent of a sort the moment God issues moral commands to human beings or makes covenants with them. Indeed, the moment God does that, God makes us part of God's moral community.

Several of our book's authors emphasize the notion of divine simplicity. This is a part of Theory A that I do not want to argue against so much as declare that I only dimly understand it. Even so, I do think the arguments advanced in favour of divine simplicity in this volume are unconvincing. For example, Gyula Klima argues (if I have caught the drift) that if a given object is composite, then in respect to one of its parts it has to be something that in respect to another part it *is not*. 'But,' he says, 'not-being in some respect is incompatible with being fully, in an absolutely unlimited sense.' But I would reply that if 'A is not B' is true, then whether or not A and B are parts of some larger composite thing C, this fact by itself does not imply that either A or B has or participates in *not-being*. My left foot is not my right ear, but again this fact by itself does not mean (as long as I exist) that I participate in not-being. Another argument: Paul Helm claims that composite things must be caused to exist. Everything composite, he says, 'is subsequent to its components and depends on them'. But I am unsure what 'subsequent to' means in this context. Am I 'subsequent to' my left foot? I certainly in some sense depend on it, but if God is composite, God cannot be separated from his parts, as I can, and so is not dependent on them in any theologically untoward way. A final argument: James Ross claims that denying divine simplicity entails 'God's incompleteness and dependence on things *ad extra*'. But I do not think it entails God's incompleteness at all since God's parts are obviously going to be essential parts of God, who is a necessary being. Accordingly, it does not entail God's dependence on anything external to God. Nor, if God is a necessary being, is any explanation required of why the parts of God are related to each other as they are. It is simply an essential aspect of reality that God's parts are related to each other as they are.

Similarly, Dewi Phillips asks whether the term 'God' refers to 'a thing among other things'. Well, I have always thought that the English term 'thing' is almost infinite in what it ranges over. A 'thing' is just anything whose name or referring term can appear in the subject position of a coherent sentence, is a property bearer and has an identity apart from other things. Is God a thing *like* other things? Of course not. Is God a thing *among* other things? Of course (or so I would say).

What clinches God's membership in the set of existing things, in my opinion, is the fact of revelation. Apart from God's sovereignly revealing himself to us, we would know nothing of God. Thus Psalm 28:1 – 'To you, O Lord, I call; my rock, do not refuse to hear me, for if you are silent to me, I shall be like those who go down to the pit.' If God were silent, some sort of Epicureanism or deism would be believable. But, as the prophet Amos affirms, God does speak to us: 'For lo, the one who forms the mountains, creates the wind, *reveals his thoughts to mortals*, makes the morning darkness, and treads on the heights of the earth – The Lord, the God of hosts is his name!' (Amos 4:13, italics added). If God reveals himself to us, and even becomes one of us in the incarnation, is it hard for me to see how sensibly to deny the claim that God is an item in the universe. Of course, as just noted, God is not an item *like all the other items*, but that is another matter.

IV

Finally, I wish to comment on Brian Davies's ten important features of the grammar of God. (I am sorry to say that I have not yet read or even seen his famous 'Letter from America'; in what follows, I am reacting to the brief statement of the ten features that we find in Dewi Phillips's essay in this book.). While some of the ten features are beyond reproach, others I find problematical. Moreover, not all of them seem to be (as Phillips suggests that they are) rules governing legitimate discourse about God. They are not *regulative*. (Or if they are, they simply amount to question-begging attempts to legislate defenders of Theory B out of the conversation.) In fact, many of the features amount to substantive and debatable theological claims.

The first feature avers that 'God cannot be said to be part of the world of space or time.' But it is hard for me to see how anybody who believes in the incarnation can say that. The third states that 'it is nonsense to speak of God as an individual, locatable in one place rather than another.' But while the part of the sentence following the comma is surely correct (apart from the incarnation, of course), I see no good reason to deny that God is an individual. Can something be a person or be 'personal' without being an individual? The fourth feature sheds light on what Davies means. He thinks of the term 'individual' as implying that if x is an individual, then there could be other members of x's set, other individuals that share x's nature. And while I of course agree that nothing other than God has God's nature (God is not just unique but absolutely unique), I see no philosophical or theological danger in affirming that God and human beings are both members of the set of *existing things* and the set of *individuals*. That is, I do not think the term 'individual' implies what Davies thinks it implies.

On the sixth feature, the one that says that 'It makes no sense to speak of God changing', I will simply note that Davies and I will have to agree to disagree. While I certainly hold to weak immutability (as defined in footnote 4), I reject the view that God never 'passes through successive states'.[7] On the seventh feature, I surely accept the first part (that God cannot be informed of things that he previously did not know), but I reject the notion that God does not experience pain. In the past 100 years, not just most analytic philosophers of religion, but virtually the entire Western theological world (with the exception of those who embrace Theory A) has moved to the notion that God *qua* God suffers. It is now a virtual commonplace. (That does not make it true, of course.) The eighth feature affirms that God cannot be the source of some things but not others. I suspect that all depends here on what is meant by 'source'. In some important and ordinary senses of that word, I would deny that God is the source of the last sin that I committed.

V

In this brief essay, I have not argued for much. It is more in the nature of a minority report in this book. Its burden is that those contemporary Christian philosophers of religion who reject Theory A in favour of Theory B can do so for principled reasons. There are people – and I am certainly one of them – who find Theory A deeply intriguing and in many ways attractive, but in the end indefensible.[8]

---

[7] Contrary to Professor Klima, it seems to me that even a perfect being can change in non-perfection related ways.

[8] I thank Professor Susan Peppers-Bates for her helpful comments on an earlier draft of this essay.

Index

accommodation, divine 155–7
al-Ghazali 135
Almond, Philip 10–11
Alston, William 99
  on divine goodness 104
Altizer, Thomas 26
analogia entis et nominum 87–9
analogia fidei 86–7
  meanings 87
analogists ("catholics"), position 82, 92
  see also reformers
analogy
  and anthropomorphism 159
  Aquinas's use of 131–3
  perfection-terms 132–3
  and reason 135
  tension in 46
Anscombe, G.E.M. 9, 19
  on knowing 31
Anselm, St 4, 62
  Proslogion 64
anthropomorphism 4, 16, 35, 41, 159
  and analogy 159
  avoidance of 42, 45, 129
  in the Bible 163
  Catholic 131
  dimensions of 130–31
  origins 129
  Protestant 137
  Swinburne on 137–41
  Wolterstorff on 141–5
apophaticism 23, 42, 163
Aquinas, St Thomas
  analogy, use of 131–3
  on belief in God 109–10
  creation, theology of 38–40, 42–3
  on divine
    knowledge 142
    repentance 156
    simplicity 144
  on essence of God 43, 70–3
  on God as Creator 107
  on God as source of moral goodness 118–19
  on goodness of God 119–24
  grammar of God 46
  on justice of God 119
  knowledge
    ontology of 35, 38
    theory of 40, 42
  mind/world identity 31–4
  modes of being 67–8
  on name of God 58
  philosophy, and Catholic doctrine 28–9
  on scientific reality 90–91
  on Scripture 82, 89
  self, conception of 32
  on simplicity of God 110–11, 142, 144
  on the soul 29, 35
  on subject/object relation 23, 33
  theology
    negative 110–11
    theocentric 37
  on truth 38–9
  works
    De Potentia 90
    Quaestiones Disputatae de Veritate 87
    Summa contra Gentiles 30, 83, 87
    Summa Theologiae 23, 58, 87, 118–19, 121, 129–30
  see also neoThomism
Aristotle 55, 121
  division of being 68
  Physics 21
Arnold, Matthew 16
Augustine, St 4
  on name of God 55–6
  On Christian Doctrine 55, 82
Avicenna 4, 79, 87, 130

Balthasar, Hans Urs von 131
Barrett, Cyril 2, 6
Barth, Karl 22, 86, 131, 134
  Church Dogmatics 27

on subject/object relation 27
Bavinck, Herman 153–5
  on divine
    attributes 154–5
    essence 155
    repentance 157
    simplicity 154
being
  analogy, and inherence theory of predication 167–70
  division, Aristotelian 68
  and essence 70
  modes of, Aquinas 67–8
  participation of, formula 70
  as predicate 65–6
belief
  in God 109–110
  nature of 10
  religious, grammar of 18
beliefs, about God 98–101
Biddle, John 113
bivalence, principle 66
Blocher, Henri 87
Boethius 55
  De Trinitate 83
Bonhoeffer, Dietrich 22
Braine, David 2, 133
Brightman, Edgar Sheffield, on God 14
Brown, James
  Subject and Object in Modern Theology 21, 35
  on subject/object relation 22–4
Buber, Martin 22
Bultmann, Rudolf 22
Burrell, David 2, 41, 129–35, 164

Calvin, John
  on divine
    repentance 156
    simplicity 147–9
  on The Trinity 148–9
canon law, revised code 21, 28
Catholic doctrine, and Thomistic philosophy 28–9
"catholics" *see* analogists
Christ, human and divine union 44–6
Clement of Alexandria 28
Clifford, William 101

coherence, Swinburne on 138–40, 157
Coleridge, Samuel Taylor
  Biographia Literaria 24
  on subject/object relation 24
compatibilism 163
constituitive reference 61
creation, Aquinas's theology of 38–40, 42–3
Creator
  creature, distinction 2–4, 20, 41–2, 129–31, 133–4
  God as 101, 106–107, 110, 123
Creel, Richard 3
  on God 14
Crombie, Ian 2

Daly, Mary 28
Davies, Brian 1, 4–5, 9, 12–16, 81, 97–122, 133, 164
  on grammar of God 2–3, 97fn1, 101, 165–6
    criticism 165–6
  on name of God 97
  on Plantinga 3
  works
    "Letter from America" 1, 18, 81, 97, 99, 101–103
    "The Problem of Evil" 118
Davis, Stephen T. 3, 161–6
  on God 14
  on God's goodness 103
  Logic and the Nature of God 161
dehellenization project, Wolterstorff 141–2, 144
deism 162
Derrida, Jacques 47
Descartes, René, *Meditations* 113
description
  task of philosophy 5–6
  types 18
  Wittgensteinian 5–6, 18
Dodds, Michael 2
Dummett, Michael 9

Edwards, Jonathan
  on divine eternity 152–3
  on divine omniscience 153
  on divine repentance 156
  Freedom of the Will 152
  influences on 152

on moral agency of God 16
Ernest, Cornelius 29
essence
   and being 70
   of God 39, 70–71, 73–7, 160
      modern vs premodern positions 73–6
evil
   God's struggle against 14
   problem of 18
      and goodness of God 103–105, 117, 124, 164
existence *see* being

Faith and Philosophy 139
Flew, Anthony 101
   and Alasdair MacIntyre, *New Essays in Philosophical Theology* 22
Francis de Sales, St 4

Geach, Peter 2, 9
Gilbert of Pourçain 154
Gill, Christopher, *Personality in Greek Epic* 32
God
   attributes
      Bavinck on 154–5
      incommunicable 149–51
   as being itself 42, 49
   belief in 109–110
   beliefs about 98–101, 123
   as body 108
   Brightman on 14
   as consequence of curiosity 12
   as Creator 101, 106–107, 123
      Aquinas on 107, 110
   Creel on 14
   Davis on 14
   diversity of 114–15
   Edwards on 16, 152–3
   essence of 39, 160
      Aquinas on 43, 70–72
      Bavinck on 155
      modern vs premodern positions 73–6
      Turretin on 151
   eternity 160
      Edwards on 152–3
      Turretin on 151
   evil, struggle against 14
   goodness, source of 125
   goodness of
      Alston on 104–105
      Aquinas on 119–24
      in Bible 120–21, 124
      Davis on 103
      Euthyphro dilemma 124
      Plantinga on 104
      and problem of evil 103–105, 117, 124, 164
      Rowe on 103
   grammar of 2–3, 9, 13, 18, 46–8, 97fn1, 101, 123, 165–6
   Hartshorne on 14
   Hasker on 14
   hiddenness 114
   immutability 15, 166
   incomparability of 114
   incorporeality of 107–108, 124
   as infinitely other 49
   interactivity with humans 146
   James on 13–14
   justice of 116, 119
   knowledge, Aquinas on 142
   language about 12, 47, 49
   mind, truth of 40
   as moral agent 16, 102–106, 112, 115–18, 122–3, 126, 164
   name
      Aquinas on 58
      Augustine on 55–6
      Christian/pagan usage 59
      Davies on 97
      grammar of 53, 55
      modern vs premodern position 74–5
      and monotheism 56–7, 73
      sense and reference 57–8
      use 58–9
   nature of 9
   omnipresence 150
   omniscience
      Edwards on 153
      Swinburne on 145–6
   as person(s) 84, 113–14, 124, 137–8, 140, 166
   Pike on 14
   Plantinga on 14–15, 104
   and reason 133–4
   reference to 7–9, 44
   remoteness of 164

repentance 156–7
revelation 165
righteousness of 115, 124
Ross on 165
in Scripture 82, 144–5, 163
simplicity of 15, 85, 92, 124, 150, 164–5
    Aquinas on 110–11, 142, 144
    Bavinck on 154
    Calvin on 147–9
    Ross on 165
    Wolterstorff on 142–3
as source of goodness 16
as source of moral goodness 118–19
as subject 21
temporality of 13–15, 95
theories of 162–4
transcendence/immanence dichotomy 161–2
triune 49, 86
Wolterstorff on 14
goodness, God as source of 16
see also under God
Google search engine 53
grammar
    of God 9, 13, 18, 46–8, 123
        Aquinas's 46
        changeability 47
        Davies on 2–3, 97fn1, 101, 165–6
    of name God 53, 55
    of religious belief 18
Grant, Sara 129–30
Gregor Smith, Ronald 21–2
Gregory of Nyssa 4
Guirez, Germain 2
Günther, Anton 28

Haldane, John 30
Hamilton, William 26
Hartshorne, Charles, on God 14
Hasker, William 3
    on God 14
Hegel, G.W.F. 52
Heidegger, Martin 22, 28, 37, 41, 49
Helm, Paul 137–57, 165
Henry of Ghent 133
Hermes, George 28
Hooker, Richard 147
Hume, David, Swinburne on 7–8

intellect, and truth 38–9
intelligibility, and knowing 31
Irenaeus 4

James, William, on God 13–14
Jordan, Mark 2
Justin Martyr 28

Kaiser, Walter C. Jr 87
Kant, Immanuel 22–3, 28
Kenny, Anthony 65, 151
    Aquinas on Mind 77
Kerr, Fergus 12, 21–35, 49, 133
Kierkegaard, Søren 22, 45
    Purity of Heart 95
Klima, Gyula 53–77, 164–5
Klubertanz, James 131
knower/known
    isomorphism 30–31, 35, 38, 40–41, 49
    relation 49
knowing
    Anscombe on 31
    and intelligibility 31
    McDowell on 31
    Putnam on 31
    as "taking a look" 30
    Taylor on 30–31
knowledge
    activist approach 36–38
    Aquinas's ontology of 35, 38
    confrontation model 29–30, 35
    contemplative approach 36–8, 49
    medieval vs modern view 36–7
    and reality 36–7
    subjectivism vs objectivism 36
    theory of, Aquinas on 40, 42
    and truth 40–41
Kretzmann, Norman 30
Küng, Hans, *The Paradigm Change in Theology* 93
Kyongsuk Min, Anselm 35–48

language
    about God 12, 47, 49
    as belief about reality 11
    games 54
    inadequacy of 12, 19–20, 47–9
    learning, requirements 76–7

and linguistic communities 54–5
  see also linguistic authority
Leftow, Brian 2
Leo XIII (Pope), *Aeterni Patris* encyclical 28, 131
Levinas, Emmanuel 22
libertarian freedom 145–6, 155
linguistic authority 54, 63–4
  examples 55
  meaning 55
linguistic communities, and language 54–5
Locke, John 152
Lonergan, Bernard 131
  Verbum: Word and Idea in Aquinas 29
Luther, Martin 4

McCabe, Herbert 2, 110, 133
McDowell, John, on knowing 31
McInerney, Ralph 2, 132
MacIntyre, Alasdair *see* Flew, Anthony
Mackie, J.L. 126
Maimonides, Moses 4, 79, 87, 129–30, 135
Malcolm, Norman 2, 6
Marion, Jean Luc 47
Maritain, Jacques 38
metaphysics, idealist school 22
Meynell, Hugo, *The Theology of Bernard Lonergan* 30
mind
  matter, distinction 23
  world, identity, Aquinas 31–4
Monophysitism 45
monotheism, and name of God 56–7, 73
Moore, Gareth 1, 2, 5–6, 12, 18, 97, 100–101
  Believing in God 10
moral agent
  God as 16, 102–106, 112, 115–118, 122–3, 164
  meaning 111–12
moral responsibility 18
mysteries, as givens 18–19

neoThomism 28–9
  philosophy/theology dichotomy 131
Nestorianism 45
New Blackfriars 1, 99
Newman, John Henry 131
Nicene Creed 84–5

Owens, G.E.L. 132
Owens, Joseph 29, 132

parasitic reference 61
  examples 62–3
Paul, St 4
Pearson, John 147
Pelz, Werner 26
person(s)
  Cartesian 113
  definition 55
  God as 84, 113–14, 124, 137–8, 140, 166
Phillips, D.Z. 1–20, 47, 49–52, 81, 92–5, 97–8, 123–7, 158–60, 165
  Wolterstorff on 3
  works
    Faith After Foundationalism 5
    Religion Without Explanation 5
    The Concept of Prayer 5
    Wittgenstein and Religion 7
philosophy
  description in 5–6
  religion, identification 13
  Thomistic, and Catholic doctrine 28–9
philosophy of religion
  American 3, 4, 13–14
  Wittgensteinian 4, 9–10
Pickstock, Catherine 47
Pieper, Josef 131
Pike, Nelson 3
  on God 14
Plantinga, Alvin 3, 153
  on God 14–15
  on God's goodness 104
Plato 13
predication
  absolute vs qualified fallacy 66–7
  inherence theory of
  and analogy of being 67–70
  formula 66
Pseudo-Dionysius 87
psychologia rationalis 21, 29
Putnam, Hilary, on knowing 31

Qur'an 135

Rahner, Karl 43, 46
reality 50
   and knowledge 36
   religious/scientific approaches 13
   scientific, Aquinas on 90–91
   and subject/object relation 37
reason
   and analogy 135
   and God 133–4
   kenotic 134
   proto-sacramental 135
reformers
   position 82, 92
   vs analogists, traditions 81–6
religion, philosophy, identification 13
   see also philosophy of religion
Religious Studies 139
repentance, divine
   Aquinas on 156
   Calvin on 156
   Edwards on 156
   Turretin on 157
representationalism 30–31
Rhees, Rush 6, 15, 19, 46–7
   on reference to God 8–9
Robinson, Howard 7–11
Robinson, J.A.T. 26
Rocca, Gregory 133
Rosmini-Serbati, Antonio 28
Ross, James F. 2, 81–91, 132
   on divine simplicity 165
Rowe, William, on God's goodness 103

Scotus, John Duns 4, 133–4
Scripture
   Aquinas on 82, 89
   God in 82, 144–5, 163
the self 25
   Aquinas's conception of 32
Shanley, Brian 118–20, 122
Socinianism 146
Socinians 113, 149, 154
Sokolowski, Robert 129–30, 134
the soul, Aquinas on 29, 35
Stump, Eleonore, *Aquinas* 29
subject
   and external reality 28
   God as 21

subject/object relation 21–2, 32, 34–5
   Aquinas on 23, 33
   Barth on 27
   Brown on 22–4
   Coleridge on 24
   literary 25
   and reality 37
   reversal 23
   Torrance on 26–7
   union 29, 35–6, 38
Swinburne, Richard 3–4, 99, 107, 116–17
   on anthropomorphism 137–41
   on coherence 138–40, 157
   on divine omniscience 145–6
   on Hume 7–8
   on negative theology 140–41
   on theism 138
   works
      Providence and the Problem of Evil 102
      The Coherence of Theism 102, 137, 139, 141

Tanner, Kathryn 134
Taylor, Charles, on knowing 30-31
te Velde, Rudi, *Substantiality and Participation in Aquinas* 130
terms
   metaphysical disagreements about 59–61
   proper/improper uses 54, 63–4
theism, Swinburne on 138
theology
   dogmatic 22
   natural 153
   negative 110–11
      Swinburne 140–41
   philosophical 21–2
   process 14, 129
   Roman Catholic 21
   theocentric 37
Tillich, Paul 22
Torah 135
Torrance, Thomas F.
   God and Rationality 26
   on subject/object relation 26–7
traditions
   Protestant 146–55
   religious 5–7

Trigg, Roger 11
The Trinity, Calvin on 148–9
truth
    Aquinas on 38–9, 89–91
    derivation 39
    of divine mind 40
    and intellect 38–9
    and knowledge 40–41
    tests for 89–91
    varieties of 39
Turner, Denys 133–5
Turretin, Francis, on divine
    essence 151
    eternity 151
    incommunicable attributes 149–51
    repentance 157

Van Buren, Paul 26
Vardy, Peter 10–12
Vatican Council, First 84, 134

Watson, Sir William 16
Watt, Ian, *The Rise of the Novel* 25
Weil, Simone 4
Whitehead, A.N. 144
William of Ockham 4
Williams, Christopher 9
Williams, H.A. 26
Williams, Stephen 8

Winch, Peter 6, 10–11
Wittgenstein, Ludwig, on description in
    philosophy 5–6
Wittgensteinianism 2, 9–10, 161
    anti-metaphysics 10
Wolff, Christian 23
    Cosmologia Generalis 21
Wolterstorff, Nicholas 4–5
    on anthropomorphism 141–5
    dehellenization project 141–2, 144
    on divine
        interactivity with humans 146
        simplicity 142–3
    on God 14
    on Phillips 3
    works
        "Divine Simplicity" 142–3
        "Suffering Love" 142
Woodhead, Linda 7
words, uses of 53–4
    see also terms
world
    discovery of 49
    homocentrism 37
    mind, identity, Aquinas 31–4
    structure 50

Xenophanes 63

Printed in Great Britain
by Amazon